EARNEST
GAMES

EARNEST GAMES

Folkloric Patterns in the Canterbury Tales

CARL LINDAHL

INDIANA UNIVERSITY PRESS

Bloomington and Indianapolis

First Midland Book edition 1989

This book was brought to publication with the assistance of a grant from the
Andrew W. Mellon Foundation.

Manufactured in the United States of America

Library of Congress Cataloging-in-Publication Data

Lindahl, Carl.
Earnest games.

Bibliography: p.
Includes index.
1. Chaucer, Geoffrey, d. 1400. Canterbury tales.
2. Chaucer, Geoffrey, d. 1400–Knowledge–Folklore,
mythology. 3. Folklore in literature. 4. Games
in literature. 5. Oral tradition—England. I. Title.
PR1875.F67L5 1987   821'.1   86-45469
ISBN 0-253-32503-X cl.
ISBN 0-253-20550-6 pbk.

2   3   4   5   93   92   91   90   89

*For
Robert and Constance Lindahl
and Lorraine Wright,
the mooste fre*

CONTENTS

Part Three
GENTIL FOLK

Acknowledgments

An American Council of Learned Societies Fellowship for Recent Recipients of the Ph.D. (1983) allowed me nine months of uninterrupted work on the book. The University of Houston's internal grant programs awarded me a Research Initiation Grant (1981) and a Limited Grant-in-Aid (1986), and the University's Department of English and College of Humanities and Fine Arts provided course reductions and research assistantships to aid completion of the manuscript.

I thank Johns Hopkins University Press for permission to reproduce in Chapter 4, below, parts of my article, "The Festive Form of the *Canterbury Tales*," which first appeared in *English Literary History* 52 (1985): 531-74.

Too briefly acknowledged:

—Alfred David and Linda Dégh, whose teaching and writings gave me the core of this book, and who offered continual advice and support during the five years required for its completion.

—Mary Ellen Brown, Barbara A. Hanawalt, and W. Edson Richmond, who carefully considered the earliest versions.

—Larry Benson, Erika Brady, David Buchan, Elissa Henken, Tom McGowan, Ann McMillan, Ben McRee, Bill Miller, Wolfgang Mieder, Lee W. Patterson, Lois Roney, and Lorraine Stock, each of whom read and criticized a manuscript chapter or an article bearing on the content of this book.

—John McNamara, who read the final draft, offering invaluable advice on methodology, medieval rhetorical theory, and social history.

—Sara Booth and Tracy Daugherty, who artfully edited the manuscript.

—Barry Jean Ancelet, Robert Bouthillier, Vivian Labrie, and Luc Lacourcière, who led me to modern folklore analogues of Chaucer's tales.

—storytellers Ben Guiney, Willy Robichaud, and Henri Sonier, who shared with me their narrative art.

—Paul Alessi and Joanne Harrison, who gave aid in the translation of the *Descriptio Norfolciensium*.

—Joan Catapano, who provided great support throughout the editorial process.

—My emotional editors—Caroline and Barry Ancelet, Sara Booth, Dana Everts, Harry Gammerdinger, Katherine Guild, Luz Maria Lopez, John McNamara, Cynthia Santos, Lorraine Wright, and Robert and Constance and Kristin and Alison Lindahl—who kept reminding me that the book was worth taking seriously, but not so seriously as to entail blindness, heart disease, and premature senility as essential ingredients in its creation.

The happiest aspect of this book is that I feel I can count each of these remarkable teachers as a friend.

ONE

Chaucer the Storyteller

Chaucer the storyteller: the phrase evokes two images. The first, like an accidental double exposure, mixes unlike worlds. Here, one of the Middle Ages' most sophisticated artists—nurtured at noble courts, trained in diplomacy, learned in Latin, French, and Italian poetic traditions—trades tales with a company composed largely of socially marginal men: a warty miller, a surly summoner, a drunken cook. In their speech and actions these pilgrims represent a way of life deemed very nearly inhuman by the fourteenth-century aristocrats who, we presume, formed the contemporary audience of the *Canterbury Tales*. Yet Chaucer retells the churls' tales with indecorous relish. And their lower-class behavior is rendered so vividly that modern readers may easily assume Chaucer knew such storytellers—and spent as much time with them as with the nobles who taught him the arts of refinement.

The second image, though unified, is equally ironic. In this romantic tableau, Chaucer—whose works have been silently read, studied, and represented by five centuries of critics—stands engaged in an oral performance. By turns he lectures and diverts his *gentil* audience. Sitting before him are the kings, princes, and ladies that are all better known today because they lived when he did. This scene is orthodox in the way it depicts Chaucer's relation to the cultural history we've learned largely through him, but striking in the sense that he *speaks* the lines so few today move their lips in reading. Our reactions to his art have been deeply influenced by the physical phenomena that attend a silent reading. We sit over his work, occasionally to "rise from its perusal" impressed by "the forcible style which brings action before the reader's eye."[1] We envisage Chaucer surrounded not by listeners, but by books—for thus have we surrounded him in our time.

The two pictures of Chaucer the storyteller disturb and fascinate the modern critic. Both have been objects of controversy for more than a century, and both are now in disfavor. Presumably, we cannot explore the implications of either image, because we know so little about medieval oral artistry. Yet even less is known about silent reading in those times, and this has not stopped us from compiling a massive body of criticism (now averaging over two hundred fifty books and articles a year), almost all of it based on the professed or implicit assumption that Chaucer's poetry was inspired by the silent reading of earlier authors and crafted to be read in silence.

If anyone has something to say about the nature of late medieval oral performance, it is Chaucer. He and his contemporaries have left behind hundreds of visual and poetic hints of his involvement in such entertainments. His friends and fifteenth-century followers portrayed him as a speaker, delivering

> vnto mannys heeryng
> Not only the worde
> But verely the thynge[2]

he described; he was the man

> That made first to distille and reyne
> The golde dew droppis of speeche and eloquence
> In-to ure tounge. . . .[3]

Artists saw him similarly. A strikingly lifelike, if highly stylized, illumination from the Corpus Christi manuscript shows Chaucer performing before a courtly audience.[4] The Lansdowne manuscript depicts him standing, open book in outstretched hands, apparently poised to read aloud to an audience not included in the illustration.[5] In his writings are dozens of passages addressing now departed listeners: "But *in this hous* if any fals lovere be" . . . "*herkneth* with a good entencioun" . . . "*ye* may . . . sorwes *here*."[6] Both *The Parliament of Fowls* and "Complaint of Mars" have been connected to historically documented ritual entertainments during which poetry was orally presented.[7] In *Troilus and Criseyde,* a young lady reads a romance aloud to a small group of noble women; in less elevated surroundings, the clerk Jankin reads from moral tracts to humiliate his wife Alisoun of Bath.[8] Perhaps the most engaging evidence is *The Canterbury Tales:* the most celebrated storytelling event in world literature testifies to Chaucer's fascination with verbal art.

This is an impressively varied amount of evidence—more impressive and varied than the occasional Chaucerian interjection inviting the reader to "turne over the leef" or follow "as I write."[9] Yet these and all other arguments for Chaucer's "orality" have been challenged repeatedly. The portraits of the poet in performance were made after his death and drew upon certain iconographic conventions bearing no necessary relationship to Chaucer's role as entertainer.[10] The words to his "listeners" may be based on a similar convention: the literary fiction that listeners are present.[11] And the *Canterbury Tales* itself may be pure fiction, one of a host of literary frame tales conceived in the study and divorced from the reality of medieval folk narrative.

Nevertheless, I believe that new critical approaches will restore, even as they deromanticize, the two old portraits of Chaucer the storyteller. The poet himself does not state outright the extent to which he was influenced by storytelling. In his time, such influences were too pervasive and obvious to require explanation. Fortunately, however, there is sufficient information from other sources to supplement what Chaucer does say and to reveal something substantial about the nature of oral artistry in his time. This study begins with the assumption that such varied and often fragmentary sources can be combined to explore Chaucer's debt to the forms and techniques of folk performance.

I will examine the *Canterbury Tales* as a folkloric document in two senses: first, as a realistic depiction of storytelling in the Middle Ages; second, as a poem which—whether or not it was read aloud—was strongly influenced by certain rules of folk oral delivery. Such knowledge should help us to both reassess Chaucer's literary achievements and judge his acuity as storyteller and observer of storytellers. It will also improve our understanding of medieval folk tradition.

A definitive study of Chaucer the storyteller would demand skills as varied and well-coordinated as those combined in building Canterbury Cathedral. It would require that various disciplines be meshed to reconstruct the social matrix of his poetry. An ultimate synthesis may be unattainable for twentieth-century scholars, but in this study I draw upon three fields essential to a sound beginning: literary criticism, social history, and folklore.

The principal literary approach I pursue might best be termed "informed new criticism"—a way of looking at Chaucer that can be traced back at least as far as George L. Kittredge, and whose more recent practitioners include E. Talbot Donaldson and Alfred David.[12] These men share the assumption that—despite D. W. Robertson's claim to the contrary[13]—medieval people were not essentially different from ourselves. Like David and Donaldson, I believe that the distance between Chaucer's time and ours is not so great as to prevent us from drawing upon our own emotions and motivations to discover those of Chaucer and his characters. Further (and here I take another position which has lately grown unfashionable), I believe that no attempt to distill the "meaning" of the *Canterbury Tales* can safely exclude the behavior of the individual pilgrims or their interaction as a group. Recent efforts to view Chaucer's creation as a product of more abstract principles have missed the core of the poem—that quality which sets it most dramatically apart from other medieval works. Much of my reading of the *Tales,* then, is based on the proposition that Chaucer is presenting *credible* actions and characters, that a great deal of observation underlies his art.

My "new critical" approach, however, carries this qualification: though I rely upon the use of subjective perceptions in judging the *motivations* of Chaucer and his fictional characters, I also stress the fact that the social milieu in which the poet and his characters lived created a set of *possibilities for action* markedly different from those available to us now. Many past readers of Chaucer assessed his characters principally according to "timeless universals of human nature" and ignored the verbal and behavioral cues that conveyed more specific meanings to the medieval audience. But no matter how much Chaucer and his pilgrims resemble us, they had to work within their unique social framework, a context that must figure largely in any solid reading of their words and deeds.

Recently developed approaches to social history will help reconstruct the societal constraints which channel the motivations and shape the speech of Chaucer and his pilgrims. I rely on a broad range of background materials representing several stages in the development of historiography. All this information has been available to Chaucerians for some time, but the uses to which I put it justify its re-examination. Most of my sources—catalogs of festive performances, Gild Hall records, court cases, courtesy books—are old indeed. The compilations of T. H. Riley and Frederick Furnivall date from the nineteenth century; in the early decades of the twentieth century, G. G. Coulton and Charles Pendrill drew upon those works to create *potpourris* of portraits illustrating everyday life in medieval London.[14] But my interpretive methods derive from a more recent approach first advanced by such historians as M. M. Postan and George Homans and further developed by J. A. Raftis and Barbara Hanawalt.[15] Their studies have affirmed that the systematic use and linkage of records can yield a more representative and ultimately more vivid view of medieval life than that provided by a collection of dramatic but haphazardly assembled vignettes. This precept, now considered a truism by historians, has yet to influence Chaucerians, who continue to use the *potpourri* approach to provide historical background.[16]

The central facet of my study, however, is folklore, a field indispensable to any fruitful examination of Chaucer the storyteller. Many respected folklorists have contributed to Chaucer scholarship: Francis J. Child, G. L. Kittredge, W. M. Hart, Archer Taylor, Stith Thompson, B. J. Whiting, Margaret Schlauch, Bertrand Bronson, and Francis Lee Utley, to list a few of the more prominent names. Presumably their efforts would have secured an important place for folklore in Chaucer studies; however, such has not been the case. Recently, Derek Brewer and others have lamented that Chaucer's debt to folk tradition is "a largely unexplored subject."[17] I

agree with Brewer, and would add that modern Chaucerians have ne-
glected folklore as much because of as in spite of the brilliant work of the
early literary folklorists. Taylor, Thompson, and Utley shared a certain
confining vision of folklore, a view—now questioned by folklorists and
medievalists alike—that has limited our understanding of the role of folklore in the late Middle Ages.

First, to the scholar of the nineteenth and early twentieth centuries,
folklore was an *item*, most often an artistic genre. The list compiled by
Archer Taylor is broadly representative: "Folklore consists of . . . tales of
various kinds . . . ballads, lyric folk song, children's songs, charms, proverbs, and riddles." The proper work of the folklorist, states Taylor, is "the
collection, classification and interpretation of these traditional materials."[18]
For Taylor and his colleagues, "classification and interpretation" consisted
primarily of comparing *plot outlines*.

Yet this approach cannot successfully distinguish medieval folklore from
medieval literature. According to Taylor's methods, most of the *Canterbury
Tales* would be classified as folklore, because the bare plots of the tales told
by the Man of Law (AT 706), Miller (AT 1361), Merchant (AT 1423),* and
a dozen other pilgrims possess hundreds of close oral analogues.[19] In the
Middle Ages the concept of authority was compelling on an artistic as well
as a theological level: it was not the writer's purpose to change the shape of
his story. Artistic prowess was measured by the skill with which the narrator
retold his tale, and, occasionally, by the interpretive values he assigned it.
Such criteria as "folk" styles and values have not been applied to Chaucer's
"folktales"—though these are precisely the criteria necessary to separate
literature from folklore in the art of the Middle Ages.

If the first part of this definition fails to recognize any differences between Chaucer's work and medieval folklore, the second part denies any
similarity. Folklore, as described by earlier generations, has a second property: it is *oral*. Taylor, Thompson, and Utley agree unanimously that
folklore is "handed down by word of mouth," "from generation to generation," and preserved either "*by memory or practice* rather than written record."[20]

The criterion of oral-memorial transmission presents a staggering im-
pediment to the student of medieval folklore. Among the thousands of
available medieval texts, only a handful are *verbatim* records of speech—and
most of these are transcripts from legal proceedings, which do not by any
stretch of the imagination present ideal or natural contexts for a serious
study of verbal art.[21] Furthermore, the oral-memorial criterion cannot ac-

---

*AT refers to Antti Aarne and Stith Thompson, *The Types of the Folktale*. Folklore Fellows
Communications, no. 184 (Helsinki, 1961). The numbers following AT refer not to pages, but
to the folktale plots listed numerically in this standard classificatory index.

curately separate medieval folklore from other forms of medieval expression. The Icelandic law-speakers recited complex legal codes which they had memorized; monks in their cloisters recited the Song of Songs. Both are acts of oral transmission from memory, and both testify to the power of the medieval spoken word, but neither can be considered folklore in its strictest sense.

Finally, despite the claims of early folklorists to the contrary, no literate culture, past or present, has developed art forms that are purely oral in nature. In any society where oral art and art literature coexist, there is some degree of interdependence between the two. Albert Wesselski has demonstrated that this rule applied throughout the Middle Ages[22]—and it has continued to hold. In sixteenth- and seventeenth-century Germany, priests would write down the oral tales of their parishioners, then shape them into entertaining *exempla* and asides to be embedded in their sermons. When the sermons were delivered, members of the congregation wrote down or memorized the plots, then reshaped them into anecdotes for oral presentation outside religious contexts. Priest and peasant shared in a cycle of transmission that blended orality and literacy.[23] This interdependent process is still at work in contemporary peasant communities, where narrators sometimes tell tales from memory and sometimes read them aloud from books.

By the same token, the medieval literary world cannot be adequately assessed by those who conceive of literature only as an optical pastime, confined to silent reading of the printed page. Oral and *aural* transmission (the term used to designate the act of reading aloud from written sources) predominated. In the early Middle Ages, silent reading was considered extremely strange, as evidenced by St. Augustine's amazement at St. Ambrose, who read while his "heart and tongue remained silent."[24] By the fourteenth century, silent reading had no doubt grown more common, but aural entertainment continued to flourish, in part because probably no more than half of Chaucer's day-to-day associates were comfortably literate.[25] Even the ability to read and write does not, of course, preclude a *preference* for aural entertainment.[26] In a social environment where the consummately literate Jean Froissart read a romance aloud to a noble—and largely literate—audience, and where the King of England read aloud to Froissart, the prevalence of aural entertainment cannot be overestimated. That similar performances sometimes took place without the aid of texts is certain. Froissart himself described sessions in which nobles told him legends and tales, accounts later incorporated in his *Chroniques*.[27]

The relationship between written and oral entertainment in the European Middle Ages was probably similar to that which obtains today among societies with comparable literacy rates. In Turkey, written and oral versions of the same romances circulate in the same area; in Yugoslavia, written and oral versions of the same epic have been created by the same composer.[28] In sixteenth-century Britain, states *The Complaynt of Scotlande,* shepherds told the *Canterbury Tales* aloud: they did not read them, nor is it likely that they memorized them; they retold the tales.[29] Two centuries earlier, the same situation applied, even among the highest levels of society. Chaucer probably got at least some of his tales from oral sources,[30] and it is equally likely that he and others sometimes repeated his stories in oral prose form.

Thus, neither of the criteria—"oral" or "item"—set forth by earlier folklorists can help explain Chaucer's folkloric relationships. Utley worked long to develop a working definition of folklore for literary studies, but the result—"literature orally transmitted"—is simply an oxymoron combining the two elements just discussed and serving no useful function for the medievalist.[31] A more accurate view of medieval folklore must be presented before Chaucer's debt to this tradition can be weighed. The difficulties encountered by folklorists in defining their field have not diminished since Utley's time, and no new attempt at definition is likely to find universal approval. Nevertheless, to avoid some of my predecessors' problems, I here undertake a general description of medieval folklore, which can best be understood through its points of contrast with a better-documented system of cultural expression.

Throughout the Middle Ages, there were two basic means of communication: the elite and the folk. Elite culture was formal and institutionalized, and—whether passed on by means of the oral or the written word—based on a method of rigorous schooling developed over centuries through manuscript traditions reaching back to the ancient past. Nearly all medieval writers—whether of legal, edificatory, or entertainment literature—were trained according to these elite traditions; therefore, nearly all surviving information on medieval culture reflects the elite view to a greater or lesser extent.

Elite culture is marked by impersonal standardization. For five hundred years, for example, every student who received the Doctor of Philosophy degree from a medieval European university was required to write a commentary on the *Sententiae* of Peter Lombard. Through such standardized methods, elite culture creates an impersonal "community" larger and less flexible than one based on face-to-face interaction. Generations of readers who had never met Peter Lombard learned from him and were in turn trained to teach his work to other strangers, in schools or through the medium of writing. This exercise had no necessary relationship to the everyday community in which it was practiced: monks and clerks in Spain, Italy, and Ireland were similarly schooled in Latin (a language foreign to most of the inhabitants of their regions) and required to master academic and religious codes whose rules greatly differed from the prevailing norms of surrounding cities and towns. Similarly, the rhetorical techniques essential to the composition of elite poetry and prose constituted one third of the *trivium,* the core curriculum of the elementary schools. Orators also used these time-honored methods, and even the most creative poetic treatises, such as Vinsauf's *Poetria Nova,* repeated with little variation the classifications in use since Cicero's time. To a broadly educated Englishman like Geoffrey Chaucer, the differences between elite rhetoric and everyday speech were startlingly great. The former had been developed by a massive scholarly community numbering far more dead than living representatives, a widespread community encompassing many more countries than Chaucer would ever see.

Even the lightest entertainment literature was marked by similar forms and rules. The "international court culture" centered in France dominated noble entertainment in the late Middle Ages. Works created to amuse this refined audience were more flexible than the edifying treatises written in more austere surroundings, but they too possessed a certain impersonality. Except in a few particulars, the courtly vernacular romances of thirteenth-century France, England, and Germany can be distinguished only by the language in which they were written. The verse forms of the late Middle Ages—*ballade, rondeau, virelai*—and the very thoughts and images they presented were the common property of noble courts throughout Europe. Thus, elite culture does not easily adapt to the community in which it is practiced, but requires instead that the community adapt to it.

Folk culture, on the other hand, is nonstandardized and centered outside the boundaries of institutionalized learning. Whether or not writing is involved in its transmission, folklore is passed on through face-to-face communication; its existence requires the presence and assent of a concrete community. As a result, the "rules" of folk culture are less rigid and more often determined by popular consensus than are those of elite culture. To explain its codes of behavior, a folk community invokes no written laws, but instead cites the actions of its most admired members. To convey the community's essential values, a folk moralist does not draw upon classical sources and elaborate ethical tracts, but rather relies on proverbs and tales. To learn various concepts of eloquence, the folk artist does not search the minds of long-dead authors whose speech is preserved in books, but witnesses his neighbors' repartee: he can judge firsthand which phrases, styles, and strategies are most effective in his own community.

In folk—as opposed to elite—artistry, teacher and student, entertainer and audience, stand in close physical proximity. And the listeners exert enormous influence on the speaker's message. Once begun, an oral story will not be finished unless it meets the approval of those present.[32] The community has an important shaping effect on the content and style of oral literature, an effect which is at once more immediate and more enduring than that wrought by a widely-scattered group of silent readers upon a written work. Members of a silent audience may have nothing in common other than the fact that all have read the same book. An oral tale, however, cannot survive unless a majority of its listeners decides to hear it again and again. Thus, though folklore may not be governed by the elite rulings of law or government, it is unofficially regulated by the prevailing tastes and attitudes of its audience. Oral folklore absorbs and carries on the *standards of its community*, becoming the shared product of teller and hearer.[33]

This community aspect of folklore is so fundamental to human activity that it occurs and recurs everywhere. Folklore is not confined to small, homogeneous groups of illiterate villagers, isolated from external social influences; indeed, such communities were extremely rare, even during the English Middle Ages.[34] An extended village family or urban gild, any London neighborhood, a manorial or seigneurial estate, the royal court itself—all had the essential attributes of the folk community, and all regularly participated in folkloric events. Such diversions as May games and Christmas mummings found their way into all these settings, though certain aspects of the performances varied, as folklore always does, with the needs and concerns of each community. The 130 richly costumed mummers who paraded before Richard II in 1377—playing dice with the king and presenting gifts to his court—may seem quite unlike the small companies of straw-hatted guisers that went from door to door on winter nights through village streets to gamble, mount plays, and exchange gifts and food. Yet both were folkloric entertainments, performing similar functions in their respective settings. In addition to providing obvious diversions, mummings afforded solace for the winter nights (we find continually that the largest and wildest folk pastimes took place during the darkest months, when people were particularly susceptible to depression). In all their contexts, mummings also served to unite the community and to reassert the interdependence of its members, whose varied tasks often separated them at other times of the year. Finally, through the gifts distributed at all versions of this festival, mummers underscored the Christian values of sharing and charity important even in modern celebrations of Christmas. Whether played out in rural communities or in the Kenyton palace where Richard received his mummers, these were *earnest games,* acts of play in which serious social messages were embedded.[35]

Folklore, then, is more than an item or a means of transmission: it is a community-based process, embodying the values and beliefs of that small closely-knit group, and generating works of art that reflect them. It is the emphasis on community which distinguishes recent folklore scholarship from the earlier models that have dominated medieval studies.[36] This re-evaluation grants folklore a major role in every human life—a role so vast, one may argue, that it would be unnecessarily difficult, even pointless, to attempt to isolate folklore and analyze it. Indeed, both elite and folk cultural processes have been essential categories of Western culture from its historically documented beginnings. They blend together in a complementary way.

But even when folk and elite culture are so closely entwined, it is important at least to *attempt* to isolate them, because the two represent fundamentally different perspectives on the world. The tension between these forces can be likened to the debate concerning Experience and Authority which engaged Chaucer and his contemporaries. The superorganic *authority of elite culture* comes from outside the boundaries of one's community, from great distances of space and time. (Indeed, authority derives its sanction from space and time, generally following the precept, "the older and more distant the source, the more venerable.") The authoritarian rules of law, science, and poetry are passed down in set form by formally trained specialists. We are asked to accept these rules without question, whether or not they accord with our experience. Only a few of us are incorporated into the elite structure which guards such codes, and fewer still will be able to change them.

The *community experience* of folk culture, on the other hand, is based almost wholly on what one sees and does. Everything, even the most distant past, takes on the shape of the palpable present. A man may tell a thousand-year-old tale, but its style, form, and content are determined by a situational esthetic; the tale must reflect the exact circumstances in which it is told. The "rules" of such a community, though unwritten, are constantly apparent in the behavior of its members.

Because folk culture relies directly on experience, it is the more pragmatic of the two expressions—and the one more often relied upon in situations of social danger. The critical world tends to associate folklore only with trite and innocent pastimes: Mother Goose, jump rope rhymes, silly stories of all sorts. If folklore were to be assigned to one or the other of Chaucer's favorite pair of categories—*ernest* and *game*—nearly every twentieth-century reader would classify it exclusively as *game*. Yet, as the *Canterbury Tales* reveals, it is remarkable how often games are found to contain earnest matter. The Host warns that one should never make earnest of game, but he knows, and we observe, that one can always *conceal* earnest within a game. The folkloric patterns I shall discuss are the most earnest conceivable games, for the pilgrims use these traditional strategies to express their most negative and heretical thoughts—thoughts which, if given any other form, would invite frightening consequences. Authority, the voice of elite culture, speaks for the powerful and helps them preserve their powers; experience, the folk mode, teaches the powerless how to survive.

Of course, experience can create its own authority, as Alisoun of Bath well knew. And, as a public official, Chaucer knew that any long-existing authority will create its own experience. But neither Chaucer nor his characters doubted the importance of the fundamental difference between the two. Similarly, Chaucer was aware of the dramatic difference between an oral storytelling session and the rhetorical rules taught in school. I contend that this difference was not only obvious but important to Chaucer, and that he translated his awareness of it into poetry.

In general, then, Chaucer's poetry has three sources: the authority of elite literary convention, the experience of folk artistic convention, and the creator's idiosyncratic vision, which is never wholly governed by such traditions. Great art, whether elite or folk, must impart a great measure of that third quality, but it must also observe at least some of the literary or folk conventions as common frames of reference; otherwise, it will fail to reach an understanding audience. The artist's background, inclination, and audience determine the proportion of folk and elite traditions in a given work. There are individuals who tend to emphasize exclusively one or the other of these two traditions. Milton, for example, was inclined almost wholly toward elite culture, which he knew exceptionally well in its ancient, medieval, and Renaissance forms. Scriptural sources, classical poets, philosophers, natural scientists, and exemplum writers furnished most of his subject matter and were the major influences on his style. Private reading and a Cambridge education constituted the generating matrix of his poetry. Robert Burns, on the other hand, relied primarily on a folk tradition, incorporating traditional Scottish customs, dialects, and verse forms into his work. Early in his career, Burns tried to adapt elite English verse styles and forms, but these ultimately had little influence on his best and most representative productions.

As for Chaucer's background and inclinations: the elite sources of his art have been painstakingly examined and re-examined. His probable schooling has been reconstructed.[37] His debt to those teachers of elite poetry, the rhetoricians, has been analyzed, although authorities are divided as to how much he relied upon or respected their teachings.[38] All his likely extant written sources, both artistic and educational, have been sifted and weighed. But even after the enormous number of lines, ideas, and stylistic traits derived directly from elite sources are subtracted from his work, an impressive body of art remains.

According to scholarly convention, the remainder—which includes most of the frame and links of the *Canterbury Tales*—is the product of Chaucer's unique genius.[39] Yet evidence suggests that Chaucer's rich imagination was further enriched by the observation and imitation of the folk culture of his time. Consider as an example the description of the Miller's talent for smashing doors with his head—a practice which is certainly not the product of medieval elite culture. Scholars have shown that this rough form of folk entertainment has a history extending from the Middle Ages into the nineteenth century.[40] The sport appears in earlier literature only in *Havelok,* a popular romance which Chaucer almost certainly did not read. Consider as well the folk speech of the Reeve. Chaucer gives Oswald some characteristics of Norfolk speech, traces of a dialect whose reflexes can still be heard in Norfolk today.[41]

There is, then, no doubt that Chaucer's unique genius drew upon folk cultural pastimes. It would be absurd to assume the opposite, that he based his description of the Miller on a silent reading of *Havelok.* All he had to do was watch and listen to find his models. Similarly, there was no extant grammatical treatise on Norfolk speech for Chaucer to consult. The poet, whose family came from a similar dialectical region, got his information firsthand, from the mouths of friends and acquaintances.[42] These close correspondences between Chaucer's work and day-to-day English life demonstrate that both Chaucer and his audience had more than a bookish knowledge of the folklore of their contemporaries, even those from lower social strata.

Through the same process of observation that taught him the customs of his countrymen, Chaucer was also exposed to their verbal arts, the style and content of their performances. It would be a mistake not to consider at least the possibility that the oral artistry of the Canterbury pilgrims may also have some folkloric relationships. Thus, folklore has a potential role not only in helping us determine the specific sources of certain details in the *Canterbury Tales,* but also in identifying sources for aspects of Chaucer's style hitherto presumed unique simply because they were without *literary* precedent in his time. If we allow ourselves to speculate on how oral folk culture may have influenced him, a number of possibilities come to mind. Many of these will always be beyond proof; some may be proven incorrect; few can be addressed at length in this book. But a survey suggests how folklore may be used in the interpretation of many mysteries surrounding Chaucer's work.

On the level of poetic diction, for example, many of Chaucer's contributions to poetry are not bookish, but conversational; they reflect the style and temperament of verbal art. Chaucer's status as the first English court poet to write exclusively in English,[43] his introduction to written English of hundreds of native oral colloquialisms[44]—these attest to his exceptionally well-tuned ear and hint at a connection with an oral, folkloric community distinctly different from the elite society.

Chaucer's imagery and narrative style present devices seldom if ever found among the learned literary traditions upon which he is presumed to have relied. His extensive use of the folk (as opposed to the literary) proverb tradition is unique among the authors of his time.[45] His particular uses of irony, assumed by some to constitute his greatest poetic achievement, have few literary antecedents but a great many oral parallels. His *fabliaux* plots are far removed from written sources but share many traits with oral narrative jokes. His style of characterization is informed by a thorough knowledge of how members of small communities interact. These examples—general as they are—give us further reason to ask if folkloric explanations may be at least as apt as previously offered elite solutions.

In Chaucer's themes lie further hints of folk cultural influence. Relativism, his most impressive addition to literary perspective, has strong folkloric affinities. His wide-ranging narrative voice animates lower-class characters, characters his contemporaries deemed unworthy of quotation, and bestows an evenhanded judgment on people of unequal birth and talents. Just as (the Manciple reminds us) a countess can be laid as low as a peasant girl, a miller (or, at least, Chaucer's Miller) can make a tale to match a knight's. The poet's great predecessors—Dante, Chrétien, Jean de Meun—presented absolute systems of values. Dante created an orderly universe, and in so doing had his enemies condemned to hell. Each of the two authors of the *Roman de la Rose* created a unified view of the world, a view which all the disparate characters merely serve to reinforce. Chaucer, however, relied on the relative and contextualized framework of face-to-face, community confrontation to allow us to judge—as *he* never does, explicitly—the merits of his characters. This perspective, new to literature but traditional in verbal art, sets the social hierarchy on its head: an ill-bred summoner bests a "worthy" friar, a cook talks back to a taverner, a manciple channels dangerous thoughts into a socially commendable tale which simultaneously describes and deplores the limitations of speech that his creator knew firsthand.

Of all Chaucer's works, the *Canterbury Tales* presents the best opportunity for the examination of such stylistic questions. The poem sets forth a whole series of "oral texts," together with their contexts; it describes both the items of folklore and the folk community which created them. In elite literature, success is measured in terms of the author's ability to communicate in a manner understandable outside the situation in which his work was first produced; therefore, literature must *incorporate* some sort of context. But in folk artistry, much of the context lies well beyond the story itself: the meaning of a folktale is often inseparable from the situation in which it is presented. The Middle Ages have passed down only a few frame tales in which the storyteller and his situation are presented together, and the *Canterbury Tales* is the most vivid of them. Much more than presenting a few details from the folkloric world—a door-butting Miller, a thick-accented Reeve—Chaucer presents an extended performance incorporating several levels of society at play. If the *Tales* can be shown to be not only a lifelike, but a realistic description of storytelling, there is much it can teach about the nature of medieval folk artistry.

The sense of realism I pursue here is not literal. I do not intend, as Manly did, to show that the portraits of the pilgrims are modeled after actual people, nor do I claim that the *Canterbury Tales* is a factual account of an actual pilgrimage.[46] But I do intend to show that the interactions and stories of the pilgrims were shaped by the author's awareness of the traditional social roles and verbal rules of medieval oral performances. This sense of verisimilitude, once identified and interpreted, can help to answer some questions concerning Chaucer's style, meaning, and intent.

In the chapters that follow, I examine the three communities of the *Canterbury Tales*. The world of the *gentils*—to which belong the Knight, the Prioress, Chaucer the Pilgrim, and Chaucer the man—owes its allegiance to the elite, authoritarian culture; as will be shown, however, even the *gentils* have their unofficial community standards for deportment and play. The churls' domain—peopled by such men as the Miller, Reeve, and Manciple—will receive far greater attention, because the poet explores this lower realm to a far greater extent than do any of his contemporaries, affording us a unique view of an artistry otherwise almost lost to us. Finally, there is the mixed world of pilgrimage, a festive framework in which the two communities, often uneasily, interact. In Part One, I measure Chaucer's cast against the social realities of fourteenth-century England, to show how the *Tales* often parallels, and sometimes fully duplicates, contemporary social structures: the various strata, their interactions, their games.

In Part Two, I concentrate on the language of the pilgrims, from their briefest speech acts to the extended rhetorical strategies of their tales. Here the vastly different dialects of *gentil* and churl are shown to clash, rendering the *Tales* a stylistic war representing the broader social conflicts of the late fourteenth century. In my final chapter, I return to Chaucer himself to show that, in addresses to his elite audience, he uses many of the same techniques with which his lower-class creatures address their betters. In the end, the *Tales* and Chaucer's career both emerge as lessons in survival, models of diction for those who cannot, for safety's sake, openly state their minds.

Such a demonstration requires a two-part methodology. Wherever possible, I employ reliable and exactly contemporary English and northern French sources. When parallels from medieval lore are scant or absent—a rather common situation—I draw upon modern folklore fieldwork for supplementary material. In citing examples so far removed in time and space from the focus of inquiry, I run a certain risk. But, as I subscribe to the belief that people in different times and places will act similarly *only under similar social conditions,* I cite only those modern parallels which arise from community situations similar in form and function to those of Chaucer and his pilgrims. In such under-documented areas, I will sometimes turn to Chaucer himself for the final judgment on the patterns of medieval folk performance. It may seem ill-advised to place the work of an ethnographer in the hands of a poet. But in cases where Chaucer's descriptions of setting, cast, and specific situation are verifiably realistic—and there remain but one or two pieces missing from the puzzle—the poet warrants such trust. To paraphrase H. Marshall Leicester, Chaucer's fiction may explain, as well as be explained by, the facts of fourteenth-century social history.[47]

When Chaucer speaks and all other sources are silent, my arguments are beyond proof, and I can only hope to persuade the reader that the points presented here are worthy of consideration, that these new approaches to Chaucer may reveal something, if not enough, of his knowledge and mastery of the second great tradition within which he worked: the folk culture of his time.

PART ONE

The Shapes of Play and Society

TWO

Frames around the Frame

The Community of Players

My inquiry begins where the poem does, with a close consideration of its cast. The General Prologue of the *Canterbury Tales* is essentially a group portrait of the performers, a catalog of *dramatis personae* unequaled in detail by any in preceding literature. Chaucer here presents a temporary community, a diverse group that has been interpreted even more diversely by four centuries of readers. To literalists such as John M. Manly, these are faithful sketches of Chaucer's flesh-and-blood contemporaries.[1] To allegorists such as Frederick Tupper, the pilgrims have no human models, but are meant to personify such abstract qualities as the Seven Deadly Sins.[2] To folklorists, however, the cast raises possibilities that fall between the two interpretive extremes. The General Prologue supplies in careful detail a context that allows us to judge the social factors underlying the performances to follow.

Oral art has a social dimension extending beyond the momentary roles of its participants. Traditional performances reflect the broader backgrounds of the players. A taletelling session is in many ways an act of community self-definition, underscoring group values, aspirations, and apprehensions. Unless the oral artist is addressing an audience he recognizes as a community, *his* community, there is little likelihood that a performance will take place at all. Unless his audience recognizes the teller, in one way or another, as *their* representative, there is little chance they will listen to his tale.[3] Reading the Prologue against the facts of fourteenth-century social history, I find that *Chaucer's cast is essentially a realistic group, a group that the poet's listeners could easily have imagined convening for the joint purposes of pilgrimage and play.* My view is shaded slightly toward the literal, but carries an important qualification: Chaucer's concern with social realism (rather than literalism) invites us to read his poem not in terms of precise events and persons, but in conjunction with social patterns representative of his age. *The General Prologue challenges the traditional theory of society,* presenting in its place a description of an important new element of public power in the poet's time.

This new group, with its concerns and antagonisms, supplies a backdrop for the shape of the pilgrims' narrative conflict.

The common judgment is that there is simply not enough historical evidence to support a case for the realism of Chaucer's cast. Pilgrimage records are too sparse to confirm either the prevalent view or my own. But I hope to turn our ignorance to my advantage: here I argue principally by analogy, because my purpose is to identify the cast not simply with the institution of pilgrimage, but more generally with a distinct segment of English society emergent in the fourteenth century. The riders who leave the Tabard Inn represent a class defined most clearly in the membership roles of the late medieval parish gild. The gild and the pilgrims share the same social structure and functions.

Before turning to the gilds, I must examine the pilgrims. Though centuries of readers, following Dryden, have seen in the cast a picture of the "Whole *English* nation," we no longer find such breadth reflected in the poem.[4] It is unlikely, for instance, that any of the pilgrims represents the lower ranks of the peasantry. The Plowman, the only possible candidate for this title, may be a freeman. Furthermore, the poet excludes the highest reaches of society: royalty and greater nobility have no role in his poem. From the Knight—the most socially exalted of the pilgrims—to the lowly Plowman, there is clearly a social spread, but it is one of limited range.

Many have interpreted Chaucer's cast in terms of the traditional concept of the three estates, which simply divided the medieval world into *Miles* (Chivalry), *Clerus* (Clergy), and *Cultor* (Peasantry).[5] If Chaucer were indeed working from this model, we might expect that the three parts would be clearly delineated and evenly represented in his poem. But it is more likely that the poet was challenging, rather than following, the three-estate paradigm; his pilgrims, like the population of London in his time, generally defy the standard classification. Only the clergy is represented proportionately, by eleven members: Prioress, Second Nun, three nun's priests, Monk, Friar, Clerk, Parson, Summoner, and Pardoner. Among the twenty-two remaining pilgrims, only two (Knight and Squire) embody the estate of chivalry, and one (Plowman) the *Cultor*. Fully two thirds of the pilgrims fall outside the schema as interpreted in its strictest sense.[6]

In reality, the mixed assemblage that leaves the Tabard Inn under the guidance of the Host consists almost wholly of one class—a group which, today, we would identify with the middle class. Chaucer expands somewhat the boundaries of this group by setting the Knight at the top of his social ladder and adding the Plowman at the bottom. And certainly every gradation of this diverse middle world is represented. The pilgrims' range of status is so great that they can with justification be divided into two general categories: *gentils* and churls. Yet in Chaucer's day this assembly represented a group unclassified in the estates system—indeed, a group that was to render that system utterly archaic.

Although one of the fourteenth-century records I will examine here speaks of a "class of middle [or average] people" (*de statu mediocrum virorum*), there was no commonly used medieval term cognate with our "middle class."[7] Medieval people continued to observe, in speech if not in practice, the tripartite division of society into *Miles, Clerus,* and *Cultor*. But the classic pattern no longer served, especially in the urban environment from which Chaucer and most of his pilgrims came. As the Middle Ages drew to a close, it became customary to enlarge the *Cultor* category to include all those who did not fit into the first two. Merchants, shipmen, and lawyers could be roughly termed "laborers," or "servants of society," so they were classed with the peasants. This solution was clearly reductionist, because it did not recognize the complexities of Chaucer's time, when commoners could buy noble titles, villeins could buy their freedom, the clergy was intimately involved in worldly affairs, and the peasants were often in open revolt against their presumed protectors, the *Miles*. The great majority of Chaucer's *Cultor* class possessed far more wealth and power than any cultivator could hope to attain; indeed, some members of this fictional third world (the Man of Law and Merchant, for example) approached the power, if not the prestige, of the *Miles*. With society in such a state of flux, class boundaries were often difficult to perceive.

Chaucer was acutely aware of this confusion. His pilgrim persona pleads to his audience, "forgive me if I have not presented my players according to their status" ("in hir degree"; 1.744).[8] Now, as I shuffle the poet's list somewhat, I ask the same favor. Any brief attempt to reorder Chaucer's society according to its real values, as opposed to its professed ones, must steer between the hazards of oversimplification on the one hand and an impractical attentiveness to variables on the other. Here I take a relatively simple approach. One of the surest measures of medieval social stratification is found in the protocol lists of noble households. These charts set out the special privileges to which members of certain estates were entitled on formal occasions: who should precede whom into the hall, who should eat with whom, and so on.[9] Such lists, of course, have their imperfections. For one, they deal only in passing with the lower reaches of society. Furthermore, they indulge the habit—common in the late Middle Ages—of according the lower clergy a nominal status disproportionate to their social power. Clergymen are often ranked above commoners who were in reality granted a greater measure of respect. Finally, the lists recognize only in the vaguest way a reality which was of the greatest importance in the late Middle Ages: a given individual was judged not only in terms of title, but also according to economic status, education, and behavior.[10] In the lists are

FIGURE 1

The Social Ranking of the Canterbury Pilgrims

Protocol Lists	Pilgrims	Class Designations
(Knight's table)		
Knight	Knight	
Unmitred Abbot	Monk	Lesser Nobility
Prior	Prioress	
	Squire	
(Squire's table)		
Sergeant of the Law	Sergeant of Law	
Merchants	Merchant	Upper Middle Class
	Chaucer*	Haute Bourgeoisie
	Host (Taverner)	Greater Misteries
Franklins	Franklin	Clerical Officials
Gentlemen	Gildsmen	
	Shipman (?)	Gentils—
Preachers of Pardon		
Preachers and Parsons	Nun's Priest	
that are *greable*	Parson (?)	
Friar (?)	Friar (?)	Middle Class
	Clerk	Lower Middle Class
	Wife of Bath (?)	Petite Bourgeoisie
	Yeoman	Lesser Misteries
	Pardoner (?)	Rural Elite
	Summoner (?)	
	Reeve	Churls
	Manciple	
	Miller	
	Canon's Yeoman	
	Cook	
	Plowman (?)	Servants

*Chaucer's standing on this list depends, of course, on the assumption that the narrative persona of the poem is identical to the real-life poet—an assumption that many contest.

injunctions granting privilege to "preachers and parsons that been *greable* [suitable]"—but it is not always easy to determine which of Chaucer's pilgrims would be "suitable" for deferential treatment.

With these qualifications in mind, I have ranked the pilgrims as they would have been ranked in a fourteenth-century household (see Figure 1). They are divided into four groups indicative of general social standing. In a noble hall, four of the pilgrims, at most, would have been given the honor of eating with the *nobility*, at a table hosted by a knight: the Knight himself, the Monk, the Prioress, and perhaps the Squire. These are the only members of Chaucer's company that could conceivably rank above the middle class, and even these represent the lowest level of the nobility. The highest-ranking pilgrim, the Knight, holds an office which stands fourteenth from the top on one medieval seating list: surely, the most exalted elements of medieval society are unrepresented in the *Tales*. If Chaucer's Monk and Prioress were nobly born, they would certainly have a status equal to or greater than the Knight's; if not, they would rank slightly below him. The title "squire" was not necessarily a designation of nobility, but Chaucer's Squire, as a knight's son, is noble without doubt.

Members of the *upper middle class* and "suitable clergy" were accorded the privilege of dining with the squire of the household. The records specifically mention, in the following order, these commons: sergeants of the law, merchants, franklins, and "yeomen of good name" (a truly baffling category, as the term "yeoman" was defined in many different ways). Among the clergy, pardoners and certain preachers and parsons are set in the same group. At this table, the Host, Gildsmen, Shipman, and Nun's Priest would join the pilgrims whose professions are precisely spelled out in the lists.[11] Chaucer the Pilgrim would find a place at the squire's table, if the fictional traveler possessed the same status that the poet did. Pardoners *should* sit here as well; in fact, in most lists they are ranked above parsons, preachers, and other representatives of the regular clergy. But Chaucer's Pardoner, so abhorrent to the fictional *gentils*, may well have been denied the honor. The Parson and Summoner would be in the same situation—both were theoretically qualified to sit with the squire, but both may have been considered unsuitable. The Parson's ascetic views, not welcome everywhere, may have denied him the privilege of the squire's table, though it is difficult to imagine this Parson dining willingly at any table where the Host and Shipman held forth. The Summoner, who cultivates the company of pimps and whores, would be unlikely to find a place where the Parson does not. Friars are not mentioned on any of the lists, and, strictly speaking, they had no place elsewhere than at the beggars' table in a noble home. But Chaucer's Huberd is known to have kept company with franklins (1.216), and his dress and manners are impeccably *gentil*. He is "lyk a maister" (1.261): his bearing implies that he, like so many friars in his time, has attained a high level of education. Therefore, I place him just above the border between *gentils* and churls.

The division between the nobility and the upper middle class is well marked on the seating lists, but the boundaries of the third category are difficult to determine. Here, the *lower middle class* represents the higher orders of the churls. The Wife of Bath's career and standing straddle the all-important boundary between *gentil* and churl. Her economic success as a

clothmaker might entitle her to a position near the bottom of the upper
middle class, but her trade (a minor mistery) and her behavior might work
to confine her among the churls.[12] Also near the top of the lower middle
class would stand Chaucer's Clerk, who could not be admitted to the
Squire's table until he completed his doctorate.[13] The Knight's Yeoman, as
"a yeoman of good name," is also among the more highly ranked churls,
and might be expected to dine with his betters on special occasions. The
Manciple, a minor institutional functionary, would be a member in good
standing of the lower middle class, as would the Reeve and the Miller, who
were numbered among the "rural elite"—powerful and relatively wealthy
representatives of the seigneurial society.[14]

The fourth and lowest category is that of the servants—those who live in
partial or total bondage. It cannot be said with certainty that any of Chaucer's pilgrims is in this lowly position, but there are three characters who
may stand on the line dividing servitude from freedom. At the very bottom
of the lower middle class is Chaucer's Cook, a poor member of a minor
trade hired to accompany the upper-middle-class tradesmen. Roger is
somewhat lower in status than the Miller and Reeve, yet he is not quite a
servant. The Canon's Yeoman, the personal servant of a religious officer,
has less freedom even than the Cook; yet the Yeoman's status would be
elevated by that of his master and make him the "better" man. The most
likely candidate for servitude is the Plowman, who—whether freeman or
bondsman—must exchange his labor for the right to farm his property.
Although such services, in the form of *benework,* were sometimes rendered
by even the wealthiest workers of the manor, most of those who performed
labor for rent were the villeins at the bottom of the social heap.[15]

The composite result of this classification shows that no more than five of
the pilgrims would fit into categories outside the stratum I identify as the
middle class. The middle world is almost equally divided into two subgroups, which represent the *gentils* and churls among the free and less-
than-noble medieval population.

Why, and under what conditions, would such a group convene? Pilgrimage itself might serve as a social magnet; by nature it tends to level class
differences. Such communal religious events are marked by a phenomenon
which Victor Turner calls *communitas,* a sense of shared religious purpose
that lowers social barriers and leads to relatively egalitarian communication
among people of varied backgrounds.[16] Chaucer recognizes this concept:
he speaks of the "sondry folk" who have come together by chance in "felaweshipe"—a fellowship to which he seeks and gains admittance (1.25–32).
Yet, as often happens in times of social upheaval, the *communitas* of the
Canterbury Tales is imperfect: awareness of social hierarchy and class conflict
attend the pilgrims throughout the journey.[17]

Communitas, then, provides only partial justification for setting the pilgrims together on the road to St. Thomas's shrine; it does not answer all the questions implicit in the interactions of the players. For example, the familiarity shared by all classes might obtain on holy journeys, but would it extend to play? It is one thing for a socially diverse group to band together for pious purposes, but quite another for its members to interact in a storytelling contest. Shared recreation requires its own brand of familiarity, one which Turner's concept of *communitas* cannot fully explain.

The fragmentary records of medieval pilgrimage merely hint at the degree of social spread found on such journeys. On a pilgrimage made in 1395 by a band of citizens from Bagnolet to the Cathedral of Notre Dame de Chartres, some members rode horses, others walked—a suggestion of varied means—but beyond that fact, there is no evidence of the group's constituency.[18] The pilgrimage records of Walsingham and Canterbury were destroyed in the sixteenth century, leaving little background against which the verisimilitude of Chaucer's group can be gauged.

The most relevant real-life analogue I have found is the parish gild, a religious and fraternal organization omnipresent in Chaucer's England, a body which reveals much about the nature and extent of social relationships within the English middle class. The richest surviving evidence pertaining to the parish gild is dated 1389, shortly after Chaucer began work on the *Canterbury Tales.* A Parliamentary Act of 1388 had required that "all gilds and brotherhoods whatsoever" submit reports specifying

> . . . the manner and form and authority of the foundation and beginning and continuance and governance of the gilds and brotherhoods aforesaid . . . the manner and form of the oaths, gatherings, feasts, and general meetings of the bretheren and sisteren . . . the liberties, privileges, statutes, ordinances, usages, and customs of the same gilds . . . and all other matters and things in any way concerning or touching the said gilds and brotherhoods. . . .[19]

Returns filtered back to Parliament in the early months of 1389; even their number, and the circumstances of their collection, tell us something of the nature of the gilds. First, they must have been considered important, perhaps even dangerous, by London officials, or such an accounting would not have been solicited in the first place.[20] Second, the parish gild, far less well-known today than the craft gild, was enormously popular in the late fourteenth century. Parliament sent out separate orders to the parish gilds and the craft gilds; returns show that parish gilds may have outnumbered trade gilds—one more reason for modern researchers to heed whatever these groups may tell us of Chaucer's society.[21] The parish gilds varied somewhat in their structures and functions, displaying a considerable range of social representation, economic requirements, religious duties, and entertainments. Yet behind this variation is a consistent core of information linking the gilds to the Canterbury pilgrims in five important respects.

1. The parish gild was, by conception and membership, primarily a *middle-class institution*. George Unwin traces the development of the London gilds to the rising economic power of the middle class.[22] As the number and wealth of the nobility decreased, the churches and chantries endowed by the wellborn fell into disrepair and were abandoned. Richer members of the merchant class gradually assumed the support of these churches; the parish gild had its roots in this practice. Occasionally, the bourgeois patrons attempted to take on the exact role of their noble predecessors: one wealthy family would maintain an entire church. With the passage of time, however, it became more common for large groups of wealthy men—aided by smaller contributions from less wealthy parishioners—to organize groups that paid for the hiring of priests, singing of masses, care of the altar, and purchase of ceremonial candles. Such groups were modeled on trade and frith gilds, and like the earlier organizations they proclaimed the communal power of those who did not fit easily into the three-estate paradigm—of those I here identify with the middle class.

It is true that institutions somewhat similar to the parish gilds existed among nobles as well. A prime example was the fellowship of the Lincoln Cathedral—a select group indeed—whose membership numbered almost all of Chaucer's noble and royal patrons: Edward III, Richard II, Henry IV, and John of Gaunt. Philippa Chaucer and several of the poet's in-laws were also members, though Geoffrey himself was excluded, probably on account of his lower birth. Such organizations were primarily social clubs. Though they did engage in some benevolent enterprises, they did not have the functions of mutual financial support that characterized the middle-class gilds.

Parish gild enrollments resemble the personnel of Chaucer's pilgrimages even to the smallest detail. A few nobles were admitted; Sir John Fastolf, kinsman of Chaucer's friend Sir Hugh, was one of ten knights among the 452 members of the gild of St. George, Norwich.[23] We also know, through the testimony of the Paston letters, that the servants of richer members took part in this gild's activities.[24] Thus the non-middle-class elements found in Chaucer's cast were also present, in kind and in proportion, among the rolls.

2. The range of *economic status* in the gild lists corresponds well with the varied means of the Canterbury pilgrims. Not all the fraternities show a wide distribution of economic power; indeed, a few were so exclusive that they catered only to the richest stratum of the upper middle class. At least three London gilds required enormous membership dues, which would clearly exclude nearly all London freemen.[25] Others, like the Poor Men's

Gild of Norwich, served only the most disadvantaged segments of the middle class.[26] These extremes of wealth and poverty are generally found in only the largest cities, such as London and Norwich, where citizens were settled in neighborhoods reflecting occupational and social divisions, and where the congregations of local parishes reflected the narrow social ranges of their neighborhoods.[27]

Yet the great majority of the gilds in both city and village showed substantial economic variation. Some clearly attempted to make membership accessible to every free man and woman. Norwich's Gild of St. George, which included ten knights, an archbishop, and four bishops as well as hundreds of people of lower birth, required an offering of a mere halfpenny for its masses. Other gilds, such as St. Magnus in London, assigned dues on a graduated scale. Initiatory and annual fees were decided according to each member's means to pay: "some give five marks, some forty shillings, some twenty shillings, some nothing."[28] In a few cases, there were no dues for anyone: applicants gained entrance merely by the assent of the established members.[29]

Also, as is the case with the cast of the Canterbury pilgrimage, the parish communities recognized economic and social divisions within their ranks. The two subgroups of *gentils* and churls identified by Chaucer in the *Canterbury Tales* were commonly found in the gilds as well. Though the fraternity of St. Magnus was very generous in establishing a policy of economic tolerance for its members, the group entertained no fiction of class equality within the gild, which, in their own words, was founded by five wealthy members and "others *of the better sort* of the parish."[30] When the lower middle class had control of a gild, a reciprocal prejudice against the "better sort" was often apparent. At St. Michael on the Hill (Lincoln), it was "ordained that no one of the rank of mayor or bailiff shall become a brother of the gild, unless he is found to be of humble, good, and honest conversation and is admitted by the choice and common consent of the brethren and sistren."[31] Thus the gilds, while truly egalitarian in an economic sense, did not fail to recognize, nor occasionally to stress, class differences. Here is an immediate parallel between the institutions of gild and pilgrimage. Both groups worked together when mutually concerned with religious and social duties, but neither could ignore the divisive forces at work within it.

3. The *occupational range* represented in the gilds was as broad and varied as that of Chaucer's pilgrim band. Again there were a few exceptions: certain parish gilds were also trade gilds, and therefore admitted only those who followed one specific calling. But most parishes—perhaps as many as eighty-five percent—welcomed a great variety of occupations.[32] Unwin has noted that Chaucer's five gildsmen, "clothed all in o lyveree / Of a solempne and a greet fraternitee" (1.363–64), must have been members of a

parish gild, because the diversity of their occupations precludes the possibility that they could have been members of a city trade gild.[33] Numerous
fourteenth-century records show occupational representation at least as
broad as that spanned by Chaucer's five. The parish of St. Magnus was
founded by a bailiff, a fishmonger, a chandler, and a vintner, and counted
several other trades—fletchers, masons, glovers, girdlers, and pursers—
among its membership. The Gild of St. Mary and St. Giles, which served St.
Giles, Cripplegate, included poulterers, painters, brewers, couriers, smiths,
and merchants.[34]

4. Membership lists indicate that the *clerical and feminine representation* of
the parish gilds also mirrors the constituency of Chaucer's pilgrim society.
Female enfranchisement was nearly universal in such organizations: sev-
enty-five percent or more of the gilds admitted women. Though wives of
male members were sometimes admitted free of charge, widows and other
relations of the men often paid full dues. According to many charters,
women had an equal role in votes and other internal decision-making processes, though modern historians tend to agree that such formulaic phrases
as "the common consent of the brethren and sistren" were more lip service
than reflections of shared political power. Women did, however, receive
special consideration in certain cases—as in the provisions for enlarging the
dowries of impoverished girls. Although males greatly outnumbered females, such women as the Wife of Bath were no more strangers to the
parish gilds than to pilgrimage.[35]

Representatives of the clerical estate, though expressly forbidden from
membership in some gilds,[36] were allowed to join and even to hold offices
in the majority. To convey an idea of the range of clerical representation in
a single gild, I again cite the Gild of St. George, Norwich, which included at
least one archbishop, four bishops, several priors and rectors, eleven friars,
two ecclesiastical teachers, and two chaplains. The entire range of the titled
clergy appears in the rolls.

Thus, in its range of status, wealth, occupation, and representation of
female and ecclesiastical elements, the parish gild closely resembled Chaucer's pilgrim cast. As one final illustration, consider the membership of the
Gild of Holy Trinity, St. Botolph's, Aldersgate, London. The emphasized
words designate occupations, estates, and proportions that are also present
among the Canterbury pilgrims:

> Headed in 1374 by a *capper* and a *weaver*, they were *predominantly of middle
> citizen rank or lower*, with *a few gentlemen, one noble patron, the lord Roos*, and a few
> liveried *merchants*. The *women* were mostly wives of craftsmen, entering with
> their husbands; among the *few who entered alone* were [*a wife whose husband was
> not a member*], a huckster, and a single woman named Juliana Ful of Love,
> occupation undesignated. The occupations of the men, so far as they are given

or can be ascertained, were as follows: 65 *clergy,* 22 *gentry and officials,* 22 citizens of *merchant* companies, some of them *liverymen,* 12 brewers, 4 maltmen, 4 *dyers,* 3 *weavers,* 3 armorers, 3 *carpenters,* 3 *cooks,* 2 chandlers, 2 *cappers,* 2 masons, 2 butchers, 2 saddlers, with 1 representative of each of the following: barber, bladesmith, chapman, cooper, cordwainer, curier, drover, glazier, gold-beater, herald, *leech,* painter, spurrier, *surgeon, taverner,* tiler, waterman, and Kentish *husbandman.* The remainder must have been of similar trades and *humbler rank,* for their names are not identifiable. . . . [In a later membership list appear] a *squire* and a *gentleman.* . . . [37]

Surrogates for the entire Canterbury cast—with the possible exception of the Shipman, Miller, and Reeve—are mentioned specifically or generally in this list. And there are some temptingly close parallels. The single knight among the gildsmen stands out in the same sharp relief as Chaucer's pilgrim knight. The name of Juliana Ful of Love suggests an immediate, if spurious, comparison with Alisoun of Bath (Juliana is single, at least for the moment). The poet no doubt knew this parish, located as it was near Aldersgate, the home of his friend Ralph Strode; there is also a good chance Chaucer knew several members on this list, as they were enrolled in 1375, when Chaucer was living in London, a decade before he began the *Tales.*

Yet the resemblance between the gild and the pilgrimage does not end with the social peculiarities of their casts: there are also parallels in motive and behavior. Gild members, like the pilgrims, banded together for a number of widely different reasons. One basic set of purposes was shared by the two.

5. Both institutions served the twin and seemingly antithetical functions of *providing religious edification and entertainment.* Parish brotherhoods, like pilgrimages, were convened officially, ostensibly for the sole purpose of the salvation of souls. Yet all the major analysts of the gilds recognize that there was a substantial social and convivial side to these organizations.[38] A gild meeting often served simply as an excuse for having a good time.

The major event on the gild calendar was the feast, held at least once annually. More playful gilds feasted four times each year. The feast gave members the opportunity to parade their finery and noble pretensions. Like Chaucer's gildsmen, clad in their matching livery, most ranking parish gildsmen wore expensive uniforms which they were required to purchase from their own pockets. This finery was guarded religiously, both by the individual wearer and by gild statutes, which required that members wear such clothing on special occasions.[39] The ostentation of Chaucer's gildsmen, with their decorative knives and their richly clad wives, who are

> . . . ycleped "madame,"
> And goon to vigilies al bifore,
> And have a mantel roialliche ybore (1.376–78)

is echoed in the records. There was much pageantry at the yearly ritual: lavish horseback processions, troupes of dancers whose costumes were financed by the gild, badges of gold and silver worn by members. Even the waiters serving at the feasts wore special badges. Fines were assessed any member who "comyth not to the Messe in hys best clothing."⁴⁰

Beyond ceremony, there was a second and perhaps more important secular function: that of providing an excuse for game. The gild feasts were aptly named "the drynkynge" by the Gild of St. Thomas (Lynn) and many others.⁴¹ Overconsumption of alcohol was expressly prohibited by several gilds—indeed, a number sufficient to assure us that such excesses regularly occurred. The Gild of Shipmen in Lynn protected its alcohol (which was, incidentally, a common medium of payment of gild fines) by requiring members to obtain special permission even to enter the chamber where the ale was stored.⁴² To complement the "drinking," there were special speakers at the feasts; the content of their addresses is unknown, but one is tempted to assume that storytelling was sometimes on the program.⁴³ There was also ample musical entertainment: minstrels were hired to accompany processions and entertain diners. Plays were sometimes performed, and dances were held quite often.

Affinities with the *Canterbury Tales* are many and obvious. The same blend of polar opposites—piety and irreverence, fast and feast—is at work in both groups. Though some have characterized the gilds as more sober than playful, and though most view the *Tales* with an opposite bias, the fact remains that gild and pilgrimage share fundamental compositional and functional traits. Furthermore, there are many specific links between the parish brotherhoods and the institution of pilgrimage. Some gilds exempted members from paying dues while on pilgrimage. Others helped finance the pilgrimages of poorer members or provided lodging for pilgrims passing through their parishes. Groups of gildsmen like Chaucer's company of five often went together to a shrine, and occasionally a very large body—perhaps the entire parish—gathered for the journey. Even when only some of its members went together, the gild looked upon pilgrimage as a shared enterprise. Members of the Gild of the Resurrection (Lincoln) formed processions to accompany departing pilgrims to the city gate, where each of those left behind presented each who journeyed with a "halfpenny at least."⁴⁴

Chaucer knew about the parish gilds—he drew a portrait of the gildsmen in his Prologue. But the functional and structural traits linking the gild to Chaucer's pilgrim band suggest that these playful religious fraternities supplied him with something more than five of his least memorable characters. The parish gild was both pervasive and new in Chaucer's time. Not only were such groups "established in half the churches of London at the time

the *Canterbury Tales* were being written"[45]—most of them had been formed
so recently that Chaucer could not help but see in them a striking and novel
symbol of the rising middle class. The great majority of parish gilds responding to the survey of 1389 (shortly after the General Prologue was
composed) had been founded since Chaucer's birth.[46]

Yet these links between the gild and Chaucer's pilgrims do not require us
to see the one as the immediate source of the other. The gild embodies, as
the General Prologue depicts, something larger than both, a major contemporary social configuration. Growing from the decay of the noble class and
a set of newfound opportunities in urban life, the two groups represent a
new middle world presaging the social realignments of subsequent centuries. Both are composed principally of those previously "unclassified" in
medieval society. Both—in admitting a knight or two, a plowman or two—
carry with them only the vestiges of the social extremes of the older order,
as if to serve notice that the estates system will no longer stand. And both
are subdivided into companies of *gentils* and churls, whose rivalry imitated
the older, more dramatic opposition of nobles and peasants. So communities similarly composed to Chaucer's cast *did* assemble regularly in fourteenth-century London, to share religion and game and conflict.

THREE

Frames around the Frame

The Role of the Pilgrim

Chaucer presents not only a social but a spiritual context for his poem. Whatever their various backgrounds, the storytellers assume the common role of pilgrim, which merges with their real-life social status to affect the nature of their game. Before we know anything else about them, we find the players gathered in "felaweshipe" for a journey to the shrine of St. Thomas, and they are miles down the road as the General Prologue ends. Here I examine the place of storytelling and play in such "felaweshipe," comparing the details of the poem to the workings of the world outside it, to measure how successfully Chaucer imitates the behavior of his contemporaries and to discover what his setting suggested to those who first heard the *Canterbury Tales*.

All evidence points to an ancient origin both for the custom of pilgrimage and for the playfulness that often attends it. As Johan Huizinga has shown, play is an intrinsic aspect of ceremonialism in "primitive" and folk religions.[1] It is true that many medieval authorities scorned the interplay of game and religion; churchmen often banned ceremonies in which the ludic element was strongly pronounced. Throughout Chaucer's era—as in 1405 at Nantes—clerics tried to institutionalize pilgrims' piety, declaring that one *must* act soberly en route to a shrine.[2]

Nevertheless, from the beginning of the Middle Ages, the integration of ludic and purely pious elements was essential to the spirit, sometimes even to the doctrine, of the Church. Pope Gregory the Great saw compromise as essential to conversion. He believed that northern European converts would find the message of the Church more palatable if they received their first Communion wine in old, familiar vessels. His manifesto of A.D. 601—instructing his missionaries not to ban festivals, but to Christianize them, "so that while [the converts] still keep outward pleasures, they may more readily receive the spiritual joys"[3]—remained a *de facto* aspect of religious observance in Chaucer's day. And nowhere was the blending of the pagan and Christian worlds more evident, and more readily condoned, than along the pilgrim's road. Indeed, in such English cities as Canterbury and Walsingham, pilgrimage centers were also the sites of sanctioned play: fairs conducted under ecclesiastical supervision. Though many monks and Lollards despised the intermingling of piety and play, the pilgrim games persisted.

A representative index of pilgrim excesses was compiled by Roger Vaultier, who examined a series of *lettres de rémission,* or royal pardons, issued in France during the Hundred Years' War.[4] Many of the offenses seem light, and some might be judged innocent, even by Lollard standards. Some pilgrims played ball games along the paths to shrines in northern France. Some gathered roadside flowers to make chaplets and necklaces reminiscent of May Day dress. Others observed sober behavior during the pilgrimage only to hold their wild parties and night-long dances *after* its completion, thus ending their journeys not at the shrine, but at the tavern. Occasionally, the clerical division between sanctity and celebration broke down entirely, creating wild mixtures of worship and play: when a company of pilgrims to Nantes reached their shrine, they "said their prayers, made their offerings and heard the service, as good folks and proper pilgrims must do," but soon began dancing within the church itself. At another church party, girls decked the nave with flowers to create a softer setting for their courting games; at a third, celebrants tossed votive candles behind the altar to clear a space for dancing, then gagged a woman who had voiced objections to their play. The offenses listed by Vaultier were not the worst that took place; all of them, after all, were judged mild enough to be pardoned. Still, they show clearly enough that the more sober clerical views of piety were widely disregarded.

Yet the traditional conception of religion as a sort of sacred play was under constant attack in fourteenth-century England. Pervasive corruption in the clerical estate convinced increasing numbers of Christians that the heart of their religion no longer resided in the clergy. Many worshippers, spanning the full compass of society, began to espouse the austere doctrines of Wycliffe and others, who proclaimed that play and even the practice of pilgrimage itself were among the inherent ills of the Church. In the highest reaches of the Catholic hierarchy, pilgrimage found enemies. In 1370 Simon Sudbury, soon to become Archbishop of Canterbury, declared that the indulgences granted at Canterbury possessed no spiritual value. As the religious community agonized, and then began to split, over the nature and worth of pilgrimage, a corresponding divisiveness became apparent in the motives of the pilgrims. In earlier days the great majority had traveled to play *and* to pray—but by Chaucer's time increasing numbers came to do only one or the other.[5]

On the "purely" pious side, there were flagellants who made pilgrimage
. an act of self-torture, and ascetics who made their way on foot, often bare-

foot. Even among the most refined, such austerity was evident. Chaucer's contemporary Le Mareschal de Boucicaut, one of the most genteel of French knights and an accomplished love poet, conducted regular penitential journeys à pied. The Countess of Clare, grandmother of one of Chaucer's patronesses, perfomed a barefoot pilgrimage to Canterbury.[6]

At the opposite extreme were those who undertook pilgrimage solely for irreligious ends. Sexual motives were common. Male travelers to the shrine at Nantes chased after the women and girls who walked with them. Men often propositioned prostitutes at the Cathedral. One record tells of a passionate pilgrim who possessed a woman within the church.[7] Theft and fraud were rife. Thorpe speaks of poor men so seized with desire to visit the bones of a saint that they stole the money enabling them to do so. Less innocent were those who did not give alms, but took them from the collection plates passed among the crowds assembled at the shrines. Others committed balder thefts, breaking the locks of collection boxes and running off with their contents.[8]

The disintegration of the pray-and-play ethic leaves its mark on the *Canterbury Tales*. Even Chaucer's clergy is polarized and can be readily divided into pious and impious camps. The Parson—labeled a Lollard by the Host—isolates himself from the other pilgrims, condemning the telling of tales (10.31–34) and refusing to speak with those who utter oaths (2.1170–71). The Pardoner, on the other hand, ridicules his own profession, openly confessing that he is in it for the money (6.439–51). The dividing line between prayer and play is perhaps most strongly evident in Chaucer's Retraction, where the poet himself asks forgiveness for "the tales of Canterbury, *thilke that sownen into synne*" (10.1086). Apparently, Chaucer's final vision of pilgrimage was not unlike the Parson's.[9] And there was a prophetic quality to both. A century and a third after Chaucer's death, the Protestant revolution presaged in the doctrine of Wycliffe brought bans on pilgrimage and the destruction of the shrine at Canterbury.

Though the *Tales* sometimes evokes the conflict that would eventually destroy the very ritual it celebrates, Chaucer concentrates on the older, more traditional view of pilgrimage, in which playing and praying intermingle with relative ease. Even the most playful pilgrims do not deny the dual nature of the journey. At an early crux in the poem, Herry Bailly addresses the Parson, "Sir Parisshe Prest . . . *for Goddes bones, /* Telle us a tale." The sober Parson becomes angry at the Host's careless use of God's name. Unperturbed, Herry Bailly prepares the company for a sermon from this "Lollard." But a certain pilgrim, perhaps the Shipman, raises his voice in protest:[10]

Nay, by my fader soule . . .
. . . heer schal he nat preche. . . .

We leven alle in the grete God. . . .
He wolde sowen some difficulte
Or *springen cokkel in our clene corn.* (2.1178–83)

In stating that it is impure *not* to play on pilgrimage, the Shipman is up-holding the traditional view of ritual, in opposition to the Parson's reformist position. Fourteenth-century records often echo the Shipman's loathing of excessive piety, even when practiced on similarly pious occasions. On Ascension Day (c. 1320) near Prades d'Aillon, in Foix, a mendicant Friar joined a company of villagers for dinner. He was asked to sing the "Ave Maria," as much to entertain the group as to bless their meal. When the Friar's performance became "too pious in tone," he—like Chaucer's Parson—was censured by his audience.[11] Neither the Shipman nor the villagers of Prades should be considered irreligious, though both could be called anticlerical. We have every reason to believe theirs was the dominant view in Chaucer's time. Certainly, a solid majority of the pilgrims shares the Shipman's conviction that play has its place as an important, perhaps necessary, foil to their holy procession.[12]

The warring voices of Parson and Shipman aptly reflect the dual nature of medieval pilgrimage; here, as elsewhere, Chaucer presents a range of behavior that falls well within the expressive compass of his time. From the breadth of plausible actions, the poet consistently chooses moderation. True, he represents the diversity of conduct recorded in the historical sources, from austerity (Yeoman, Clerk, Plowman, and Parson) to ostentation (Gildsmen, Monk, Wife of Bath). He also includes all the motives to which the records bear witness: piety, pleasure, sex, and theft. Yet Chaucer does not carry his characters' motives to the behavioral extremes so often attained by real-life pilgrims. None of his creatures is a self-flagellant, and none commits the criminal outrages found frequently in the records. The Parson's devoutness is exemplary, but his remonstrations are moderate. He is generally aloof, but seldom a scourge to his fellows, and he has only one negative exchange with another pilgrim. The Knight most closely resembles a penitent: his rust-stained shirt is a uniform of humility, but it carries with it no self-inflicted pain. And though he is strongly committed to sacred ideals, he resembles the Shipman in his refusal to tolerate expressions of extreme solemnity. Late in the journey, as the Monk is presenting a dreary *sic passunt gaudia,* warning the pilgrims that no man can trust "blynd prosperitee" (7.1997), the Knight breaks in to state as politely as possible that the company will not listen to such mournful *exempla* (7.2767–79). Among the other pilgrims as well, excess is often expressed in speech but seldom translated into action.

The choice of moderation can be ascribed in part to the poet's attempt to balance the functions of play and prayer, to reassert the double purpose of the religious festival at a time when many were speaking against it. Playful aspects of pilgrimage dominate in the storytelling and dialogue, but devotion also exerts its presence. The pilgrims do not lose sight of their ultimate physical and spiritual destination, even as they wander by the way. Their play often becomes rough, sometimes openly contentious, but it never reaches the pitch of strife between religious and secular elements that often marred the festivals enacted in Chaucer's age. A truly communal sense of piety does prevail, when it must—when games become fights that threaten to overwhelm the group. When the Host goes too far in his abuse of the Pardoner, and the two men are on the verge of blows, the Knight restores order with a simple Christian ritual: he has the antagonists exchange a kiss of peace that puts an end to their cruel play (6.962–68). Similarly, the Parson (who, we recall, was censured early in the journey for excessive piety and told to keep his thoughts to himself) may often be ignored, but he is not ultimately abandoned. The company assents to hear his sermon at the proper time: as the storytelling draws to a close. Piety is always welcome, in its place.

This interweaving of what the modern world often perceives as antithetical elements displays Chaucer's thorough understanding of the medieval festival. The juxtaposition and balance of worldly game and otherworldly gravity was a ruling principle in popular plays and holiday celebrations which the poet witnessed—a principle common in daily practice and public ceremony, but absent from the elite literary tradition of the English court. In the Corpus Christi dramas, solemn and playful elements alternated, sometimes within the framework of a single play; in the keeping of Christmas and other holy days, parody masses and volatile games complemented the solemn observances held in churches and homes. But England's elite poetry has no such thematic structure; Gower's *Confessio Amantis,* written for Chaucer's king and court, sets together both sacred and profane, but in an allegorical relationship that will suffer no joy in the latter. In abandoning the courtly esthetic and appropriating a traditional ritual pattern, Chaucer was exercising an impulse both theatrically apt and ethnographically accurate.

We may identify a humanistic philosophy behind Chaucer's choice of moderate behavior, and a sense of realism behind his balancing of sacred and profane; but whatever their underlying impulses, these two elements in combination force the reader's attention to narrative style. By creating oppositions unresolved by action, Chaucer creates *narrators,* not combatants, for his poem, people who express their differences in words—who tell about crimes, but do not commit them (thus the Pardoner's confessional prologue); who talk about, rather than practice, sexual infidelity (thus the Wife of Bath's Prologue); who engage in oral rather than in physical battle (thus the *fabliaux* of the churls). The behavioral extremes of the *Canterbury Tales* are found within the tales themselves. As the characters extend themselves into their stories, their words take on the strength of actions, and their various styles become increasingly varied and important. In a manner unknown in previous literature, the diction, subject matter, and theme of each pilgrim's tale comes to represent that pilgrim's individual position in the festival at hand and in society at large. The poetic strategies that make the *Canterbury Tales* the most closely read poem of the English Middle Ages have their parallels, perhaps their roots, in the folk esthetic of English medieval pilgrimage.

Chaucer's emphasis on language rather than deed leads to a second consideration: his pilgrimage provides a perfect setting for festive behavior, but would the poet's contemporaries perceive the pilgrims' road as an apt stage for storytelling? Herry Bailly explains very specifically to his flock the purpose of the game he has devised. Taletelling provides a necessary diversion from the hardship of the road, producing an earned *solace* for the trials encountered by the penitent.

> For trewely, confort ne myrthe is noon
> To ride by the weye doumb as a stoon. (1.773–74)

Glending Olson has shown that Herry Bailly's theory of entertainment was shared by many of Chaucer's contemporaries.[13] More relevant here, however, it was shared by the more traditional religious leaders of the age. Responding to a Lollard's charge that pilgrims conduct themselves irreverently, Archbishop Arundel echoes the words of the Host:

> ... thou considerest not the great [travail] of pilgrimes: therefore, thou blamest that thyng that is praysable. I say to thee that it is right well done, that pilgrimes have with them both singers and also pipers: that when one of them that goeth barefote, striketh his toe vpon a stone, and hurteth him sore, and maketh him to blede: it is well done that he or his felow begyn then a song . . . to dryue away with such mirth, the hurt of his felow.[14]

Like the Shipman, Arundel argues against those who do not seek play's remedy for the hardships of pilgrimage. The entertainer is respected for his ability to dispel the traveler's pain.

Though the Archbishop speaks of song rather than story, Herry Bailly's preference for the latter was not merely suitable, but ideal: oral tales were so characteristic of medieval pilgrimage that the words "pilgrim" and "storyteller" were nearly synonymous. Fourteenth-century listeners would respond sympathetically to the fact that pilgrims tell the *Canterbury Tales;* it is a detail that affirms the poet's recognition of one of the fundamental facts of life in his time.

Pilgrim and storyteller are linked in a variety of sources. The Lollard Thorpe, speaking against the revelry of pilgrims, attests to the cultivation of oral art along the road: "if these men and women be a moneth out in their pilgrimage, many of them shall be an halfe yeare after, great iangelers, tale tellers and lyars." William Langland observed the same behavior among pilgrims to Rome and Santiago:

> Pylgrimis and palmers plyghten hem to-gederes
> To seche saint Iame and seyntys of rome,
> Wenten forth in hure way with meny un-wyse tales,
> And haven leve to lye al hure lyf-tyme. . . . [15]

John Capgrave of King's Lynn, author of *A Solyce of Pilgrimes,* explains that one of their major pastimes, and greatest virtues, is to retell the stories they have heard on their travels. *Mandeville's Travels,* perhaps the most popular pilgrims' guidebook ever written, expresses similar sentiments. John Bromyard, however, strongly condemned the pilgrims' obsession with these same *nociuis et detractoriis . . . narrationibus.* [16]

Some of these descriptions may be read by the modern analyst as references to lies and exaggerations rather than to crafted narratives. Yet the critics of the Middle Ages saw no need to distinguish between the two. From the earliest mentions of oral fiction in European culture, the folktale was considered to be synonymous with "lie, empty talk, garrulity": *Indecorum et satis indecens* were the chroniclers' terms for the *falsis fabulis rusticorum.* [17] The equation of folktales and falsehood was a medieval commonplace, a matter of doctrine, to which the narrators themselves often responded. An anonymous eleventh-century German author was clearly referring to fictional entertainment when he said, "I am guilty of lying-sagas, of lying-tales." [18] The linking of lies and folktales was so common that it may account for their shared presence in the English word "tale," which possessed the two meanings of "artful fiction" and "malicious falsehood" for centuries before Chaucer's pilgrims told their stories. [19]

This double meaning has persisted in folk communities to the present day. In the 1960s, when Karoly Gaál ascended into the Burgenland of Austria to search out *Märchen* tellers, well-to-do villagers informed him that the people who told such stories were cheap, idle "liars." [20] The storytellers themselves, as well as their most avid listeners, also know tales as "lies," but in such cases the term is more an invitation than a prohibition. "Let us lie a little bit, Gyuri," one Hungarian will tell another when he wants to hear a *Märchen;* "Okay, let us lie a little," responds the narrator as he begins his fiction. At the end of his tale, the teller often adds, "I lied, for they listened to me." [21]

Thus, storytelling has long occupied the same marginal position assigned to the concept of play on pilgrimage. To such sober clerics as the pilgrim Parson, the Canterbury cast violates St. Paul's order to "refuse profane and old wives' fables, and exercise thyself rather unto Godliness" (I Tim. 4:7; cf. 10.32–34). In his catalog of vices the Parson sets lies and entertaining tales together under the deadly sin of *ira*:

> Another lesynge comth of delit for to lye, in which delit they wol forge a long tale. . . . (10.609)

> . . . After this comth the synne of japeres, that been the develes apes; for they maken folk to laughe at hire japerie as folk doon at the gawdes of an ape. (10.651)

The Parson's doctrine echoes that of most medieval ascetics. Chaucer's pastor, like Thorpe, lacks economy of language. Thorpe inveighs against "tale-tellers" and "liars"; the Parson censures "japeres" and tellers of "lesynges." All four terms are interchangeable. A tale is a form of blasphemy. The nature of fiction is to misrepresent the truth of God.

Yet there are few pilgrims who, like the Monk, "have no lust to pleye" (7.2806) the narrative game. Like modern narrators, most of Chaucer's company lie with delight, and they lie very well. In *The House of Fame*, Chaucer ranks pilgrims (their "scrippes bret-ful of lesinges"; 2123) with the greatest liars. In the *Canterbury Tales*, he ranks them with the greatest storytellers. In both cases he is merely repeating the common judgment of his age.

The reason for the pilgrim's role as master narrator is simple: from the earliest recorded descriptions, the traveler has been the archetypal storyteller, and the archetypal traveler has been the pilgrim. Research has verified that storytelling is by tradition the property of the traveler. The wandering medieval minstrels have their wandering descendents. In recent years the best-known tellers have come from migrant working communities of craftsmen, soldiers, and fishermen; and from groups of landless peasants engaged in lumbering, herding, and seasonal agricultural labor. Invariably, itinerants are singled out as the finest storytellers, and itinerant communities found to be the richest sources of narrative repertoires.[22] Traveling gives the teller greater opportunity to tell tales, greater opportunity to hear them, and a constantly shifting audience on whom to hone his talents.

Like latter-day narrators, most of Chaucer's characters, even when not on pilgrimage, were well accustomed to the road. According to Du Boulay, "at least thirteen [pilgrims] not including Chaucer himself were regular travelers by profession or taste," and among these were nearly all of Chaucer's finest narrators: Knight, Reeve, Wife of Bath, Clerk, Pardoner.[23]

The association between travel and storytelling is not merely incidental to the nature of oral fiction. The folktale is not simply told by travelers, it is *about* travelers, on both narrative and spiritual planes. It was not coincidence that when Chaucer began to write a poem about travelers crossing a familiar landscape on a spiritual quest, he drew upon folktales for the first time in his poetic career. Nor is it accident that fifteen of the pilgrims' tales have analogs in modern oral tradition.[24]

To explain: though the folktale is on one level a lie, it is also the vehicle of certain social truths and individual desires. An accomplished oral artist will adapt his narrative material to suit his environment and the needs of his audience, as well as to express his own views. The narrator must cater to consensus; otherwise, his audience abandons him. Unsatisfied listeners walk away from a poor teller, or drown him out with noise, or—like Herry Bailly and the Knight in the *Tales*—simply tell the bungler to shut up.[25] Therefore, the teller's craft is a compromise between his listeners' expectations and his own imagination. The narrator serves as a physical and artistic link between audience and tale. He is the flesh-and-blood traveler acting as representative of the fictional traveling hero.

The taleteller's first compromise with reality is to open his fantastic fiction with a scene set in a fully plausible environment. Unlike Dante's metaphorical *camina*, or the surreal scenes that descend from the heavens into medieval dream visions, the setting in which a folktale begins is, as a rule, ordinary and well-known. In Chaucer's folktales, the opening scenes are familiar sights to all travelers: a rural estate (Clerk's Tale), a castle (Squire's and Merchant's tales), a village (Miller's Tale), a farmhouse (Nun's Priest Tale). Similarly, a master folk narrator generally begins by duplicating the environment of the listeners. A great many tales told in Hungarian spinning rooms, for example, begin with a scene set in a spinning room.[26] Likewise, the figure of the Ashlad, or Cinderella—the poor child who lies resignedly in the ashes of the hearth—has been introduced on thousands of occasions to groups seated beside a fire, as if *they* were the protagonists of the tales thus told.[27] The technique of putting the audience in the hero's place gives the listeners a double identity and serves as their springboard to fantasy. They undergo an imaginative process reminiscent of the dreams depicted in Hollywood films of the 1930s and 1940s: as the sleeper lies in bed, a second ghostlike sleeper takes form, sits up in bed, walks to the door. The folktale listener remains seated by the spinning wheel or the fireside as his or her double in the folktale cast departs for imagined glory.

In light of this fact, it is worth noting that five of Chaucer's narratives (those of the Knight, Man of Law, Wife of Bath, and Summoner) begin on the road, as imaginary travelers duplicate the real travels of the pilgrims. Like the audience assembled for the story, the protagonist of the Summoner's Tale is introduced to us as a wayfarer; indeed, he bears the traditional symbols of the pilgrim: "He wente his wey, no lenger wolde he reste. / With *scrippe and tipped staf,* ytukked hye . . ." (3.1736–37). In other tales (such as the Reeve's) the protagonists are wayfarers; in yet others (such as the Friar's) the action is centered on the road. The Pardoner, who tells his tale at a tavern, sets his fiction at a similar roadside inn.

All who listen sympathetically to a folktale see themselves in the hero, but no one is *identified with the hero* more strongly than is the narrator. Though the tale is community property, the narrator is the momentary owner and, more than any other person present, can be said to share the identity of the hero. The teller reflects this sense of identification by portraying himself as someone who is a little closer than his audience to the magic of the tale. As his story ends, he often claims in a joking way to have been present at the action described in the final scene: "As I was there when all that happened, they sent me here to relate it to you. I have finished."[28] Thus the oral narrator proclaims himself an emissary from the chimerical world he describes. All experience the hero's wanderings vicariously, but the narrator "has been there," in the magic world, to a greater extent than anyone else. The traveler, a wanderer over the earth, is the ideal storyteller, by virtue of both his real experience and his audience's expectations. Like the hero of his story, he has been to places they have not; he is best qualified to tell about the world beyond the immediate setting where they listen, where the initial actions of the magic tale unfold.

Through such conventions, the best folktales approach paradox: the unbelievable becomes nearly believable. Chaucer preserves this sense in the telling of his first tale. The Knight, the most traveled, hence the best suited to begin, opens his story in the distant East, where he himself has often been. Having just returned from a campaign to Lithuania, which then embraced what had once been Scythia, he describes a journey from Scythia to Athens:

> [Theseus] conquered al the regne of Femenye,
> That whilom was ycleped Scithia,
> And weddede the queene Ypolita,
> And broghte hire hoom with hym in his contree
> With muchel glorie and greet solempnytee. . . .
> And thus with victorie and with melodye
> Lete I this noble duc to Atthenes ryde,
> And al his hoost in armes hym bisyde. (1.866–70, 872–74)

In the late fourteenth century, this route was controlled by the Ottoman Sultanate, where the Knight had also fought. His campaigns probably did not take him within two hundred miles of the journey his tale describes. But to his fellow pilgrims, the Knight had come *close enough*—surely he knew this region better than they. Furthermore, the character seen first in this tale is Duke Theseus, a noble, traveling warrior, like the Knight—and guided, like the Knight, by wisdom (1.865; cf. 1.68) to many victories. As the pilgrims ride listening to the Knight, the Knight describes Theseus' ride. It is on that journey that Theseus encounters the scene—a group of mourning women kneeling "in the heighe weye" (1.897)—that triggers the ensuing action. In his opening lines, the Knight combines his distant travels with his listeners' current context.

What is true of the traveler is most true of the pilgrim. Because he wanders the physical world on a moral and spiritual quest, the pilgrim has become a common *subject*, as well as a teller, of tales. In many medieval and modern folk stories, the pilgrim appears as a benefactor to guide the hero to the solution of his problems (cf. AT 756). English legends of the Battle of Brunanburh state that a band of pilgrims, returning cured of their afflictions from the shrine of St. John of Beverley, inspired King Athelstan to pray at John's shrine before the battle and obtain holy help for his victory two days hence.[29]

Often the folktale hero becomes a pilgrim himself, and his pilgrimage becomes his principal test. Such a test may take many forms. In the medieval legend of Alexander of Metz (AT 888), husband and wife take the pilgrim's road at different times—he to prove his faith, she to prove her fidelity. In the legend of Count Hubert von Calw (AT 974; DS 530, 529) the pilgrimage is a test of values, and the Count ultimately chooses to live as a wanderer rather than return to the company of his hypocritical peers. In the well-known Tannhäuser tale (DS 171), the test once more concerns faith, but here the hero fails.[30]

Magic and miracles, defining properties of the folktale, are especially common on the road of the pilgrim. Most *Märchen*, as I have noted, begin in ordinary surroundings. There is no magic at home; only when he wanders does the hero find wonders. This tendency is intensified when the hero takes the pilgrim's road: magic and miracles crowd his path. British legends speak of a heavenly light that shines out along the road to Glastonbury when a crime is committed. This miracle commemorates the time when St. Indractus and his company were murdered while on pilgrimage to St. Patrick's tomb; their bodies were discovered and their murderers killed through similar miraculous acts.[31] Chaucer knew such stories: it is on a like journey that the pilgrim described by Chauntecleer is granted a magical dream informing him of a friend's death (7.2984–3049). Finally, in *Märchen*, not only the pilgrim's road, not only his actions, but his *tales* as well, possess magical virtue. Simply by recounting the story of his own sins and misfortunes, the holy man can convert sinners from their evil ways (AT 756A, KHM 206).

The folktales retold by Chaucer's pilgrims sometimes speak of pilgrims too. They provide examples of both the devout and the erring pilgrim. Both types encounter miracles in the course of their quests. In the Man of Law's Tale (AT 706), a penitential pilgrimage to Rome reunites Alla with his faithful wife Custance; this "coincidence" asserts that on pilgrimage, as in a fairy tale, the impossible can come to pass. Three misguided pilgrimages end less happily. The Knight's Tale puts Palamon on a "pilgrymage / Unto . . . Venus" (1.2214–15), a petition that fails because Palamon has invoked a deity that cannot answer all prayers. In the Pardoner's Tale (AT 763), a hubristic pilgrimage to conquer death destroys three wastrels. The Friar's Tale is another parody of pilgrimage, setting a churchman on an unholy quest with the devil as companion. In these three tales, the miracle of the pilgrimage is a negative one, reflecting the impure motive of the pilgrim.

Both literally (because the teller chooses tales which reflect his own experience, then adds his personal touches to them) and metaphorically (because, through the conventions I have discussed, the teller is identified with the action of his tale), the oral narrative represents its narrator, and vice versa. Both by experience and by association with the story, the best taletellers are travelers. The Canterbury pilgrims are archetypal travelers and, like the real-life pilgrims described by Thorpe, "great tale-tellers" as well. Chaucer's choice of pilgrimage as a setting for oral stories is consonant with everything we know about the spirit of the folktale.

Three widespread phenomena of Chaucer's day—the parish gild, the dual nature of pilgrimage, and the concept of pilgrim as storyteller—are themselves simply manifestations of deeper social, religious, and cultural realities of the English Middle Ages. Each is representative of contemporary patterns of thought and behavior, patterns Chaucer preempts and plays upon to give shape and meaning to his poem. We know that the poet observed the workings of these phenomena: the traits most characteristic of the gilds as they functioned, and pilgrimage as it proceeded, in his time, are portrayed with telling accuracy in his verse. Parish gild, pilgrimage, and pilgrim artist comprise the frames around the frame of the *Canterbury Tales*.

FOUR

Chaucer and the Shape of Performance[1]

The road as stage, the pilgrim players: both aspects of Chaucer's setting incorporate the folkloric structures of fourteenth-century thought and society. Yet the *Canterbury Tales* presents far more than the general conditions for generating stories: it gives us a game, described in some detail, with well-delineated rules, clearly executed roles, distinct and consistent patterns of interaction. Is this game Chaucer's invention? If not, from what source did he derive it? Does the game itself—*as a game*—have a shaping role in the poem? Critical interpretations of the structure of the *Tales* range from the exasperatingly vague to the excruciatingly specific.

At one extreme are the allegorical readings that address the poem as if it were a riddle, the least obvious solutions often found the most intriguing. For seventy years various critics have claimed that the pilgrimage was contoured as a foil for theological doctrine, that the characters and their stories symbolized, for example, the Seven Deadly Sins.[2] Later, the shapes of Gothic architecture were invoked as blueprints for the deep symbolic structure of the poem.[3] As these imaginative reconstructions multiply, Chaucer's own concrete and explicit setting—a company of pilgrims engaged in a festive storytelling contest—becomes lost in a crowd of icons and symbols.

At the opposite pole are literal interpretations that view the poem as a chronicle, much as fundamentalists read the Bible. Frederick Furnivall, for example, counted miles and days to reassure us that, yes, it was indeed possible that the Cook would have had enough time during the eight-and-a-half-mile ride between Ospringe and Harbledown to drink himself into the stupor that caused him to fall from his horse.[4]

My approach is more abstract than that of the literalists, but more firmly rooted in social reality than the answers most recently in favor. *Chaucer shaped his poem to simulate the structure of the medieval festival, fitting the patterns of action within the frame and links to a model of oral group performance thoroughly familiar to his contemporaries.* The audience's knowledge of such oral shapes influenced their response to the poem, which—whether or not it was read aloud—became a model oral entertainment in their eyes.

It is puzzling that, of the innumerable critical works devoted to the *Canterbury Tales,* there is not one which closely examines its possible structural relationship to the patterns that governed the presentation of oral arts in medieval festival.[5] Critics have closely examined the debt of Renaissance artists to festive forms. Citing many of the rituals I will discuss, C. L. Barber has demonstrated their influence on Shakespeare's comedies, and Mikhail Bakhtin has presented an imaginative assessment of their importance to Rabelais.[6] Why not a similar study of Chaucer? Perhaps because festival form is not merely conspicuous in the *Canterbury Tales,* but inseparable from the work itself. Barber and Bakhtin demonstrate how Renaissance authors *preempt folk forms and reshape them into literature.* I contend that Chaucer *reshapes literature into festival,* crafting a frozen representation of a lively play form never before (or since) rendered in writing, a world fully consonant in its rules and interactions with celebrations witnessed and enacted by the poet's contemporaries. Shakespeare's comedies may be festive, they may incorporate festive structures, but in their larger form they adhere to the conventions of Renaissance drama. Rabelais' prose may be festive, but (according to Bakhtin) it is not based principally on festival, nor is it imitative of festival in its overall structure: Rabelais used festive modes to shatter, rather than refashion, preexisting molds of all kinds, oral and literary. Chaucer's narrator, on the contrary, claims to be reporting act-by-act the progress of a game. I contend that Chaucer the Pilgrim and Chaucer the poet stand here in formal accord. Whether or not there was ever a pilgrimage-*cum*-storytelling-contest that proceeded exactly in the manner of the *Canterbury Tales,* there were many contemporary celebrations that shared the poem's pattern.

If, in creating his poem, Chaucer has also *re-created* a consummately medieval festival, the tale he tells must have specific artistic and social dimensions, and these two factors must hold each other in constant balance. Festive art, the antithesis of closet art, must appeal broadly. There are no Emily Dickinsons among the practitioners of oral poetry: the concerns of the audience must surface in the artist's plan. Therefore, festive art not only entertains, but also gives voice to the concerns of an entire group, providing a mixture of social critique and compensation fantasy.[7] Accordingly, to demonstrate that Chaucer has re-created the medieval festival, I must first show that he has chosen festive actions appropriate to the social status of his performers. I will examine the players and moves of historically documented games, and derive their most broadly representative social and artistic patterns. The evidence presented here comes principally from nine festivals well-known to Chaucer and his contemporaries; it is likely that Chaucer witnessed or participated in specific enactments of most of them. I will identify the nine most common shaping features of these games, then describe each rule in some detail, and show how Chaucer incorporated each into his poem.

All nine festivals were mounted by groups similar in social background to some or all of the Canterbury pilgrims. The performances took two basic forms, determined by the status of the players. Such *noble and bourgeois* entertainments as the *Cour Amoureuse,* the love debates, the London Pui, and the courtly Mayings were large and elaborate contests in which poets strove for the favorable judgment of a mock prince. A close look at one reveals the form common to all four:

> The *Cour Amoureuse* was monumental both in size and formality. Over six hundred members are listed on one of its registers, about seven hundred on another, all ranked according to a rigid system. Membership was exclusively male, though ladies were present at the meetings and played an important role in the proceedings. On St. Valentine's Day, following a series of masses, the group assembled under the direction of the Prince of Love, an accomplished minstrel. Then ensued a competition among *gentil* poets, whose work had earlier been screened for entry by the twenty-four ministers of the *Cour.* The subject matter was love, and the entrants' goal was to please the ladies who were called upon to judge. The winning poet was awarded a crown and chaplet made of gold.

There is evidence to connect Chaucer to the *Cour,* the Pui, and the courtly Mayings.[8] Though all such links are speculative, the *Canterbury Tales* shows he knew their general rules. Among his fictional players, the Knight, Squire, Monk, Prioress, and Franklin would share a familiarity with these elite games.

The *Mixed-Class* entertainments—the Feast of Fools, Boy Bishop ceremonies, Riding of St. George, mystery plays, Christmas guisings and Lord of Misrule performances—were massive events in which commoners took on the roles of their masters, ruling as kings-for-a-day over the entire play society. The *Festum Stultorum* is broadly representative:

> The Feast of Fools was mounted by members of the lower clergy in open mockery of their ecclesiastical superiors. The deacons and choirboys chose from their ranks a "Bishop" to perform his role in the most absurd manner possible. The festivities began with a church service marking his investiture. Within the church, he delivered bawdy sermons and read a parody mass, which often contained the ludicrous "Prose of the Ass," performed in Latin as the congregation called out a derisive response in the vernacular. Outside the church, celebrations continued, assuming even wilder forms whose indecencies "would shame a kitchen or tavern," and involving the participation of the entire community. The outside revels also featured oral performances, most often "verses scurrilous and unchaste."[9]

Such feasts took place throughout England and embraced the entire range of its citizenry, but the principal performers and primary beneficiaries were members of the lower classes, people whose positions in life corresponded with those of the Reeve, Miller, Manciple, and Summoner. Thus, medieval performance, like Chaucer's pilgrimage, engaged two distinct classes of players: *gentils* and churls. The accompanying chart (Figure 2) describes the two performance types, which differed according to this broad social division.

In the first seven of their nine shaping traits, the *gentil* and churl festivals resembled each other closely. First, both featured an *autocratic ruler*, a Master of the Revels, who governed absolutely within the festive frame. This leader was a temporary despot whose preemptive powers made him a formidable, if playful, counterpart of the real king. The merchant membership of the London Pui chose a prince to serve as uncontested judge of their song competitions. He was endowed with royal stature by the contesting poets, who addressed their *envois* to him and strove for his approval.[10] The Floure and Leafe rivalry was probably ruled in similar fashion. One of Deschamps' *ballades* exalts John of Gaunt's daughter, Philippa: to the poet, the leader of the floures is not merely a duchess, but the very "Queen of Love, who surpasses all in wisdom and honor."[11]

Among the *gentil* celebrations, only the *Cour Amoureuse* recognized multiple leaders. The Prince assumed the autocrat's position, but he was a minstrel, more a decoration than a ruler. The real power was vested in an oligarchy of ministers who controlled the festivities and a company of noble ladies who judged the entries. Yet it is important to note that the *fiction* of rule by one mock prince was preserved even at the *Cour,* as revealed in a surviving poem addressed to the Prince:

> Noble, so powerful prince,
> valiant Pierre d'Auteville,
> holding, as sovereign, in your hand
> the Court of Love. . . . [12]

A like penchant for dictatorship is apparent in mixed-class entertainments. In his play role, the Boy Bishop enjoyed great authority—and an audience with the real-life King of England. The Pope of Fools also ruled supreme in his mock domain: he was empowered to raise funds for mounting dramas which he directed.[13]

Chaucer's Herry Bailly is an autocrat of the same playful stamp. From the beginning of the ride, the Host claims control over the artistic and behavioral destinies of the pilgrims: he sets the rules and determines who tells the tales. The Host's relatively low social status among the pilgrims has its medieval parallels—as when the minstrel Hauteville reigned as Prince of

FIGURE 2

Festive Structures in Medieval Life and Literature

TRAITS	GENTIL CELEBRATIONS (NOBLES AND BOURGEOIS)				MIXED-CLASS CELEBRATIONS	
	Cour Amoreuse (Feb. 14)	London Pui	May Day (Floure and Leafe)	Love Debates	Mystery Plays (York, N-Town, Beverley)	Feast of Fools
1. Autocratic ruler	Prince d'Amour	Prince du Pui	Queen of Love	Queen of Love	—	Pope (Bishop, Archbishop) of Fools
2. Amateurs as major performers	noble and *gentil* poets	*gentils* perform their songs	noble and *gentil* poets	noble and *gentil* poets	lead roles *sometimes* professional; others amateur	occasional pay for leader; other roles amateur
3. Measures to enforce participation	noncompetitors buy supper for all	dues waived for competitors	?	?	fines for nonparticipants	townsmen force participation of clergy
4. Rigid formality	quasilegal written charter	quasilegal written charter	patroness and retinue have specific tasks*	debates duplicate legal procedures	very formal written charters	choosing of Pope and retinue; special masses, sermons
5. Processionality	?	horseback procession to Prince's home	procession to the fields	?	massive procession preceding plays	parade through street after mass
6. Mingling of sacred and profane	religious observances precede *Cour*	gild dedicated to holy works, maintaining altar	?	?	pious plays, *interludi* sacred and profane mingle in performance	masses and revels mingle
7. Wider festive context	masses, supper, games	holy feast and supper for poor precede competition	tourneys, jousts, dances	dances, other amusements	masses, parades, revelry	Christmas celebrations
8. Competitive elements	*individuals* compete for crown	*individuals* compete for crown	*teams and individuals* compete	*individual* competition and judgment	*group* rivalry among tradesmen	social *factions:* laity vs. clergy, intra-church fights
9. Hierarchical structure	17 ranks *duplicate* social order	*duplicates* social order	queen and court *duplicate* social order	queen and court *duplicate* social order	participants' place in parade and plays assigned to gilds *duplicate* social order	lowly Pope and retinue *invert* social order

?   Indicates insufficient evidence for the presence of a given trait

—   Indicates that the trait is not present

*   Indicates the hypothetical reconstruction of the Floure and Leafe ceremony, according to Bédier, Kittredge, and Pearsall

FIGURE 2 (Continued)

TRAITS	MIXED-CLASS CELEBRATIONS (continued)			FESTIVE FICTIONS		
	Boy Bishop	Lord of Misrule and Mummings	Riding of St. George	Canterbury Tales	Decameron	Sercambi's Novella
1. Autocratic ruler	Boy Bishop	Captain of mummers; Lord of Misrule	St. George	Host (Herry Bailly)	rotating dictatorship	Leader (Aluizi)
2. Amateurs as major performers	occasional pay for leader; other roles amateur	amateur players	amateur players	amateur players	all tellers perform as amateurs	teller not paid
3. Measures to enforce participation	forced participation of clergy	fines for nonparticipation	gild members must attend or pay fine	noncompetitors must pay bill for all players	—	—
4. Rigid formality	choosing of Bishop, retinue; masses, sermons	specially delegated roles, regimented performances	elaborate procession with delegated roles	Host dictates rigid rules to company	each dictator chooses theme	Leader appoints storyteller, entertainers
5. Processionality	parade through street after mass	guisers ride and march in procession	all participants join in procession	pilgrimage	—	pilgrimage
6. Mingling of sacred and profane	masses and revels mingle	masses and revels mingle	religious gild funds masses	pilgrimage and profane tales	—	pilgrimage and profane tales
7. Wider festive context	Christmas celebrations	Christmas celebrations	masses and feasting on St. George's Day	pious frame indicates sacred procession	—	—
8. Competitive elements	social *factions*: laity vs. clergy, intrachurch fights	social *factions*: lower classes mock superiors	?	*individual and factional* competition (trade vs. trade, class vs. class)	—	—
9. Hierarchical structure	lowly Bishop and retinue *invert* social order	lowly king (abbot) and court *invert* social order	lowly servants play St. George and retinue, *invert* social order	Host attempts to *duplicate* social order as *gentils* defer to him; churls attempt to *invert* social order	—	Leader appoints treasurer, stewards; no evidence of class status of appointees

Love over real-life lords at the *Cour*. As Master of the Revels, the Host shares a pedigree with the mummers' captain, the May Day king, and a host of anonymous autocrats who have governed folk performance as far back in time as it can be traced.

Second, in medieval celebrations the featured performers were *amateurs who comprised both the cast and the audience*. The festive play world gave the stage to those who would not normally mount it. Sometimes, as at the Pui and the *Cour*, accomplished minstrels attended the rites, and occasionally they held positions of esteem. Nevertheless, professionals did not figure in the central performances. At the *Cour* and in the love debates the nobles contended for honor; at the Pui the wealthy *gentils* competed. Men who customarily paid others to entertain them here entertained their peers. The knight Boucicaut, who had servants read to him on Sunday afternoons, was among the composers of the *Cent Ballades,* and he presented these pieces as questions of love at the Papal Palace in Avignon.[14] The late Middle Ages marked the birth of one kind of renaissance man—the *gentil* who also served as occasional artist.

Mixed-class feasts were also primarily amateur affairs: only a handful of players were compensated. The Paston family of Norwich retained a servant, William Woode, "to pleye Seynt Jorge" in the Riding, but Woode also worked day-to-day as a Warden in the Paston household.[15] By and large, the roles of audience and participant were even less distinct for the lower classes than for the *gentils*. As Bakhtin has stated, festival "does not know footlights, in the sense that it does not acknowledge any distinction between actors and spectators."[16] From time to time—as during the Prose of the Ass, when the Pope of Fools read his profane sermon to all assembled in the church—one performer set himself apart from the crowd. But the pattern of the churls' celebration allowed for a looser period of entertainment during which the entire group performed variously and severally, or in unison: after the sermons of the Boy Bishop and the *Rex Stultorum,* the crowd carried its rough artistry into the streets.

Chaucer himself was one of the Middle Ages' accomplished amateur artists, of the same status as the merchants who performed at the Pui and the untitled *gentils* who submitted poems to the *Cour*. It is not surprising, then, that the composer of the *Canterbury Tales* describes a festive amateur performance. In keeping with the festive rules, Chaucer's audience and cast (with the exception of Herry Bailly, the Master of the Revels himself) are one and the same. E. K. Chambers once suggested that the Canterbury pilgrims tell tales only because there are no professional entertainers in the company.[17] But Chambers has misread the purpose of this traveling game: it is simply festival decorum that the entertained must also entertain.

Third, the autocrat's powers were most pronounced in his *strictures to ensure the players' participation.* The edict of Chaucer's Host—"And whoso wole my juggement withseye / Shal paye al that we spenden by the weye" (1.805–6)—finds a perfect echo in the bylaws of the *Cour Amoureuse:* any minister who failed to submit songs was required to host a dinner for his fellows.[18] Both the *Canterbury Tales* and the medieval celebration offer systems of rewards and punishments designed to cajole every member of the audience into the spotlight. For the lower classes, urging often turned into coercion. In Beverley even the gildsmen who did not act in the mystery plays were called upon to attend, wearing uniforms. Fines and dues were also levied by the King of Fools and Lord of Misrule: their subjects were required to play—and to pay for their fun.

Fourth, medieval games were marked by a *rigid formality* that would seem forbiddingly constrained in modern play contexts. In the twentieth century, only the driest of "festivities" (college commencements, for example) are structured as severely as were the most playful pastimes of Chaucer's England. The Canterbury game is no exception. In addition to setting an enormous fine for failure to join in his game, Herry Bailly passes down general rules for participation, specifies a prize and the means of funding it, appoints certain storytellers, and reserves the right to stop a teller in the middle of a tale (1.788–809, 828–41). He works out a system of protocol for the pilgrims to follow. At the journey's outset, though many outrank him in real life, they sheepishly—"by oon assent" (1.817)—acknowledge his privilege to "seye his voirdit as hym leste" (1.787). As the journey progresses, the Host maintains his rigid authoritarianism. Though from time to time he is challenged, even overridden, the pilgrims' defiance is directed not at the festive rules themselves, but at Herry Bailly's failure to apply those rules correctly (a point to which I will return).

Gentil celebrations were often governed by written statutes. The charter of the *Cour* orders ministers to register and seal the verses submitted for competition. The subjects of the poems, even the exact words of the refrains, were dictated to the entrants. If the *Cour's* codes can be taken as representative, punishments for noncompliance were severe. Anyone guilty of composing

> . . . ditties, complaints, rondeaux, virelais, ballades, lays [or similar pieces], rhymed or in prose, to the dishonor, diminution, or blame of a certain woman or women in general . . . will have his coat of arms erased. His shield will be painted the color of ashes, as if he were an infamous man, an enemy of honor, and dead to the world.[19]

This ruling raises questions concerning Chaucer's punishment as described in the *Legend of Good Women* (F 431–41): to atone for having created a faithless Criseyde, he must write poems in praise of virtuous ladies. Though many have read this sentence simply as a product of the poet's imagination, the *Cour* would have punished the author of the *Troilus;* the Pui, with its like set of prohibitions, would also have censured him.[20]

A similar sense of protocol attended mixed-class revels. Surviving "missals" attest that the parody mass celebrated during the *Festi Stultorum* was as elaborate as the regulation mass itself: the text requires, for example, that during the performance of this sometimes rather orthodox service, the celebrant bray three times at specific moments, and that the congregation respond by braying, providing comedy on cue.

Fifth, the *Canterbury Tales* and fourteenth-century festivals share a sense of *processionality* which conjoins the act of entertainment with the parade. In the *Tales,* the procession provides the major motivation for the game: stories are told to soften an otherwise hard and joyless road. Tales and songs made the journey more pleasant for the traveler. Yet it was an intrinsic aspect of medieval performance that, even without a goal to move toward, travel was inseparable from entertainment. Medieval performances—particularly those involving the entire community—were seldom stationary affairs.

Of the nine games examined here, not one can be said for certain not to have included a procession. Among the *gentil* celebrations the Floure and Leafe was introduced by a morning procession into the fields, and the London Pui included a horseback progress to the home of the newly chosen Prince. The Feast of Fools and the Boy Bishop ceremonies ended with cavalcades in which the mock potentate was carried through the city. And the Corpus Christi pageant often included two processions: one, the more pious ecclesiastical march, in which the town's governmental and trade officials went with church officers through the streets; the other, the plays themselves, in which it seems the procession traveled to the performers, as the audience visited dozens of fixed stages.[21] Both processions were so highly valued that at York (1426) it was ruled that they be held on separate days, so that one parade would not engulf the other.[22]

Like the mixed-class festivals, medieval pilgrimage oscillated between the poles of utmost formality and utter chaos. Shorter processions tended to be formal. Local pilgrimages in fourteenth-century France, for example, featured groups of riders followed by pilgrims afoot, all proceeding in rank, *cierges* in hand, toward a nearby shrine.[23] On the longer processions it was likely that at some point the ranks would break into an ungoverned flow, often a near riot, which was as much a part of the festivities as were the measured marches. Similarly, the investitures of the Boy Bishop and Pope of Fools were marked by processions down the church aisles during which hierarchical decorum was observed. Afterward, however, the crowd became riotous and moved formlessly through the streets. Orderly and disorderly parades would alternate.

The length of the Canterbury pilgrimage dictates that it follow the long form just described. Chaucer does occasionally indicate that some order is being imposed on the ranks. We know, for example, that the Miller plays the bagpipe for the company and that his music leads them out of Southwark. Here is a partial image of procession, one that is reinforced to some extent by the observation that the Reeve rides always at the end of the group. At St. Thomas's watering hole, however, the Host breaks up this parade, gathers the group in a flock (1.824), and initiates a less orderly progress, which loosens as the journey wears on and reaches a peak of disorder when the Cook becomes drunk and falls off his horse, just before the last secular tale is told.

Sixth, in all the medieval celebrations, *sacred and profane elements intermingle* in an easy and complementary fashion. Even the most secular (the Court of Love, presenting erotic themes in governmental guises) and the most anticlerical (the Feast of Fools, observed in patent mockery of the Church) entertainments openly embraced the most conventional aspects of piety. Masses and sincere prayer marked these otherwise unholy rites.[24] Similarly, the overtly religious events possessed a second, secular, impious side. After the Boy Bishop's mass, prayers were supplanted by obscene songs as celebrants filed from the church.

Chaucer's poem opens with a melding of sacred and profane—invoking in one breath spring breezes, mating birds, and the holy blissful martyr, Thomas of Canterbury. The subsequent tales freely interweave piety and play. This combination is characteristic not only of the nine games examined here, not only of the *Canterbury Tales,* but also (as I stressed in Chapter 3) of medieval pilgrimage in general, where piety was penetrated with nearly every gradation of play—from simple levity to open blasphemy, from gambling to sex acts in sacred places.

Seventh, even the most elaborate medieval games were simply parts of greater celebrations, fragments embedded in a *wider festive context.* Each feast was a mere motif in a complex ritual design, and each must be seen within its frame to be fully understood. In general, the framing event was a foil to offset the celebration: the more austere events were temporally flanked by revelry, the more playful events by austerity and order. The wildest celebrations were set in the midst of the holiest seasons. The Feast of Fools, the Feast of Boys, and the reign of the Lord of Misrule were fixtures on the church calendar, small and relatively uncharacteristic segments of the long, devotion-filled chain of Christmas holidays. The Riding of St. George occurred at the end of the Lenten season, on the day (April 23)

dedicated to the patron saint of England—in the very time of year that
Chaucer's pilgrims begin their ride.

The *Canterbury Tales,* like its real-life medieval analogs, is a celebration
within a celebration, a profane event embedded in a sacred procession.
Beginning with a seasonal allusion, the poem places the pilgrimage at the
onset of spring, in the neighborhood of Holy Week and St. George's Day, a
time when both spiritual faith and secular life are revitalized by the return
of warmth and greenery. The pilgrims' play and their holy destination are
both appropriate to the season. The allusion to St. Thomas which opens the
poem and the sermon on sin which ends it are as true to the nature of
medieval play as are the raucous tales which fall between these sacred
markers. Like those contemporary games which were framed by pious activities, Chaucer's poem emphasizes the impious side of things, thus providing a contrast to the larger, more serious celebration the pilgrims are keeping. Herry Bailly's first address to his guests, as they end their supper the
night before the ride, describes the dual nature of the journey they will
soon undertake:

> Ye goon to Caunterbury—God yow speede,
> The blisful martir quite yow youre meede!
> And wel I woot, as ye goon by the weye,
> Ye shapen yow to talen and to pleye.... (1.769–72)

The Host, like the great majority of his co-celebrants, sees no ambiguity in
this juxtaposition. As Canterbury is reserved for praying, the road there
favors playing. And as the journey lengthens, the Host does all in his power
to maintain a mood of levity: he calls repeatedly for merry tales and con-
demns excessive religiosity wherever he finds it. The pilgrims generally
affirm that the playful make the best prayers.

The seven traits examined thus far apply equally to the games of the
gentils and those of the churls, but the remaining two break down according
to class lines. Until now, in this chapter and elsewhere, I have stressed how
Chaucer created a middle world mediating the extremes of society and
behavior. His cast excludes most gradations of nobility and peasantry, his
pilgrims generally foreswear pious and impious excesses. Yet, as some of
the gild records have suggested, this newly formed middle-class community, not yet officially recognized in Chaucer's time, was marked by
internal tension. The more *gentil* members sought the power and privilege
traditionally accorded the nobles, and the churls sometimes claimed the few
concessions the older order had granted the peasants. In the *Canterbury
Tales* both groups exploit the play roles of the venerable three-estate system. The *gentils* imitate the behavior appropriate to noble games; the churls
adopt performance patterns characteristic of the peasants.

Eighth, medieval games were marked by strong *competitive elements.* There was a marked tendency among the *gentil* celebrants to compete for a prize: often a crown of gold or of leaves, as at the *Cour* and the Pui. There was an acknowledged winner and a prescribed means by which he was chosen. Entrants played hard, and not always fairly, for this prize: the Pui's statutes dictated punishments for prejudicial action on the part of the judge, and the bylaws of the *Cour* went to great lengths to ensure that entries were honestly submitted.[25]

The churls, however, competed as a rule not individually, but by factions. Individual competitions sometimes occurred, but these generally *preceded* the feast. The Boy Bishop and Pope of Fools were chosen from among many candidates well before the celebration; the festivities began with the winner's investiture. Within the feast the real contest was one of class and occupational rivalry. Such fights were often the unsanctioned side effects of play. Nevertheless—as Le Roy Ladurie has shown—they constituted perhaps the most important aspects of the performance, as far as the lower classes were concerned.[26]

At the *Festi Stultorum* and the Feast of Boys, the competition was often between the laity and the permanent clergy. At Rheims in 1390, the vicars and choirboys dressed themselves in bourgeois fashion; in reprisal, offended laymen mounted plays satirizing the clergy. At Auxerre, a similar rivalry was institutionalized, as laymen and lower clergy competed in the singing of "doggerel songs." The winning faction often subjected the losers to intense mockery.[27] Occupational rivalry surfaced continually on Corpus Christi Day. Members of each gild tried to outdo all others, both within the dramatic framework and outside it. Trade competition often surged into violence. At York in 1419 the Carpenters and Cordwainers attacked the Skinners, using axes to hew apart the torches carried by the latter to light the Corpus Christi procession. Later, there was a four-year wrangle between York's Cordwainers and Weavers. The issue was precedence in the procession: the Cordwainers, who felt slighted by protocol, refused to bear torches. The quarrel led to the arrest of many tradesmen and was submitted to civic arbitration before it was resolved.[28]

In the *Canterbury Tales*, the Host—a man of no small social standing, who wants to be a respectable "play" lord to his betters—favors the *gentil* approach. He sets up a prize and announces rules favoring individual competition. And the *gentils* respond, with characteristic grace. The Knight temporarily renounces the privilege of his rank and signals his submission to the rules. Like real-life entrants in *gentil* contests, he is interested in the prize. His remarks reveal a competitive bent, but affirm his intent to compete in *gentil*manly fashion:

> I wol nat letten eek noon of this route;
> Lat every felawe telle his tale aboute,
> And lat se now who shal the soper wynne. . . . (1.889–91)

Other *gentils* begin their tales humbly, lamenting their lack of artistic skills, a rhetorical ploy also found in extant poems from the *Cour* and the love debates.[29]

True to *their* rules, however, the churls bolt: they tell their stories not for the free lunch but for blood. The Miller, Reeve, Cook, Manciple, Friar, and Summoner appear on stage not merely as artists, but as verbal duelists, using their tales as vehicles for thinly-veiled blows against occupational and class rivals, in a manner reminiscent of the mixed-class celebrations. In general, the fights between pilgrims of roughly equal status are the most overt and intense. Furthermore, the intensity of their competitions is generally proportionate to the intensity of the rivalry between the trades represented by the duelists. Thus, when the Miller faces off with the Reeve, it is not merely personal animosity, but a long-standing trade conflict between the estate of reeves and the estate of millers which lies at the root of their fight. Similar occupational rivalries lie behind the slurs traded by Summoner and Friar, and Cook and Manciple. Their quarrels evoke the fights held on Corpus Christi, when intertrade conflict was an essential, if unofficial, motivating force for the players.

Ninth, the churls' readiness to fight is rooted in the fact that all the games were marked by *elaborate hierarchical structure*. In these festivities, the "craving for symmetry" which Johan Huizinga finds everywhere in medieval culture is clearly evident.[30] The *Cour* was divided into seventeen orders, from *grands conservateurs* to "gardeners," each play role yielding powers commensurate with its title. The *Cour* duplicated the actual machinery of government and society—the entire upper and middle portions of French society were mirrored in play. The Prince of the Pui, the patroness of the Floure and Leafe, and the Boy Bishop were all given play roles corresponding exactly to the functions of the leaders for whom they were named.[31]

Such duplication pervades the entire social range of performance. In the mumming performed before Richard II, the masked procession represented the most powerful elements of upper-class society and marched in ranks which followed the dictates of protocol. First came the knightly estates: squires, riding two by two, preceded knights riding in similar fashion, heralding the Emperor; then followed the clerical procession, with a Pope and a retinue of twenty-four Cardinals. In the processions preceding the mystery plays the entire town marched in uniform, with the lowly Porters in the lead, followed by other groups in exact ascending order of municipal importance. At Beverley the most powerful gilds also acted the most important plays, with the Gild Merchant, which controlled the town, significantly assigned to mount the *Last Judgment*.[32] Deference to rank entered even into the wage scales of the paid performers. At the Coventry Corpus Christi plays, the player of God was the most highly paid actor, followed by the players of Souls, Common Men, the Worm of Conscience, and Judas. The same connection between social and metaphysical hierarchies is seen in the plays assigned the gilds: "play" life imitated day-to-day life as closely as possible. At York, the shipwrights, fishers, and mariners staged the *Noah* play; the goldsmiths the *Magi;* the bakers *The Last Supper.*

One important factor, however, divides the *gentils'* play hierarchy from that of the churls. While the elite games *duplicated* the social order, placing players in roles correspondent to their real-life status, the churls *inverted,* even *subverted,* that order. The Pope of Fools was chosen from the lowest ranks of the inferior clergy, the Boy Bishop from the choirboys, St. George from among the servants—and their retinues as well from among other lowly groups.

Although mixed-class feasts mocked the highborn, the mockery itself presented a hierarchical conception of society. This fact cannot be over-stressed; interpreters of medieval festival often fail to note the importance of hierarchy even for the churls. In an otherwise impeccable depiction of carnival, Bakhtin declares:

> The suspension of all hierarchical precedence during carnival time was of particular significance. Rank was especially evident during *official* feasts . . . [which produced in effect] a consecration of inequality. On the contrary all were considered equal during carnival.[33]

In emphasizing freedom, Bakhtin distorts the nature of the game. *Relative* license was indeed extended to the lower classes during carnival, but abso-lute, ungoverned freedom was not. The freedom of festival, like that of yoga, is based upon constraint. Mixed-class celebrations featured the same formal aspects that governed *gentil* pastimes: both had their autocrats and enforced participation. Even as, during the Feast of Innocents, choirboys marched down the aisles proclaiming the fall of the mighty (to the strains of *Deposuit potentes*), a new Bishop—a boy bishop, granted rank and privilege over his fellows—came forward to assume the mitre and reinforce the paradigm of hierarchy. Festive churls did not destroy hierarchy; rather, they rearranged its content, from the bottom up—much as when the Pope of Fools wore his holy breeches on his head.

Such inversions were not only desirable but necessary for the lower classes. Festival presented their only opportunity for sanctioned social as-cent. It was a time when a miller *could* "quite" a knight, as Chaucer's Miller does. The subservience of the churls at all other times made them not only relish, but demand, exalted treatment on holidays. And the lowly were generally granted greater power at festival than at any other time. This power extended from the license to act like clowns and louts to the more directed animosity of imitating and ridiculing their social superiors, and to requesting and receiving clear concessions from the upper classes. Such obligatory charity marked the Boy Bishop ceremonies: the chosen boys were not only granted the pleasure of ruling for a day, but were also given money, lavish meals, and the permission to skip classes the following day, as the rest of the community resumed its ordinary work. And at the Feast of Fools, the Bishop who surrendered his role to the play Bishop was required to host a sumptuous feast for the mobs that mocked him. Clearly, these were real as well as "play" rewards.

Furthermore—and this is perhaps the most important point—the churl denied such holiday offerings would feel no inhibitions about seizing them outright. At wedding feasts in northern France, the hosts customarily offered wine to the crowds, whether or not the watchers had been invited to the wedding. In 1427 at Magnieux, a group of peasants, when refused this wine, started a riot; another such scene in 1381 ended with a death. A record dated 1375 from Chalon-sur-Marne records the tradition (*acoustumé et de longtemps*) that newly married nobles must give their servants wedding gifts; in 1391 a servant denied his due killed the bridegroom.[34] Similar violence, most often taking the form of riots, and occasionally leading to murder, is found in various fourteenth-century accounts of the *Festi Stultorum*. Defiance of uncharitable *gentils* also occurred on pilgrimage. In 1431 four hostelries near the shrine of Our Lady of Walsingham were burned to the ground. The explanation advanced for the arson was that pilgrims were enraged by the high cost of lodging.[35]

The Canterbury pilgrims follow the performance paradigms appropriate to their respective estates. Chaucer the Pilgrim, like Chaucer the poet, is a *gentil* who introduces the players in customary fashion: his list of *dramatis personae* reads in nearly exact descending order, just as do the two surviving membership lists of the *Cour Amoureuse*. When the festival begins, Herry Bailly reinforces that order, setting up his game strictly along *gentil* lines. He manipulates the straws in his hand so that the Knight—the most exalted pilgrim—may tell the first tale. Attempting to use this planned accident to create an elite hierarchy, the Host invites the Monk to tell the second tale. In seeming irony, but true to the nature of medieval performance, it is the highborn pilgrims who bow before the less-than-worshipful Herry Bailly. The Knight, Man of Law, Squire, and their peers "wol nat rebelle" against his pleasure (5.5), but proclaim his requests their obligations (2.41).

The churls, however, have another game plan. True to his pedigree, the Miller defies the Host's attempt to keep him in check. As Herry Bailly asks the Monk to tell a tale to follow the Knight's, Robyn steps in and says he has a noble tale himself. The Host, trying to maintain gentility's control, says that some man better than the Miller should speak next (1.3130). This proves too much for the Miller—he must endure servitude at all other times, but not on holiday. The Host's condescension only strengthens the Miller's resolve: if refused his holiday rights, he will simply seize them.[36]

As the celebration continues, the two factions continually evince their predictable behavior. The Squire, Merchant, Franklin, Man of Law, and Prioress all speak only when spoken to, using the most deferential language in addressing their often indelicate leader. But the churls seldom acknowledge the man's existence. Like the Miller, the Reeve, Cook, and Summoner all break into the session without so much as speaking to the Host, let alone asking his permission.[37] The Summoner, Pardoner, and Friar interrupt other pilgrims, defying the Host and assuming his leadership functions. From the Miller's Tale to the Manciple's, the churls mount a revolt against the Host, rendering the *Tales,* in effect, a double celebration: an abortive *gentil* entertainment and a churls' brawl, both at once.

Over this mixed event the Host rules precariously, in both modes. He is the exalted Prince of the Pui, sometimes delicate (as in his address to the Prioress, 7.445–51), sometimes speaking "lordly as a kyng" (1.3900). But as the festivities wear on, he assumes more and more the ludicrous aspects of the Pope of Fools. His gaucheness, malapropisms, and anticlerical jokes partake of the slapstick of the *Festi Stultorum.* Herry Bailly's mock panegyric to the Physician is set in a comic style common to surviving texts from mixed-class festivals. Just as the Host praises the most ignoble tools of the doctor's trade—

> I pray to God so save thy gentil cors,
> And eek thyne urynals and thy jurdones,
> Thyn ypocras, and eek thy galiones,
> And every boyste ful of thy letuarie;
> God blesse hem, and oure lady Seinte Marie! (6.304–8)

—the office of the Feast of Fools magnifies the most asinine qualities of the ass:

> Behold the son
> Yoked below his massive ears!
> Extraordinary ass!
> Lord of Asses!
> That strong jaw . . .
> Pulverizes the fodder . . .
> He consumes barley grains
> Together with their ears;
> Wheat from chaff
> He separates on the threshing-room floor![38]

In both texts, the more extravagant the rhetoric, the sillier its object is made to seem. Herry Bailly expends similar mock praise on such *gentil* clerics as the Monk (7.1924–64). But he is less subtle in deriding churchmen of lower rank (the Parson and Pardoner, for example), and he is openly abusive to his secular inferiors (Miller, Cook, Reeve).

But in the end, the Host's balancing act fails. To salute one's betters while slandering inferiors is not festival decorum. Because Herry Bailly never relinquishes his real-life social position, he cannot control the churls. When he insults the Miller (1.3130, 3134–35) and the Cook (1.4344–55), both in terms of their class status, he is asking for trouble. And when, in a passage worthy of the Prose of the Ass, he proposes to enshrine the Pardoner's testicles in a hog's turd (6.947–55), he very nearly forfeits his role. His speech is a quintessential festive inversion, momentarily substituting the Pardoner's sexual "relics" for St. Thomas's shrine, and invoking the comic principles present at the Feast of Fools when dung rather than incense was burned in church censers to convert the sacred to the utterly profane. But the Host himself is not the appropriate person to mock the Pardoner. Unlike the Bishop of Fools, he is not a lowborn man assuming temporary control over his equals. Instead he has been pulling rank, assuming he can have the best of both worlds: the authority of the *gentils* and the churls' tongue. It is necessary here that the Knight step in to reimpose order. This *gentil*, who has acted in a manner consistent with his class, merits the respect he demands in telling Host and Pardoner to kiss and make up. He displays the deference wise nobles extended to churls on holiday and reasserts the festive equality of the two men. After this, the Host never regains his former stature. The Knight, breaking his promise not to interrupt any man's tale, shuts up the Monk; even the lowly Manciple prevails over Herry Bailly, convincing him not to make the Cook perform (9.25–68).

Just as the General Prologue proclaims the end of the three-estate society, the dissolution of the Host's rule prefigures the death of the medieval festival, which is deeply rooted in the estates system. At the poem's beginning, Chaucer the narrator attempts to offer an idealized picture of medieval society, but adds much information revealing that medieval ideals are no longer being observed. In the General Prologue class distinctions are blurred: the riders are seldom what they would have themselves seem. The humble attire of the Knight clashes with the pretentious dress of the Miller and Gildsmen. The older estates model is not adequate to describe the society of these fourteenth-century pilgrims, who take advantage of new-found wealth and social freedoms to dress and act in ways that reflect their aspirations rather than their origins.

Similarly, the medieval festive forms which Chaucer uses to shape the *Canterbury Tales* are absolutely dependent on the estate system. Medieval festival flows from the premise that *gentils* and churls can and should be distinguished. If bourgeois Herry Bailly can pretend to be a noble, but cannot defer to his inferiors at Holiday, a festival can become a riot. Just as violence resulted when mass celebrations were repressed, the *Canterbury Tales* tends toward dissolution as the Host is overridden and the pilgrimage wears toward its end.[39]

No surviving work of medieval literature could have given Chaucer the festive outline of his poem.[40] No contemporary social theory could have supplied the structure or details of the internal divisions in his pilgrim community. But the records of medieval festivals mark the same rules, roles, and tensions that surface in the *Canterbury Tales*. Chaucer drew upon the traditional play forms he had witnessed all his life and crafted them into a lifelike shape of performance.

FIVE

The Substance of the Game

Thus far I have sought to know my subject by its shadow (the broadest contours of its social context), then by its skeleton (the rules that give it shape). These forces provide the matrix of the poem, but concrete detail fleshes it out and forms the most immediate cause of its appeal. Accordingly, the final chapter of this section studies one of the game's more specific aspects: how the tellers use traditional tactics to personalize their tales.

It has long been recognized that at least fifteen of the pilgrim narratives share the plots of well-known folktales from medieval times. This finding supports, but does not of itself ensure, the broader conclusion that the *Canterbury Tales* possesses strong affinities in folklore. As I noted in Chapter 1, content alone does not render a work folkloric in nature. Traditional patterns must be present on other levels. Here I extend the concept of setting further into the poem, to the narrative interactions of the pilgrims: the relationship between the teller who steps forward from the audience and the audience he rejoins at the end of the tale. A few of Boccaccio's frame tales display interaction between teller and audience and some sort of accord between teller and tale, but nothing in Chaucer's literary tradition has prepared us for the extent of the interpenetration of audience and story displayed in the *Tales*. Sometimes working in collusion, sometimes splitting into angry factions, the pilgrims are constantly pulling each other over the narrow line dividing fantasy from fact. An identical phenomenon has been observed in group storytelling sessions studied by folklorists, and there is no reason to believe this tradition did not exist before scholars recorded it—and long before such authors as Ibsen and Stein made similar techniques commonplace in the world of letters.

The folktale world is a "lie," but we have seen how skillful narrators give it the semblance of truth: the teller claims to have seen the chimerical wonders he describes, and often presents himself as having recently returned from the banquet celebrating the marriage of the wonder-working hero to the disenchanted princess. One of the best tactics for endowing lies with a sense of truth is to draw the audience into the fiction, to depict them as characters in the narrative. In certain traditional storytelling situations, every member of the audience becomes an actor in a giant, dramatized frame tale. The group leader, often a master taleteller, becomes the hero Prince, who in both story and fact sets out on a journey for The Most Beautiful Tale. He will reward the finest story told that day. By turns he confronts each member of the audience, allotting each a fictional identity— princess, ogre, dragon, wise old man—which is then acted out by the desig- nated performer. It is not uncommon in such a situation for group mem- bers to carry aspects of their real identities—occupations, physical traits, roles within the group—into the fictional world. The magic of the story overlaps and often overwhelms reality, as those who fail to perform satisfac- torily are pronounced "trapped" within the tale frame.[1]

In other narrative situations the tale often ends as it begins, in a setting similar to the physical surroundings of the audience. At such junctures narrator and audience conspire to blend the tale world with its real context and act out their parts in both domains. As mentioned earlier, many Hun- garian folktales, when told in spinning rooms, close with a scene set in a spinning room. Here is a typical ending:

> The heroine, previously tortured and exiled by a cruel mother-in-law, has survived in the wilderness with magical help. Now she returns to the palace from which she was exiled. She enters a spinning room filled with women, including the cruel mother-in-law. A rotating storytelling session is in progress. When the heroine is called upon to speak, she narrates her autobiography as if it were a fiction. She uses the third person, with good reason: her tale will reveal crimes committed by the mother-in-law; to present such acts as "lies" is safer than to make an open accusation. Excitement grows as the listeners begin to realize that this is the true story of the teller. The audience gasps as the heroine reveals her mother-in-law's crimes. When the woman finishes her story, the mother-in-law is killed, and the heroine is reunited with her hus- band.[2]

An expert narrator will manipulate this story situation to an intense pitch, inviting the real-life listeners in the spinning room to take the part of the fictional audience. They respond dramatically, exclaiming their wonder as the once-told tale comes to life in its second form. Folklorist Linda Dégh witnessed one such performance in the 1950s: the audience was so persua- sive in its role-playing that she immediately assumed their excitement was a reaction to the outcome of a story they had never heard before. Dégh was later to discover that the tale was well-known to the group; the listeners simply relished the opportunity to lend their acting skills to the impact of the denouement. Such narrative occasions place fantasy and reality in com- plex interrelation. The "true" audience joins the narrator in her "lie," which focuses on a character who tells a further "lie"—though ironically this last lie is (at least in the logic of the *Märchen*) an absolute truth.

A similar juggling of the markers separating life from fantasy is one of the *Canterbury Tales'* most remarkable and realistic traits, a device employed so skillfully that the frame, the tellers, and their tales intertwine in a texture of allusion which has enmeshed critics throughout the past century. Those who view the poem as naturalistic drama and expect the pilgrims to respond to everyday motives and cues have been confused by the role-playing of the Pardoner and enticed by possible biographical elements in the Miller's Tale. But such elements *are* realistic—not in terms of the everyday world of medieval people, but in accordance with the game world of traditional narrative.

In the *Canterbury Tales* narrator and audience often try to break into the fantasy world, or to trap others within it. Of course, the pilgrims recognize the difference between play and reality. Chaucer's tale world can, and often does, work by the more rational rules of analogy, wherein real-life characters are simply *compared* to fictional heroes and heroines. Herry Bailly, for example, compares his wife Goodelief unfavorably to the heroine of Chaucer's Melibee (7.1891–1923). The Clerk, however, goes a bit farther toward melding the two worlds when, after dedicating his envoy to the Wife of Bath (4.1170), he goes on to imply that his fictional heroine once lived (4.1177: "Griselde is deed"). The Clerk has brought the audience into the tale before he has properly ended it. His purpose is to set up a strong contrast between the living Wife of Bath and the fictional Griselde. His final, playful words introduce fantastic elements reminiscent of the *Märchen:* those who would presume to follow Griselde's example risk being devoured by Chichevache, the cow that feeds on patient wives. But the Clerk's frivolity simply renders his moral more concrete. He has suspended the grave fantasy world of Griselde; then, with references to a living Wife of Bath and a once-living Griselde, he opens his narrative to the real world. Finally, he combines both realms in a parody coda.

After the Clerk has ended, the Merchant follows in kind, if at first more rationally, comparing Griselde favorably to a real person, his own wife. He then launches into a fiction that conveys his perceptions of his wife. During the lengthy opening scene, in which counsellors advise January on the virtues and problems of marriage, the fictional Justinus makes reference to the flesh-and-blood Wife of Bath:

> The Wyf of Bathe, if ye han understonde,
> Of mariage, which we have on honde,
> Declared hath ful wel in litel space (4.1685–87)[3]

In its effect the Merchant's ploy resembles the Clerk's. By opening the adventure of May and January with a debate on marriage, the Merchant sets his story directly in the context of the pilgrims' ongoing concerns.

Then, by making his fictional characters respond to the arguments of the real-life pilgrims, he places the living audience in the center of his fabricated council.

Even more complex are the strategies of the Miller, Reeve, Friar, and Summoner, each of whom tries to "trap" an opponent in a scandalous tale. Chapter 8 will examine their narratives in detail. Here I wish only to point out that the pilgrim narratives sometimes become so vivid that offended parties jump into the stories and try to stop them. When the Friar's Tale reveals itself to be a slur on the profession of summoners, the pilgrim Summoner breaks in to reinterpret the action (3.1332). Later, when the Summoner exacts a fictional vengeance on friars, Huberd the Friar explodes. The Summoner's story features a friar who promises to say masses for those who give him food and alms, but later erases their names from the mass rolls. At this point in the narration, the real-life Friar cries to the Summoner, "ther thou lixt" (3.1761)—and, of course, Huberd is right. In terms of both official doctrine and the players' rational understanding, this tale, like all others, is a lie. But the vividness of the Summoner's description, the heat of Huberd's anger, and the extent to which previous tales have blurred the borders of truth and illusion—all combine to work the Friar into a state of mind that exchanges fiction for purported fact.

As I have mentioned, taletellers include elements of autobiography in their stories. The narrator's self-involvement is often unconscious: every teller of every tale somewhere, somehow talks about himself. Certainly the stories of the Wife of Bath, Clerk, Merchant, and others can be perceived, and have long been analyzed, in this way. But here I speak specifically of a conscious and calculated modeling of an alter ego, a character created by the narrator to act as a second witness to the "truth" he wants his tale to convey.

Robyn the Miller's narrative introduces just such a witness: Robyn the Knave who, as Robert Pratt has noted, bears a telling resemblance to the Miller. In addition to their name, the two share physical strength, a trait described in two nearly identical phrases: the Miller is "a stout carl for the nones" (1.545), the knave "a strong carl for the nones" (1.3469). Both demonstrate their strength by breaking down doors. These allusive connections are minimal but secure.[4]

But there are further suggestions of the identity of the two. These hints, found not only in the story proper but in the overall performance context, explain the motive for Robyn's fictional self-duplication. Before the tale is told, the Reeve, upset by Robyn's professed intent—to tell a "legende" in which a carpenter is cuckolded (1.3141–43)—tries to prevent the performance. Oswald shows a paranoid concern over the possibility that he, as a carpenter, and more particularly as a potential cuckold, might be made the butt of this dirty joke. Robyn scoffs at the Reeve's paranoia. But the Miller's words, spoken ostensibly to allay suspicion, are really calculated to intensify it. "As long as your wife provides you with what you want," says the Miller, "there is no reason to probe into her affairs"—

> An housbonde shal nat been inquisityf
> Of *Goddes pryvetee,* nor of his wyf.
> So he may fynde Goddes foyson there,
> Of the remenant nedeth nat enquere. (1.3163–66)

—the implication being, of course, that such probes may uncover unpleasant secrets. It is as dangerous to violate one's wife's secrets as to inquire after God's.

But immediately after counselling the Reeve to repress his dangerous curiosity, Robyn begins his own graphic probe into cuckoldry. Among the characters he presents is Robyn the knave, whose special task it is to search out and reveal secrets. The Miller's alter ego stalks through the house, hiding where "the cat was wont in for to crepe" (1.3441), observing Nicholas the clerk and relaying intelligence to John the carpenter.

Later, in another of the story's conspiratorial moments, we are reintroduced to the phrase "Goddes pryvetee," earlier used by the Miller to "allay" Oswald's suspicions. Nicholas speaks with John the carpenter, presenting him with secret information about a coming flood; this is the lie through which the clerk will cuckold the carpenter. "I give you this secret," says Nicholas,

> But Robyn may nat wite of this, thy knave. . . .
> Axe nat why, for though thou aske me,
> I wol nat tellen *Goddes pryvetee.* (1.3555, 3557–58)

But Robyn the knave must have been stealing about, spying upon his master as well as upon Nicholas, for—if we assume his identity with Robyn the Miller, and recall the convention by which the teller proclaims himself witness to the events in the tale—Robyn has "come back" from the fictive world to tell us this story. Though the Miller has said men should not inquire into "Goddes pryvetee," his alter ego has done so—and the pilgrim Robyn (narrative tradition invites us to conclude) has likewise fathomed the "pryvetee" of Oswald's wife.

Pratt reads the relationship between Robyn the knave and Robyn the Miller in terms of absolute, rather than storial, identity. According to Pratt, the Miller's Tale is a disguised account of something that actually transpired earlier in the lives of Oswald and Robyn. Oswald is "sely John" the carpenter, whom Robyn once served as a knave. Pratt's interpretation is an example of how a "naturalistic" reading can distort the nature of reality itself. Can one assume, easily or otherwise, that the Reeve is capable of John's extreme credulity, or that the account of John's actions—as he lies in a tub stocked with provisions, suspended far above his workshop floor—is a realistic one? I see the story as naturalistic in a different sense; it adheres to the workings of the storyteller's world. Robyn indeed wants the Reeve to seem a cuckold, but he has no evidence. Only through fiction can he portray the paranoid Reeve (presented in the guise of the equally paranoid John) as cuckold and himself (in knave's disguise) as witness to the fact.

The final instance of role-playing to be examined here is the most controversial and complex: that of the Pardoner. Like the Miller, the Pardoner "plays himself" in his fiction, the difference being that the Pardoner's is no pseudo-autobiography. The choreography of the performance is relatively simple, but it is sufficiently vague to invite confusion.

After the Physician has told an excruciatingly "moral" tale, Herry Bailly, seeking some narrative relief, turns to the Pardoner and asks for "som myrthe or japes" (6.319); however, the well-bred pilgrims—to whom the Pardoner's profession, sexuality, and antisocial actions are anathema— flatly reject this suggestion. Perhaps afraid of the ugly intensity a "mirthful" tale by the Pardoner might reach, they ask instead for a "moral thyng." After stopping at a tavern (perhaps with the rest of the company[5]) to drink some ale and eat a cake, the Pardoner responds. First, he describes his own bad business: how he uses verbal art and demagoguery to lure people to repentance while he, a heretic, practices the very sin of greed against which he so vehemently inveighs. The Pardoner then launches his tale—by all critical accounts a masterful exemplum—in which greed leads three drunkards to murder each other. Finishing this sermon before a crowd stunned by his tale, he pronounces a moving benediction. Then, after a brief pause, he lapses into a tasteless epilogue, in which he demonstrates the methods by which he sells pardons to gullible listeners. He calls upon Herry Bailly (as the one "moost enveluped in synne"; 6.942) to step forward and kiss the "relics" which he has already revealed to be forgeries. The Host responds with violent humor directed at the Pardoner's most vulnerable trait, his dubious sexuality: "I wolde I hadde thy coillons in myn hond. . . . / They shul be shryned in an hogges toord!" (6.952, 955). For the first time on the pilgrimage the Pardoner is speechless, with fury. The Host responds that he will not "pleye" with such an angry man. It takes the intervention of the Knight to end the hostilities; this *gentil* commands that the two exchange a kiss of reconciliation. This they do, and the pilgrimage resumes.

No pilgrim has received more critical evaluation than the Pardoner, and a substantial proportion of this literature has centered on the "problems of naturalism" which his performance presents. Again, I think the emphasis on "dramatic realism"—in this case introduced by Kittredge's enormously influential essay and followed by sheaves of commentary from others[6]—has often worked to obscure the sense of the tale as seen within the framework of the poem. Again, an argument based on "traditional play realism" can help solve some of the problems.

Of the many critical voices raised in explaining the Pardoner's Prologue and Tale, only a few—most notably George Sedgewick's—have called attention to the fact that the Pardoner is delivering a *performance*. Even in a context where everyone is required to perform, this fact is important, because—as Alfred David has noted—the Pardoner makes his living telling stories.[7] He is the one thoroughly professional oral artist of the lot.

Many have questioned the propriety and realism of the Pardoner's confessional Prologue. Is it not too much an act of self-damnation to be acceptable as anything other than an internal monologue? The Prologue, however, fills a definite narrative need. The Host has asked for an entertaining, joking performance—one that the Pardoner, we have no doubt, is capable of delivering—but the appalled *gentils* have demanded that the man "play himself" (or, rather, what he should be) and tell a "moral thyng." The Pardoner decides that he will indeed play himself. By making his profession part of his performance, he is following an oral tradition dating back beyond the Middle Ages. Just as the Carpenters' Gild performed the play of *Noah* at York, and just as twentieth-century migrant workers make migrant workers the heroes of their tales, the Pardoner leans upon his calling to strengthen his story.

Unlike most folk performers, the Pardoner renders a stunningly cynical self-portrayal. He has his reasons, however. He is not going to yield the *gentils* a moral thing without showing them the evil uses to which such lessons can be put. And, further to mock their naive notions of morality, he induces them to take part in his fraud. What follows is a lesson not only in his own power of deceit, but in the *gentil's* potential for self-deceit. While introducing his own role, the Pardoner introduces the audience to theirs: they are to play the simple congregation he normally addresses. His diction is calculated to force the audience into this new role, following his lead. He speaks of himself in the habitual present, serving up what is, in effect, a *performance of a performance,* both a description and an enactment of his typical oratorical strategies. When the Pardoner speaks confessionally of his methods—"in Latyn I speke a wordes fewe, / To saffron with my predicacioun" (6.344–45)—he is securing his role. The fact that he *is* now performing softens the effect of his self-damning words. A confessional *role* is less direct and upsetting than an actual confession. Like a folktale told in the first person, the Pardoner's Prologue creates the distance necessary for the audience to contain its shock at the events portrayed. The vividness of his role-playing also makes it easier for his audience to assume their parts.

He works them into his fictional context through second-person address. By the time he has delivered such speeches as this—

> Goode men and wommen, o thyng warne I yow;
> If any wight be in this chirche now
> That hath doon synne horrible, that he
> Dar not, for shame, of yt yshryven be,
> Or any womman, be she yong or old,
> That hath ymaad hir housbonde cokewold,
> Swich folk shal have no power ne no grace
> To offren to my relikes in this place (6.377–84)

—the Pardoner is probably gesturing and speaking in the manner he describes: "Myne handes and my tonge goon so yerne / That it is joye to se my bisynesse" (6.398–99). The pilgrims may be appalled, but they are also fascinated by a startlingly forceful performance.

Once he has set up the proper *emotional context* for his tale, he begins the story in the *physical context* of the pilgrimage. The group is in or near a tavern, and the Pardoner has a draft of ale in his hand. He finishes his drink (6.456) just before he starts his story (6.463). Thus, though the pilgrims are expected to play the roles of churchgoers, they are reminded that in the midst of their holy voyage they have encroached upon a place of sin. The setting provides physical evidence that no one is ever too far from temptation. The Pardoner has now given the group two complementary roles which combine to suit his purpose: they are to play *simple Christians, well aware of their potential for error.* And they know that their guide on this journey, a religious official who freely admits his own evil, is well-suited to lead them in both directions. Like the Clerk and the Merchant, the Pardoner has brought the real world into his tale, but he has done this so thoroughly and on so many levels that it will require enormous narrative skill for him to maintain a fiction so permeated with ugly reality.

The Pardoner is more than equal to the task. His tale of the three drunkards' encounter with death is haunting and inexorable. The pilgrims—who may, like the Pardoner, be nursing drafts of ale—are presented with a storial demonstration of how one sin leads easily to another. To strengthen the frightening connection between the audience and the unhappy protagonists of the tale, the teller concludes with another direct address of his congregation of "tavern pilgrims." After calling brief attention to the fact that he has been performing ("And lo, sires, thus I preche"; 6.915), he ends with a moving reference to a pardon that transcends any he can sell:

> And Jhesu Crist, that is our soules leche,
> So graunte yow his pardoun to receyve,
> For that is best; I wol yow nat deceyve. (6.916–18)

Like the other storytellers, the Pardoner has narrated a lie; furthermore, as he has openly admitted, his profession is more a lie than his tale. Yet it is an unsettling fact that all these lies can lead to the sincere contemplation of what his audience conceives to be the holiest truth.

At this point I think we may assume, with Sedgewick, that the audience has been stunned to silence. The Pardoner as well seems stunned at the effect of his performance. He has carried off the ultimate lie: all the early reminders of his fraudulent role have been temporarily forgotten, and he has in a way been accepted as a conveyer of moral truth to a group once appalled by his very presence. He now jokingly extends the play to demonstrate how severely they have been deceived. When he invites the "sinner" Herry Bailly—the man who branded him as a homosexual and asked him for bawdry—to kiss the false relics, his sermon, like any well-told folktale, ends by reentering the immediate surroundings of the listeners. Like the Clerk, the Pardoner has here reopened the narrative to embrace the real world, but the contrast between his pious tale and his own enormous impiety precludes an artful closure. The illusion of solemnity now exploded, the Host also explodes, and the pilgrims, having both heard and taken part in a powerful performance at their own expense, resume their ride.

The narrative ploys of the Pardoner, Miller, Merchant, and Clerk possess parallels in twentieth-century oral tradition. The reader may feel justifiable doubts about the presentation of evidence so far removed from Chaucer's age. Yet we have historical evidence from Chaucer's time that travelers were well-known taletellers, and literary evidence from Sercambi and Boccaccio that stories were exchanged by rather large groups of people, sometimes in a competitive manner. Furthermore, there is a record of an actual group of long-dead travelers—the Scottish shepherds of the sixteenth century—who amused themselves by telling the *Canterbury Tales*.[8] There is no record of how the *Tales* were told in this context, but—just as Chaucer's fictional pilgrims and modern taletelling communities mix reality and fiction—the shepherds may have performed not only the stories but the frame as well. If the Scottish account tells us nothing more, it strongly affirms that the best critics of oral tradition—the tellers themselves—considered the *Tales* sufficiently "oral" to retell it two hundred years after Chaucer's death.

PART TWO

Conventions of a Narrative War

SIX

The Social Base of Angry Speech in Chaucer's London

I have sketched the broader outlines of Chaucer's folkloric world and established the presence of a series of frames within which his pilgrims, like fourteenth-century oral entertainers, defined and practiced their art. My task now is to delimit more clearly the poet's traditional linguistic territory, the folkloric rules of word use which helped shaped his craft. I believe that the most appropriate prologue to an interpretation of what Chaucer *did* say is an assessment of what he *could* say. What follows, then, is an inquiry into the power of the word in late medieval England, specifically the power of the angry word—for when words are pushed to their expressive limits they expose the boundaries of acceptable speech.

No other sort of language crosses social barriers more effectively than insult. Through the agency of verbal abuse, friends and strangers formerly at peace become enemies, and common differences of opinion are aggravated into violence and murder. By its nature, insult defines one's social limits: when angry words cross class boundaries, the speaker becomes a trespasser stepping momentarily from one realm of status into another.[1] There is no better indicator of a culture's sense of propriety than what it considers its insults to be, and no better way of measuring the relative power of two social groups than to find how often, how heatedly, and how successfully one retaliates when insulted by the other.

Fortunately, the records of insults from Chaucer's time and place are remarkably full: they allow us to determine what his contemporaries thought about verbal abuse, and how common law and the common citizen reacted when confronted with angry words. The names of Chaucer's friends, patrons, and associates—Ralph Strode, John of Gaunt, Nicolas Brembre, John Northampton—appear repeatedly among the slander cases examined below. The world described in these records is Chaucer's world, and, as I will show, the boundaries imposed on everyday speech therein also apply to Chaucer's poetic speech. I draw upon records of insult from fourteenth-century London to establish the relative importance of slander in day-to-day city life, the channels through which it traveled, and the values expressed in such encounters. After showing that verbal abuse can be regarded as an accurate measure of social identification and social control, I will demonstrate how Chaucer's pilgrims put their language to the same general uses that fourteenth-century Londoners did.

To define the information available for study, I invoke the anthropological concepts of *official culture* and *real culture*. Official culture is that view of human behavior perpetuated through such formal documents as proclamations and laws. Real culture is culture as it is actually practiced, aside from, and often in opposition to, the prevailing official views. Official culture stands in relation to real culture as the elite value system stands in relation to that of the folk. I seek a real, unofficial measure of verbal abuse: a social record of insults, along with the reactions to them and punishments for them, as they occurred *in vivo*, rather than a legalistic ideal view of what one may or may not say under certain conditions. In short, I study slander and its penalties as reflexes of folk culture.

Both the legal climate of fourteenth-century London and the surviving court records favor such an unofficial approach. Except in extreme circumstances, slander was punished only in ecclesiastical and local courts, from which no records remain. The cases examined here were defined by "no certain law"[2] and therefore reflect verbal values that transcend, and occasionally defy, legal precedent. It was thus through a system of folk justice that such cases came to court.

Though tribal and national law codes of the early Middle Ages prescribed enormous punishments for slander, its legal status changed in the course of the Middle Ages. By the fourteenth century, the king's courts, the most exalted English legal body, entertained only one very restrictive statute touching on slander: *scandalum magnatum,* or the defamation of governmental officials, an act designed to punish those whose words were perceived as threats to national security. Legal historians agree that *scandalum magnatum* was very rarely invoked.[3] Thus, in Chaucer's time, slander was adjudged almost solely in minor courts, by the neighbors of the accused. The manor, the borough, and (in London) the wardmote were the common governmental units for rendering judgment.

Why did defamation actions, unlike other legal processes, descend to the lower courts as the judicial system grew more complex? Slander is always a serious matter in small communities, where oral reports are the primary determinants of one's standing as a citizen. Only the members of such a close-knit group can judge fully the effects of defamatory speech. Slander was restricted to local jurisdiction because it was most effectively judged and punished by the groups within which it operated—and within which it was likely to cause the most harm. The primary intent of such local jurisdiction was to preserve the social balance of small communities. What we now consider standard legal measures (for example, the use of a lawyer to represent the plaintiff) occurred very rarely in slander cases—in general only when a face-to-face encounter was likely to lead to bloodshed. Local courts ensured that verdicts and penalties would remain community matters. My interpretation finds support in the structure of these courts. In contrast to the king's courts, in which over half of the jurors were strangers to the accused, lower court juries consisted solely of men who knew the defendant.[4] It was assumed that the persons best able to judge the damages of defamation were those who best knew both accuser and accused—those who, in effect, made their reputations.

This conclusion—that the judgment of slander was a community affair aimed at preserving local social balance—is further substantiated by a second general observation. Today slander is almost always punished as a tort—a dispute between two parties which is settled when one compensates the other, in accordance with the judgment of the court. But in the Middle Ages, *slander was not merely a tort, but a crime against society* punished by fine, imprisonment, or public humiliation—a debt discharged not to the offended party, but to the group as a whole. This distinction is important not only in determining the gravity of slander (a crime is generally considered more serious than a tort), but also in establishing its folkloric nature—for in the local courts crime was a matter of consensus, not a question of individual rights. Most often the defendant and plaintiff had to return from the courtroom to live as neighbors in the same district. Hence, the best way to reach an amicable and long-lasting settlement was to leave judgment to the neighbors of both, thus ensuring a decision which validated the mores of the neighborhood and enlisted general approval.

If punishment defines the crime, the intent of London's slander actions was to preserve social stability (and therefore the social order in general) rather than the good name of any one person who might suffer abuse. Individual privilege was seldom even a concern of the jurors. Among 108 surviving cases in London's *Letter Books* and *Pleas and Memoranda Rolls,* we find 122 punishments meted out (many of the convicted received more than one punishment), but only three in which guilty parties were forced to pay damages to plaintiffs.[5] The standard penalties were prison sentences, fines, and removal from public office. In over 97 percent of the actions the debt incurred for verbal abuse was discharged to society; therefore, we should consider the offense a crime.

Further evidence rests in the language of the verdicts, which emphasize the public nature of the offense. In 1378, when Thomas Knapet spoke "disrespectful and disorderly words" of John of Gaunt, the court clerk stressed that not only Gaunt but all London was put to shame by this act, because the words were spoken "to the great scandal of the said lord, and to the annoyance of all good folks of the city." Several transcripts openly speculate on the grievous consequences that might ensue if slanderous words were believed. In 1383, Hugh de la Pole was put on the pillory for spreading rumors "in deceit of the whole people, and to the scandal of the City of London; the more especially as the same city, by such lies so fabricated, might very easily be everywhere defamed." These crimes are clearly community matters.[6]

There are other indications of the public nature of slander. It was adjudged not by the actual damage incurred, but by its *ultimate conceivable social consequences*. When William Spending, tailor, was tried for "speaking evil and shameful words against Robert Croul, Tawyer," he was convicted on the grounds that "discord *might have arisen* between the two misteries of Tailors and Tawyers."[7] Slander judgments were intended not merely to correct social imbalances, but also to prevent them by assigning punishments before violence occurred. A final sort of evidence argues that the goal of these actions was social balance: after the verdict was returned, the offended party had the power to intercede and effect the suspension or reduction of the sentence. Thus, in the case just cited, the tailor's sentence was suspended "at the request of the good men of the tawyers." Though the offended parties received no monetary compensation for their grievances, they retained the privilege of arranging an amicable settlement. The outcome was not a financial but a social gain, which gave the plaintiff a distinct advantage in subsequent interactions.[8] When the antagonists returned to their communities, the offender was at the mercy of the plaintiff. One abusive word would cost him dearly. Such decisions reveal the jurors' attempt to ensure that insults would not be repeated.

Slander was not merely a crime, but a crime of considerable gravity, as shown by four types of evidence. First, the *penalties* incurred were enormous. Of the 51 fines recorded, 37 were for forty pounds (roughly the equivalent of $10,000 in modern American currency) or more.[9] The jail sentences, ranging generally from forty days to one year, were serious, and the public penances were commensurate with penalties for fraud, theft, perjury, and prostitution. And in none of the cases was it necessary to establish damage to the offended party for the penalty to be inflicted on the offender. The *pervasiveness of slander jurisdiction* provides a second measure. Apparently, there was no place sufficiently secret, no audience sufficiently small, to allow one citizen to slander another with impunity. Five of the cases punished offenses that occurred in private homes.

Multiplicity of jurisdiction further confirms the power of insult. Successful slander actions in one court were sometimes considered slanderous activities by another. In 1382, an unnamed offender was committed to prison because . . . he obtained in the Court Christian a mandate of excommunication against the good men of the said ward on the pretext that they had maliciously defamed him. . . . [10]

Here, a citizen's attempt to clear his name in church court was interpreted as slander by the civil court. In another case with similar overtones, a cleric entered a civil court "and declared that the whole court was excommunicate."[11] He was committed to prison. Overlapping legal interests made slander a problem for both church and state, a problem the average Londoner found difficult to avoid.

Finally, the magnitude of slander can be gauged by the fact that *medieval Londoners, for all intents and purposes, considered words and deeds to be of equal significance.* The records characterize and penalize words in exactly the same manner as they do the corresponding actions. This decision of 1299 is representative: "if [the offenders] be convicted of having committed trespass, either by *deed or word*, against Sir Henry le Galeys, while Mayor of London . . . they shall be bound to pay the Commonalty of London 100 pounds."[12] A statement of intent was equivalent to a criminal act: "Thomas Goudsyre, brewer, was committed to prison for *saying* that he would not sell the gallon of ale at the price laid down by the proclamation."[13] In extreme cases, a simple expression of opinion was considered punishable:

> . . . no man, great or small, of whatsoever estate or condition he be, shall speak from henceforth, or agitate upon any of the opinions, as to either [Nicolas Brembre or John Northampton, rival former mayors of London, the former of whom had been dead for three years when this proclamation was issued], or shall by sign, or in any other manner, shew that such person is of one opinion or the other.[14]

The penalty for violating this statute was prison "for a year and a day, without redemption." Chaucer, who had been Brembre's employee, doubtless had an opinion of the man; but here, as at other times, he must have observed a politic silence. Though summoned many times for debt and once for abduction (or rape), he was never to our knowledge called to court for verbal abuse.

To modern critics, medieval London appears to have been a remarkably verbal culture; the spoken word had powers to exalt and damn that extend almost beyond our comprehension. A dishonest word could in effect deprive the speaker of his or her human rights, and, in a certain metaphorical sense, of his or her humanity. The insult quoted most frequently in the London records is not "thief," "ribald," or "whore"—all of which are very common—but "false man." This term was used by the jurors, as well as by the slanderers, to describe a liar. Its implication is that a liar is not quite a real man—that, by speaking words that are untrue, a man becomes something distinctly other, or less, than a man. If one insults another, one of the two is inevitably a "false man." If the slander is unjustified, the speaker is false by virtue of his words; if the insult truly describes the offended party, *he* is the false man by virtue of his deeds. Only by careful choice of words and actions could people disprove the negative traits ascribed to them by others and establish their antagonists as "false." Such was the case in 1365, when William Gedelyne, pouchmaker, charged his former master with spreading the rumor

> ... that [Gedelyne] was a man of ill-fame, who had robbed his master. ... As no one would employ him, [Gedelyne] had been forced to seek work at York, where his *behavior disproved the scandals* moved against him. ... [His master then] declared ... he would submit to judgment if four good men of his mistery could be found who would declare him guilty. [Four fellow tradesmen then testified against the master, who] publicly did penance for his false statements by standing on a stool in the great hall.[15]

Here the spoken word shows double force: the word of his master was enough to keep Gedelyne from getting a job, and later the word of four pouchmakers was sufficient to prove the master guilty. This, like other cases, was judged by neighbors of the accused, its outcome hinging on two factors: two men's overall reputations, and how they had comported themselves in previous potentially slanderous encounters. Every previous aspect of their public lives served as contributing evidence. Slander judgment may have been the nominal privilege of the court, but the verdicts had been preordained in the defendant's neighborhood.

Records attest that the courts and certain powerful individuals used slander actions for purposes of social control. As I have shown, such actions had the express purpose of maintaining social stability—and the balance constantly reaffirmed by the courts was the superior status of the noble, rich, and powerful. In 85 percent of the cases, social inferiors were punished for offending people of greater rank. Though some may read such cases as instances of *scandalum magnatum*, we most often find that it was not the governmental machinery, but the power of the upper classes, that was at stake:

> [Alice Godrich had slandered William Walworthe] to the great scandal of the offices which the said William had heretofore held in the city. ... [Ralph Strode, lawyer for Walworthe] asked that the same Alice might be chastized, that so, such scolds and she-liars might dread in the future to slander reputable men.[16]

In another action Richard Whytington, Alderman, brought to court a woman who had "defamed" him, claiming that he owed her money,

"Whereas in real truth, and according to her oath . . . she confessed that, the account being strictly balanced and everything taken into consideration she owed more to the same Richard than the said Richard owed to her."[17] In these and many other cases, the initial motivation was a private dispute, but offended parties relied on their higher legal or social status to transform a common quarrel into an act of class warfare, invoking the concept of hierarchy to settle matters in their favor.[18]

The extremes of society are seldom represented in slander actions. Servants (a term used in the records to designate both apprentice tradesmen and the personal servants of magnates) were rarely represented. Only three clear cases in which servants were offenders appear among the 108; similarly, the king, court, and nobles were considered the offended parties in a surprisingly small number of cases.[19] The tendency which Barbara A. Hanawalt discovered among the criminal cases in the Ramsey Abbey villages also holds true in the London courts: the great majority involved disputes among the highest levels of *local* society.[20] London suits most often concern quarrels between average citizens and their *immediate superiors:* in nearly 85 percent of the cases the defendants are "middle-class" citizens, accused by people of noble birth, superior social standing, or greater wealth.

Almost invariably the person of higher rank was the plaintiff, and also the winner, of the suit. In her study of village crime, Hanawalt found that verdicts were determined by status. The London courts show a similar tendency. In only four of the 108 cases are persons convicted for insulting their legal inferiors. Also confirming Hanawalt's findings for crime in rural England is the fact that the punishments vary according to the status of the convicted. One of the cases quoted above amply demonstrates the inequities involved: William Gedelyne, former apprentice of William de Ely, was able to prove that his master had slandered him and caused him to lose his job. Ely's sentence was to do "penance for his false statements by standing on a stool" in the Gild Hall. Here, for a grave insult, for which damages to the defendant can be clearly established, the social superior received a light sentence. No money was awarded the plaintiff, no fine paid the city, no jail sentence served. The only punishment dealt out was the mildest act of public humiliation found in any of the records. Penalties for those who insulted their social inferiors were small in number and mild in nature. Clearly, the major effect, as well as the intent, of the actions, was to reinforce the control exercised by powerful citizens over weaker enemies.

In summary, London slander actions operated according to three principles: 1) the maintenance of social order, which hinged at least in theory on the preservation of the social hierarchy; 2) the settlement of personal disputes, which were described in terms of threats to the social order; and 3) a bias toward the powerful, who were the principal, and nearly the sole, beneficiaries of these actions. These findings suggest an unwritten law, to be strictly observed by all who wished to stay out of trouble: "if you must slander someone, slander a social equal or inferior who does not hold a position in government."

The only other extant evidence of slander in medieval London are the *trade gild records*. Well-organized groups with quasi-official governmental powers, the gilds were chartered by the king and had to retain the crown's good graces to maintain their privileges. They were also, to some extent, subordinate to the city government. From early in the fourteenth century, city statutes gave gilds enormous self-governing powers, including the right of search and seizure in members' homes, so that wardens could regulate standards within the group.[21] In return for this power, craftsmen were expected to maintain the quality of their wares and stay out of trouble generally; if they did not, the entire gild would suffer the city's anger. Fines incurred for violating these self-regulatory statutes were deposited not in gild coffers but in the civic chest. A trade irregularity such as sales fraud was judged as a crime against the public at large, perpetrated "in deceit of the people."[22] These acts were punished in much the same way slander was, with fines, public humiliation, and prison terms.

If the city at large would suffer from trade irregularities, one particular urban group would suffer most: the offender's fellow tradesmen, whose names might be tainted by association with the criminal. Many charters state that the misbehavior of one tradesman redounds to "the very great scandal, as well of the good folks of the said trade, as of the City."[23] Among the offenses judged most grave by the city were internal disputes and public displays of hostility. To maintain its good name and charter, a craft was required to exercise strong controls over members' interactions. Because trade solidarity was a matter of importance, even of survival, for all craftsmen, it behooved the wardens to apply an equal justice to all gild members. As angry journeymen could appeal their grievances to the city, it was incumbent upon the misteries to provide some means of allowing for the redress of social inferiors *within* the gild, so as to avoid the dangerous situation of making internal dissension public. Therefore, records should reveal two things about a gild which was functioning properly: 1) city rolls should contain a comparatively small number of cases of intratrade slander, because these matters would be dealt with by the gilds themselves; 2) gild punishments for verbal abuse should show a far less rigid degree of social stratification than do the city records, because the key to social control in the gilds was not to reinforce hierarchy but to ensure amiable relationships within the group.

The records confirm these two hypotheses. First, in the civil courts, we find only 7 clear cases of slander within a given trade, as opposed to 41 instances of intertrade slander. Second, slanderers punished within the gild were treated with less regard for status than were the offenders called to city courts. In 25 percent of the gild suits (as opposed to less that 3 percent of city cases), superiors were actually convicted. Fines meted out within the gilds were fairly distributed: superiors and inferiors paid equally for their crimes. We find no clearly graded relationship between social status of offender, social status of offended, and size of fine.[24]

Strong internal controls, added to a sense of trade solidarity, inspired most members of the gild to direct their animosities outside the craft itself. Civil records confirm the strength of group solidarity, which often transcended status boundaries within the trade. When John Brugge, apprentice skinner, was taken to court for beating skins in the highway "contrary to the ordinance of said mistery," his master, Nicolas Bethewar, cursed the court with "opprobrious words" for sentencing Brugge, and the two went to jail together. Similar loyalty was shown in 1378, when the mayor and his sheriffs ran to quell a disturbance between the Goldsmiths and the Grocers. The Mayor accused an apprentice of inciting the trade fight; this apprentice happened to be the servant of one of the sheriffs present: Nicolas Twyford, Goldsmith. Twyford interceded to defend his apprentice and began to insult the mayor. Here a master abandoned his position as lawmaker to fight beside a fellow tradesman, and was sent to jail with his servant. Such accounts, taken together with evidence of frequent and violent battles between bands of rival gildsmen, demonstrate that camaraderie and internal controls caused craftsmen to channel most of their aggressions toward members of other trades.[25]

The trade gild records, when read together with the findings from civil cases, allow us to modify the unwritten rule that guided would-be bad-mouths in their day-to-day activities: "If you must slander someone, slander a social equal or inferior who is neither a public official nor a member of your craft." To discover if this rule really held, I measured my findings against certain cases of abuse which never made it to court: quarrels that led to the violent deaths recorded in the coroners' rolls. Nearly sixty percent of the rolls I examined mention an argument or quarrel preceding the murder.[26] The arguments—sometimes even the exact words of the antagonists—are frequently recorded. J. J. Sharpe has noted "how quickly, in those days, a word was followed by a blow from some lethal weapon."[27] It was apparently very common for two men to be speaking in friendly terms, and then to turn violent when one's misplaced remarks angered the other. The social penalty for insult was dramatically high, the legal penalties paltry in comparison. Perhaps the most vivid demonstration of the power of the word occurred in 1301: Alice le Quernbetere, walking home drunk in midday, insulted some workmen,

> ... calling them "tredekeiles" ["pavement stompers"], whereupon one of them drew her by the hand to himself and told her that she should work and tread the ground with them, and maliciously bumped her on the ground . . . ; she thereafter got up and went to the house of Elena Hellebole, her mistress, of whom she rented her house, and complained of the men; . . . thereupon the said Elena went to the men and called them Ribalds and other opprobrious names; . . . a man came by, whose name they knew not, and reprimanded the said Elena who abused him, calling him a thief, and he calling her a whore; . . . thereupon she threatened him saying that before the night the matter should be squared. [*CCR*, Case A29]

Elena then got two men, one of whom was her tenant, and "prayed them to avenge her" against the stranger. The men found him in a tavern and beat him to death. Here strangers, tenants, a servant (Alice, who instigated the riot, seems to have been Elena's servant as well as her tenant), and a lady of some repute are all shown acting violently against each other, with no stronger provocation than unpleasant words.

I examined coroners' records systematically to see if they would reinforce my previous findings. I expected to discover far more violence between rival trades than among members of the same trade; this, in fact, is what the records revealed.[28] Furthermore, the high incidence of "gang murders" involving warring gilds illustrates the leading role of trade solidarity in channeling aggression.[29] Often, members of one trade conspired to kill an opponent from another. In 1355, a gang of goldsmiths lay

> ... in wait for men of the mistery of saddlers in order to beat them, on account of a quarrel that had arisen between men of the mistery of Goldsmiths and that of the Saddlers. . . . [Twelve goldsmiths fell upon a single saddler and butchered him; *CCR*, Case E14.]

A second finding bearing on my argument is that violent crimes were committed against social equals and inferiors far more often than against superiors. In 43 cases, the victim was an equal or inferior, in only six a superior. Yet there was one surprising fact: there were 40 cases of killings of equals, but only three murders of inferiors. Indeed, Londoners seem to have murdered their inferiors less often than they did their superiors.[30]

What is to account for this imbalance? I assume that superior social position gave Londoners free reign to deal out verbal and physical violence against servants; therefore, the mighty could channel their hostilities successfully without having to resort to murder. Civil slander records show that social superiors could punish inferiors through legal channels, though inferiors had almost no opportunity to respond in kind. Even in those rare cases when a man of lowly status won a legal decision against his superior, the penalty was so light that the inferior gained little real reparation with his victory. Apparently, there was no hope for success against a superior, no real challenge attending an action against an inferior. Hence, there was only one social being whom a Londoner could both challenge and defeat: his equal. The civil courts cared little if a citizen insulted another of equal rank: fewer than eight percent of the slanders involve such fights. Men who could not win fights with superiors often turned their rage against those most likely to prevent their advancement. Thus, a clerk might kill a fellow clerk who had reported him to their mutual superior.[31] In other rolls, the struggle for advancement is not so clearly stated, but there is no doubt that an equal posed the only threat to which law and society allowed one to respond.

Chaucer's contemporaries faced severe restrictions on what they could say and whom they could freely address. If the *Canterbury Tales* is realistic on the level of language, similar restrictions should govern the verbal behavior of the pilgrims. I now summarize my basic points and show how the pilgrims' speech reflects the patterns of the medieval records.

1. *Although the official culture of fourteenth-century London considered slander a crime only in exceptional circumstances, the unofficial social value placed on slander was extremely strong and negative; an evil word was considered equal to an evil deed.* The pilgrims are fully aware of this precept, and even the most churlish of them use great caution in their verbal conduct. Despite the fact—noted by Bertrand Bronson—that the *Tales* is principally a study in negative relationships ranging from "tacit to violent dislike,"[32] the incidence of open abuse is remarkably low: only six percent of the statements made by one pilgrim to another can be considered direct insults.[33] Though most of the pilgrims' remarks convey criticism, and some border on slander, the speakers tend to insinuate rather than declare their views. The great majority of potentially abusive remarks are delivered indirectly, in a code language to be fully described in following chapters.

The power of the negative word is also evident in the pilgrims' intense reactions to insult. The angry exchanges of the *Tales* incorporate a great many personal and social factors. Each pilgrim has specific strengths as a debater and special areas of sensitivity. Nevertheless, the players are fully aware of the delicacy of the spoken word, and this knowledge governs their interactions. When, for example, the Miller announces his intention to tell a bawdy tale, the Reeve cries out that even a fiction can be a slander: "It is a synne and eek a greet folye / To *apeyren* any man" (1.3146–47)—it is not only sinful, but dangerously foolish to speak disparagingly of others, even

within the confines of a joke. Later, the Wife of Bath shows how seriously
she regards even the mildest criticism. The Friar has politely suggested that
the Wife cut short her reminiscences and begin her tale: "Now dame . . . so
have I joye or blis, / This is a long preamble of a tale!" (3.830–31) She
responds by using the beginning of her tale to pillory friars.

Perhaps the most graphic dramatization of word power occurs toward
the end of the poem. The Canon, whose crimes are gradually disclosed by
his reluctant Yeoman at the subtle prodding of the Host, tries to put a stop
to the "slanders":

> And thus he seyde unto his Yemen tho:
> "Hoold thou thy pees, and spek no wordes mo,
> For if thou do, thou shalt it deere abye.
> Thou sclaundrest me heere in this compaignye.
> And eek discoverest that thou sholdest hyde." (8.692–96)

The Canon accuses his Yeoman of slander, but as I've shown, no true
statement, however damaging, was considered punishable in Chaucer's
time. Indeed, even the Canon is aware of this fact: he distinguishes between
slander and "what one should conceal." He knows enough of what his age
considered slander to know he has no case. Thus, when the Host urges the
Yeoman to disregard his master's threats and "telle on," the Canon chooses
to abandon his apprentice forever, rather than witness the demise of his
reputation in the form of verbal punishment: seeing that "his Yeman wolde
telle his pryvetee, / He fledde awey for verray sorwe and shame" (8.701–2).

The fervor with which the various pilgrims "quite" the tales of their
fellows may seem the most improbable verbal slapstick to those who have
not examined the broader social context of the taletelling match. Words
make the pilgrims' reputations—and it is words they must use, both defensively and aggressively, to guard their names, their honor, their very livelihood. The *leitmotif* of Chaucer's Human Comedy—the concept that words
make the man—is based on a deadly serious social reality of his time.

2. *Slander actions reflected the interests of the powerful; the social system that so
strictly punished unseemly words was able to prevent most subversive speech and
actions.* Chaucer's poem portrays one of the least hierarchical situations in
medieval England: holiday time, when the lower classes were allotted many
more privileges than they would normally have. As I have shown, the
pilgrim churls wholeheartedly seized these rights—but the right to insult
their betters was not among them. Even when savagely insulted by their
superiors, the pilgrim churls hold their tongues. The first angry exchange
of the poem illustrates this point. Labelled a fool by the Host (1.3135), the
Miller does not return the insult directly, but instead speaks around it so
subtly that he seems to change the focus of all his abuse to the Reeve,

Robyn's social equal. Later, the Reeve, Cook, Friar, Summoner, and Host rage angrily, but never against members of higher classes. The upper-class pilgrims often use insulting language against their inferiors, but no pilgrim openly insults his superior. Even within their play, the churls observe caution: more deferential statements are made to social superiors than to any other status group.

3. *Coroners' records affirm that verbal and physical violence were most often directed at one's occupational competitors.* The intense trade rivalries witnessed in accounts of verbal abuse and violence are perfectly paralleled in the quarrels of the pilgrims. All the major disputes of the poem are based, at least in part, on occupational differences: Miller vs. Reeve, Host vs. Cook, Manciple vs. Cook, Friar vs. Summoner, Host vs. Pardoner, Wife of Bath vs. Clerk and Friar. In four of the duels, the rivalry represents trades in hot competition in Chaucer's England.

The majority of specific insults exchanged in the *Canterbury Tales* refer pointedly to trade affiliation. Though I shall consider this point again in succeeding chapters, I wish to stress now that, throughout significant portions of the poem, the language of verbal abuse *is* the language of trade rivalry. There is, of course, a high incidence of sexual slurs, as when the Host impugns the sexuality of the Pardoner (6.318, 948–53) and (more playfully) the celibate status of the Monk and Nun's Priest (7.1945, 3451). But even in such extra-occupational slurs, occupational undertones are seldom lacking. The Host's jibes at the clerics refer directly to their chosen calling. "God, yeve hym confusioun / That first thee broghte unto religioun!" says Herry Bailly to the Monk (7.1943–44). Even in gratuitous asides made by pilgrims not involved directly in trade quarrels, a man's trade is both a prominent means of identification and a prime subject of abuse. The Host uses trade slurs to mock the Reeve's long, didactic musings: "The devel made a reve for to preche / Or of a soutere a shipman or a leche" (1.3903–4). The stereotyping practiced by the pilgrims has a rich history in folklore, and has been demonstrably a device by which millers, carpenters, and other craftsmen have identified and insulted each other for centuries.[34]

Not only the prevalence, but also the magnitude of fourteenth-century trade quarrels is reflected in the *Tales*. The common critical opinion of such fights as that between the Reeve and the Miller is that they are insufficiently motivated. Perenially, scholars search out the "real" reasons for these vehement attacks—and sometimes assume the jibes have to do with past events not described by the poet.[35] But there is no need to invent a new poem; an understanding of Chaucer's language grows surely from an understanding of his society. The bloody fights between goldsmiths and saddlers, mercers and fishmongers, and the fierce loyalties that caused hostilities to be vented on rival professions, demonstrate that the quarrels of the pilgrims are more than adequately explicable on their own terms.

4. *The most violent outbursts of hostility—those most likely to lead to murder—were directed toward the group least affected by the prevailing system of social identity and control: one's social equals.* We have seen how the *Tales* reflects English society's treatment of superiors, inferiors, and occupational rivals. But the most vehement verbal duels—those pairing off Reeve and Miller, Cook and Manciple, Friar and Summoner—are fought between those of similar status. And it is remarkable how closely the churls' shows of anger follow the social channels apparent in the records. Court transcripts and coroners' rolls testify how often violent dislike of superiors was redirected toward equals—how a tradesman denied advancement would kill a fellow worker rather than seek redress from his master. Similarly, in the *Tales,* the Miller, too discreet to attack the Host openly, turns on the Reeve, a man who in real life would be competing with Robyn for the *gentils'* favor. In the Miller's Tale, principally through the characterization of Absalom, Robyn does indeed voice his scorn of the Host's noble pretensions—but in so doing he utterly humiliates his equal, the Reeve. The rules of word use support the social hierarchy by inducing "half the working class to kill the other half."[36] Merely to slap a *gentil* wrist, a churl must destroy his fellow. The *Canterbury Tales* reflects a social reality that could not have been learned from any source other than unofficial tradition.

Beyond the close correspondence between the speech patterns of Chaucer's characters and those of his real-life contemporaries, these facts convey one important message: the spoken word carried a great deal more authority in Chaucer's day than it does in ours. This finding runs contrary to the tacit—and often unconscious—assumption prevailing in modern criticism: that Chaucer and his characters could say exactly what they wanted, when they wanted, to whom and by such means as they chose. D. W. Robertson remarks, a bit defensively, that "Slander was much more seriously regarded by London citizens than it is by modern Chaucerians"[37]—but the historian cannot doubt the veracity of this claim. And if a word was powerful in Chaucer's time, a reputation was proportionally delicate. To believe that Chaucer or his pilgrims would freely use their words and thus risk their reputations is to misconstrue the meanings and forms of their speech.

SEVEN

Thine Own Tongue May Be Thy Foe

The Insult Strategies of the Pilgrims

The medieval spoken word had an almost palpable presence: rather than vanishing upon utterance, it followed—even pursued—the speaker, announcing his status, verifying his reputation, defining him as a social being. As a fourteenth-century Londoner, Chaucer lived daily with the knowledge of this verbal power. Words were his business, not only in his capacity as poet, but also in his role as a public man judged as much by his speech as by any other factor. When he undertook to write his most realistic poem, and chose to people it with characters modeled in part on living acquaintances and enemies, Chaucer translated his knowledge of verbal behavior into poetry. The Canterbury pilgrims act within the constraints of the traditional rules set forth in the previous chapter, and *react* to these restraints by conveying their negative opinions in the folkloric speech patterns that allowed medieval man to have his say without paying too much for it.

My purpose here is to show that many of Chaucer's pilgrims use a certain type of speech in their dialogues—a language that was not taught in rhetoric books, cultivated in courtesy books, or employed in any of the literary traditions available to the poet. This folk rhetoric evolved verbally in face-to-face encounters. To put the subject in its context, I first discuss the alternatives to folk rhetoric: the ideal language of *gentil* conversation on the one hand, and openly abusive remarks that courted trouble on the other.

GOOD SPEAKING

The pervasiveness of insult in the materials so far examined should not obscure the fact that medieval people placed great value on respectful language. In refined circles, language was one of the most easily measured determinants of status. In his *Chroniques*, Froissart recounts a visit to England in 1395 and remarks on the speaking manners of the courtiers, finding them "particularly courteous and easy to talk to."[1] In its structured gentility, the court of Richard II rivaled those of his contemporaries in France.

Across the Channel, the biography of Jean de Boucicaut describes one knight's high esteem for spoken eloquence. Boucicaut, coauthor of the *Cent Ballades* and founder of the order of *l'Escu vert à la dame blanche,* was noted as a poet and protector of ladies. He followed the calling of eloquence as religiously as he prayed and honored women. Boucicaut, like Demosthenes—or so says the fifteenth-century chronicler—cultivated verbal grace, inspiring many imitators: "his exceedingly beautiful speech—gentle, benign, well structured, and free of falsehood—captured the hearts of many."[2] Boucicaut's speech did not come naturally—it was *"grandement estudie."* If, on the other hand, a highborn man of Chaucer's time spoke in a manner inappropriate to his position, he was perceived, at least to some extent, as less than *gentil.* Olivier Clisson, a Breton count often present at the English court, had the highborn's scorn of the lower classes, but the speech of the inferiors he despised—for which reason he was dubbed "the Churl" by his disgusted peers.[3]

Yet if good speaking was esteemed by the nobles and gentry of the late Middle Ages, contemporary sources do not dwell on its content. The "courtesy books" of Chaucer's time leave no doubt that eloquence was considered more a product of avoiding foul words than of cultivating fair ones. Dozens of such manuscripts exist.[4] Succinct behavioral manuals, these "books" were intended for daily recitation to *gentil* children and were structured in rhyme to facilitate memorization. Even in written form, they evoke the oral culture of their time. They borrow heavily from contemporary *sententiae,* and often retain the ring of folk proverbs: "A byrd in hand, as some men say, / Is worth ten flye at large"; "Seke the pes, & lyfe in es." Like the latter excerpt, most of the precepts are set forth as imperatives or prohibitions: "Do this; don't do that."

An examination of six such manuals dating from the fourteenth and fifteenth centuries reveals an almost obsessive concern with the spoken word. Of 194 pieces of advice set out in these poems, 55—more than a quarter—are devoted to the proper use of language. Of the 55, only six speak positively of word use, encouraging young men and women to cultivate language for beneficial ends. Four of these enjoin the saying of prayers, perhaps the only speech act to which the Middle Ages always assigned a positive value. The remaining two give only the vaguest advice:

With fayr speche thou may haue thy wylle. . . .

It is also necessarye for Fathers and Maysters to cause their Chyldren and seruantes to vse fayre and gentle speeche, with reuerence and curtesye to their Elders and Betters. . . .

The remaining 49 injunctions are negative, telling people not what to say, but what not to say. The special nature of this training is revealed in a survey of the most common admonishments: *Don't speak too much* ("Haue few wordes, & wysly sette"), *Don't speak out of turn* ("Intrippe no man . . . in his tale"), *Don't swear or call people insulting names* ("Swere noon oothis; speke no ribaudie"), *Don't repeat what you hear*[5] ("Telle neuere the more thoug thou myche heere"), *Don't tell tales or jokes* ("Voyde slaunderous and bawdy tales"). But the largest category of all is composed of general admonitions to *take care what you say:* "while thou spekist, be not richelees"—"Keep thy tonge"—"Offe whome thou spekes, where & when, / A-vyse the welle, & to what men"—"Thin owne tunge may be thi foo. . . ." The consequences of verbal misbehavior are outlined in some of the epigrams. One word may ruin you: "For suche wordys thou myggt out kaste." The warnings of the courtesy books accord well with my findings from the slander cases. In any potentially dangerous situation, no words were good words. Pleas for laconic speech were not simply Polonian platitudes: even Boucicaut, that most proper knight, recognized the greater value of silence. To speak little was essential to his eloquence.[6]

Chaucer's pilgrims—or at least some of them—are aware that courteous conversation is restrained. In the General Prologue, many pilgrims are cited for verbal prowess of one sort or another, but only four—Knight, Prioress, Clerk, and Parson—are presented as exemplars in the art of proper speaking.[7] Not surprisingly, the speech of each is considered virtuous because it is spare. These four are notable primarily for what they do not say. "Though that he were worthy," the Knight "was wys": "He nevere yet no vileynye ne sayde / In al his lyf unto no maner wight" (1.70–71). Similarly, the Prioress' good speech knows no excess: "Hir gretteste ooth was but by Seinte Loy" (1.120). The Clerk says "Noght o word" more than is necessary (1.304). Finally, for the Parson, who teaches the gospel "truely," words are only given value through their consonance with acts. "First he wroghte, and afterward he taughte" (1.497). His day-to-day speech was noted for the pointedness and leanness which characterized his behavior; he was not "of his speche daungerous ne digne, / But in his techyng discreet and benygne" (1.517–18).

It may seem strange that none of the four tells a spare tale, but elite conversation and elite fiction operate by different rules. All four *gentils* exercise eloquence within their tales, but these are safe areas for such expression. The tales of the three religious speakers have moral themes, and are thus especially safe. The Prioress tells a saint's life, richly colored with rhetorical figures and addressed more to the Virgin Mary than to her fellow pilgrims; the Clerk presents an ornate novella with strong religious overtones; the Parson's "myrie tale in prose" proves to be an almost interminable sermon. These speakers attribute their eloquence not to their own talents, but to some authority that stands beyond reproach. The Clerk gives Petrarch credit for his masterful tale, the Prioress invokes the aid of the

Virgin, and the Parson's tale consists principally of quotes from Jesus and the Apostles. For all three, eloquence is fundamentally a matter of repeating the proper authority.

Outside the context of these moral teachings, the three have almost nothing to say. True to the rules of the courtesy books, they do not speak until spoken to. Only when asked do they tell their tales; then they fall silent again. Only the Parson says anything other than "Sir, I will obey your will"—and he does so only to upbraid the Host for swearing at him. These members of the clerical estate follow other courtesy book *dicta*, avoiding conversation with those who do not speak well and maintaining a humble bearing.[8]

The fourth good speaker, the Knight, is considerably more urbane than the others. His speech, like his tale, is laced with courteous expressions and delicate euphemisms. His tale, the longest of the pilgrimage, is a moral romance with Boethian overtones. Yet outside the shell of this story, he speaks with great authority, and very few words. His influence on the others is enormous: besides the Host, he is the only pilgrim who stops a tale or a fight. He performs these two acts tersely, in only twenty-two lines. And most of these (thirteen in number) are devoted to softening an insulting blow he has dealt the Monk.

Though the Knight effects some dramatic and difficult acts with his words, his style is impeccably restrained and *gentil*. He addresses even his inferiors with deference: "Sir Pardoner" (6.963), "Sire Hoost, that been to me so deere" (6.964), "good sire [Monk]" (7.2767). His orders to the pilgrims are succinct and, when verging on coercion, formulaic:

[Beginning his tale:]
Now . . . herkneth wat I saye. . . .   (1.855)

[Stopping the fight between the Host and Pardoner:]
Namoore of this. . . . (6.962; cf. 7.2767, where he
                              uses the same words on the Monk)

But after barking these unmistakably authoritarian statements, he uses an almost sycophantic deference to render them palatable:

[To Host and Pardoner:]
. . . ye . . . that beene to me so deere,
I prey yow. . . .
. . . I prey thee, drawe thee neer   (6.964–66)

In ordering the Monk to silence, he stresses that his low opinion of the Monk's Tale is *only* an opinion:

. . . litel hevynesse
Is right ynough to muche folk, *I gesse.*

I seye for me. . . .
    . . . as it thynketh me   (7.2770–71, 2778)

The Knight's verbal decorum is best shown in the ambiguous phrase "right ynough," most aptly translated "quite enough," and most often meaning "more than enough." It is his favorite slogan. He uses it three times when giving orders: once to the Pardoner and Host (their quarrel is "right ynough") and twice to the Monk ("That ye han seyd is right ynough . . . / And muchel moore"; 7.2768–69). This ironic phrase serves a double function: to let the offender know that what he has done so far is pardonable, but also to warn him subtly not to persist in it.

Besides these four acknowledged experts in good speaking, there are some who aspire to a similar gentility but lack the authority or the know-how to succeed. The Friar, repeatedly cited in the General Prologue for his "fair langage," makes his first appearance decorously, if contentiously, by delicately upbraiding the Wife of Bath for her lengthy speech and anti-clerical statements. But after the Summoner explodes angrily at him, the Friar cannot contain his speech. By contrast, the Franklin—a most *gentil* pilgrim, at least by pretension—never says a villainous word; but his lengthy introductory speech (5.673–94) irritates the Host, who orders him to get on with his tale. In both cases, the dangers are obvious: the Friar, by speaking out of turn, and the Franklin, by speaking too much, violate the *dicta* of the courtesy books and receive angry responses. They demonstrate once more the fact that good speech must be both politic and spare.

From the words of the Knight and some of his near-equals, a few techniques of good speaking can be deduced. The bywords are deference, caution, and succinctness. The speaker simply names the addressee by the most dignified title commensurate with his rank, then says little. The techique of *amplificatio*—of expanding a statement with ornate appositives—was cultivated by rhetoricians in formal written and oral discourse. Chaucer's *gentil* conversationalists, however, avoided amplification, *except for the purpose of taking the sting out of criticism.*

In their dialogue, *gentils* undertake lengthy speeches only when using three basic techniques. *Deferential criticism*, the politest form of reproof, is demonstrated in the Knight's speech to the Monk (7.2767–79, soon to be examined more closely). *Qualified praise* appears in the Franklin's words to the Squire. As tactfully as he can, the Franklin stresses that the Squire has artistic potential, but needs much more practice:

I preise wel thy wit . . .
    . . . considerynge thy yowthe . . .
    . . . ther is noon that is heere
Of eloquence that shal be thy peere,
If that thou lyve. . . .   (5.674–75, 677–79)

In a *deferential insult,* the speaker grants the butt of his criticism a higher status than himself, but finds fault with him anyway. The Man of Law introduces his tale:

> I kan . . . no thrifty tale seyn
> That Chaucer, thogh he kan but lewedly
> On metres and on rymyng craftily,
> Hath seyd hem in swich Englissh as he kan. . . .   (2.46–49)

Most instances of deferential criticism and qualified praise are uttered by that distinct minority of pilgrims who hail from the highest reaches of gentility. The folk rhetorical style, soon to be examined, does not normally embrace these figures, but substitutes in their place *conditional insult* and other, more negative tactics. The Host's unintentional parody of a speech by the Knight illustrates how unsuccessful are the tactics of deferential criticism when mixed with folk rhetorical style. After the Knight has cut off the Monk's Tale, Herry Bailly tries to regain his status as group leader by backing up the Knight's decision. Here is a juxtaposition in which characters of greatly different status say essentially the same thing. The Host's remarks echo the content of the Knight's, but the former's translation to another realm of discourse is laughably inept:

1) (Knight's) Deferential criticism vs. (Host's) open criticism—
   Knight: That ye han seyd is right ynough, ywis,
             And muchel moore. (7.2768–69)
   Host: Ye seye right sooth; this Monk he clappeth lowde.   (7.2781)

2) Subjective qualification vs. open criticism—
   Knight: *I seye for me,* it is a greet disese,
             Whereas men han been in greet welthe and ese,
             To heeren of hire sodeyn fal, allas!   (7.2771–73)
   Host: He spak how Fortune covered with a clowde
             I noot nevere what. . . .   (7.2782–83)

3) Indirect criticism vs. open criticism, and

4) Subjective qualification vs. peremptory judgment—
   Knight: [3] . . . litel hevynesse
   is right ynough to muche folk, [4] *I gesse.*   (7.2767–70)
   Host: [3] I sholde er this han fallen doun for sleep. . . .   (7.2797)
             [4] And wel I woot the substance is in me,
             If any thyng shal wel reported be.   (7.2803–4)

Herry Bailly's bumbling critique only belies his lack of expertise in a foreign rhetorical style. The Host's ineptitude is shared by his peers and inferiors: of all the less exalted pilgrims only the Clerk (no doubt as a result of his extensive schooling) has the ability to carry off such politic criticism, though he shows little inclination to practice it.[9]

The deferential language of the highborn pilgrims and the balder speeches of their inferiors have only one rule in common, but it is an important one. Both use *amplificatio* only to negate: to retract an insult or soften the blow of criticism. In their tales, sermons, and saints' lives, the *gentils*—like Geoffrey de Vinsauf and the other rhetoricians—may use *amplificatio* to praise, to brighten. In the context of conversation, however, *amplificatio* has an automatic negative association.

PLAIN SPEAKING

In light of the negative relationships that pervade the *Canterbury Tales,* there is an extremely low incidence of openly abusive speech. The pilgrims seem to be well aware that such language led to punishment in the courtroom or death in the streets. By my count, the direct discourse in the links of the *Canterbury Tales* comprises 319 speech acts, but no more than nineteen abusive remarks. All are provocative, but at most only three were sure to bring on trouble in a face-to-face encounter.

Eight of the insults are *curses,* abuses punishable only when uttered in the courtroom—or when addressed by servants to their masters.[10] As the courts that dealt out such penalties reflected folk mores, I assume that such speeches as the following were not among the most serious things that could be said in anger:

1) [Reeve, of Miller] I pray to God his nekke mote to-breke (1.3918)
2) [Summoner to Friar] I bishrewe thy face (3.844)
3) [Summoner, of Friar] this cursed Frere (3.1707)
4) [Canon's Yeoman, of Canon] Syn he is goon, the foule feend hym quelle! (8.705)
5) [Canon's Yeoman, of Canon] sorwe have he and shame! (8.709)
6) [Host to Cook] God yeve thee sorwe (9.15)
7) [Manciple to Cook] the devel of helle sette his foot [in your mouth] (9.38)
8) [Manciple to Cook] foule moote thee falle (9.40)

Most of these are especially safe, as they are aimed at equals or inferiors. As Chapter 6 explained, the power structure looked coldly upon the lower classes: conceptually, it was nearly impossible to insult a person whose very rank in life was an insult to gentility—fair grounds for foul words. Only two of the preceding quotes—the Canon's Yeoman's curses of the Canon—are potentially dangerous, for here a servant insults his master. But the Yeoman speaks only after the Canon, exposed as a fraud, has been forced by shame to abandon the company. The servant thus avoids the hazards that attended face-to-face encounters.

Four more abusive remarks fall under the vague heading of *general imprecations.* These, like the curse, are extremely provocative. But they were not legally punishable, and were far from the worst that one could say, because they were not directly damaging to one's reputation.

[Host to Pardoner]
9)   Thou woldest make me kisse thyn olde breech (6.948)
10)   I wolde I hadde thy coillons in myn hond (6.952)
11)   They shul be shryned in an hogges toord! (6.955)
[Summoner to Friar]
12)   amble, or trotte, or pees, or go sit doun! (3.838)

Such words are more likely to reflect poorly on the speaker than on the object of abuse, unless (as in the Pardoner's case) the person insulted shows obvious anger. The real danger attending these speeches is the possibility of provoking the hearer to violence. Herry Bailly's remarks are doubly safe because he outranks the Pardoner, by virtue of both his role as Host and the Pardoner's "unsuitable" behavior (as discussed in Chapter 2). The Summoner's slur is a bit more dangerous: though the most conservative theorists of the fourteenth century might rank him above the Friar, Huberd is clearly the better educated, more powerful, and wealthier man.

The insults left to be examined are, by contrast, extremely damning and dangerous, though on the surface most of them seem mild in comparison to those already listed. But to underestimate their impact is to misunderstand the importance of the literal in fourteenth-century England. The most offensive thing one could say was something that others might believe to be true. To wish a man's testicles enshrined in a hog's turd is certainly a negative gesture, but it would cause little ultimate harm, provided that one did not claim that his testicles *were* enshrined in a hog's turd, and that no one believed that they were. Sylvia Thrupp has noted that the most recurrent insult among the records of London's merchant gilds was "harlot"—a term which had not yet acquired its modern connotation of "whore" or "loose woman," but at that time simply meant "lowlife," "rascal," "disreputable man." Thrupp decries the lack of color in the recorded insults of the merchants:

> There was little originality in the merchants' language of abuse, which revolved about such points as probity, fortune, intelligence, ancestry, on which they felt themselves to be jockeying for public esteem.[11]

But there is an important factor which Thrupp does not take into account. As literal insults were the most offensive, the gildsmen's more colorful exchanges never appeared in court: the cases she examines are, after all, those in which verbal dueling had passed the stage of playfulness, or even anger—and had entered the realm of legal punishment. The truly expert practitioners of deprecatory language did not appear as defendants in such cases, because they never got caught.

Thus, a survey of the insults punished in the fourteenth and fifteenth centuries reveals that the literal slurs drew the most fire. "False man" and its variants ("false brother," "false thief," and the like) head the list, followed by "thief," "knave," "liar," "harlot," "whoremonger," "ribald" (the term had no necessary sexual connotations), various sorts of animal abuse ("worm," etc.), "Scot," "traitor," and "boy." None of these terms requires any imaginative exercise on the part of the speaker, and only the ethnic slurs and animal abuse even venture upon the figurative.[12]

Four of the remaining, more dangerous insults fall under the category of name-calling. These may have led to violence under certain conditions, but would have been safe in the situations in which Chaucer places them. The Host calls the Miller a "fool" (direct insult 13) and labels the Parson a "Lollere" (14); the Manciple brands the Cook a "stynkyng swyn" (15) and a "dronken wight" (16). Though I have found no evidence that any of these terms was particularly abhorrent, one of them could have been. "Stinking swine" is similar to several terms of animal abuse—such as "worm" or "beste"—which appear from time to time in the records. In speaking thus to the Cook the Manciple is asking for trouble. He realizes this and makes a retraction, dismisses his insult as a joke, and tenders the Cook a conciliatory offering of wine.

Penalties attending the three other slurs would have depended on two factors: the truth of the assertion and the relative status of the parties involved. Slander was defined only as a lie. If proved true, no insult, however vicious, was punishable.[13] The truth of an insult being adequate defense for making it, the Manciple's description of the Cook as a "dronken wight" is perfectly safe. Similarly, the Host, in calling the Miller "a fool," was dealing with a man who by his own admission was drunk. As drunkenness was acknowledged to cause a state of mental incapacity, the Host, though close to slander, has made a remark that would have been considered true.[14] His insult of the Parson—"this Lollere heer"—seems also to have been safe. Contrary to present scholarly opinion, a Lollard was not a heretic (if so, the improper use of the term would have been punished severely), but an "idle babbler of church doctrine," a sort of pedantic clerical fool.[15] "Lollard" was clearly a pejorative term, but also a subjective one which could be interpreted as true. As Bailly's slur of the Parson is supported by one pilgrim (2.1178–90) and challenged by none, the Host seems to have the necessary consensus to render his words safe. A second guarantee that these insults could have been dealt with impunity rests in the fact that they are all addressed to inferiors.

The three insults left to be examined are all potentially of the gravest sort. Two charges of lying are exchanged by the Friar and Summoner, and Herry Bailly charges the Cook with fraud. All three, particularly dangerous because they are literal and possibly true, will be discussed in detail later in this chapter.

Before moving on, however, I wish to stress two points. First, the rare incidence of pointed insult indicates that direct verbal confrontation was not a favored means of fighting for the pilgrims—or, by extension, for everyday people in Chaucer's London. Second, even abusive language is relative. A careful speaker can say whatever he pleases as long as he can work his words into a fitting context. This strategy sums up the essence of verbal dueling in the Middle Ages, for the victor was he who made his insult felt without having to pay for it.

THE FOLK RHETORIC OF THE PILGRIMS

"A wrong is unredressed when retribution overtakes the redresser," states Poe. No medieval churl would dispute him: all knew that the momentary satisfaction of speaking one's mind could lead to ruin. To give their speech both weight and safety, common people in similar social situations throughout the world must devise means of saying what they mean without paying a disproportionate price. "Signifying," common in the oral tradition of modern black ghetto cultures, is just such an indirect insult technique, and similar systems are employed in all other places where the spoken word exercises proportionate power.[16] Such folk rhetoric is used primarily for the speaker's protection, but it also possesses esthetic value. Among the "signifiers" of modern black ghettos the ability to deliver insults that are subtle and clever is regarded as an art as well as a survival skill.

The common men of the *Canterbury Tales*—such men as the Miller, Cook, and Summoner—speak a common language, though their shared verbal strategy is extremely rare, as far as medieval elite sources are concerned. Nothing similar exists in the French or English fiction with which Chaucer was familiar. Yet I am sure that Chaucer did not invent this method of "talking around an insult." Evidence from court cases suggests he heard it first in the London streets, and applied it later in fictional situations similar to those in which it was naturally found.

Borrowing the language of elite rhetoric, I call the minimal units of folk rhetoric "figures" or "colors." The two systems, however, have little in common. The rhetoric books seldom recognize the essential problem posed in the *Canterbury Tales*: the necessity of disguising angry speech. Hence, they offer few solutions for the pilgrims' most pressing needs. Geoffrey de Vin-

sauf, the elite rhetorician most cited by Chaucer, offers three insult techniques, none of which would serve the pilgrim churls. The first relies on
inflections of voice or gesture. This, according to the master, is how one
addresses an enemy:

> Forestall him; be willing to hail him as master. In the meantime, mock him
> none the less with gestures that belie your words. Mortify him by making the
> beak, or wear a distorted smile, or wrinkle your nose. In pursuing this ap-
> proach we ought not to use the mouth but to turn up the nose.[17]

This is simple slapstick, a tactic reminiscent of the "donkey ears" that modern children flash behind their teachers' heads. Vinsauf offers a second,
more refined suggestion, an aural strategy having to do with the ambiguity
of certain words and the way they are pronounced. For example, to raise
doubts about a person's accomplishments, choose phrases with potential
second meanings, such as " 'He is an extraordinary man.' This statement
implies that he is a very good man, but the hint that he is a very bad man
indirectly peers out at us."[18] This second tactic is certainly smoother than
the first, and Betsy Bowden has argued that such aural ambiguity is a major
ingredient of Chaucer's art.[19]

Finally, in his *Ars Versificandi,* Vinsauf states that *circumlocutio* can sometimes be used to defame. To speak about William de Guines (the king's
butler, who apparently had a reputation for impropriety), a man might hail
him not by his proper name, but as follows: "That wine-servant of the king,
that shame and insult, dregs of all wine-servants, and polluter of the king's
household."[20] This device demonstrates more than any other how poorly
the art of elite rhetoric would serve the average Londoner. Literarily speaking, this circumlocution is a success: it calls a spade a spade without mentioning his name. But in an oral context, to call a man to his face "the dregs
of all servants" would be asking for punishment. Such "circumlocution"
would not allow the speaker to escape the anger of the insulted or the
penalties of the court, unless the speaker were much more powerful than
the addressee—in which case the speech would be unnecessarily, absurdly
delicate.

In some instances the figures taught by Vinsauf, Matthew de Vendome,
and Alberic of Monte Casino do run parallel to the folk rhetoric used by
Chaucer's pilgrims. Both systems, for example, employ the simile, though
often in different ways, as I will explain. Only one of the tropes to be
examined here (again, the simile) can be identified purely in structural
terms. All others are definable primarily by shared semantic function. Like
other forms of folklore, indirect insults must be read not only *as texts,* but
also *within their contexts,* to be fully understood. Hence, my classifications
stress the uses rather than the shapes of these figures. A single phrase may

have more than one function and may thus serve to illustrate two or more techniques.

1. *Deflected apology.* Medieval rhetoricians thoroughly cultivated *diminutio*, the poet's self-disparaging remarks, in which he tastefully apologizes for his lack of artistic skill. According to the masters, the value of this device was to present the speaker in an aspect of humility which could only reflect to his credit, no matter how well, or how badly, he performed: his piece was bound to be better than he claimed it was. Following elite rhetorical tradition, most of Chaucer's *gentils* slight their own talents as they begin their tales: the Man of Law, Squire, and Franklin apologize for their lack of poetic skills; the Monk asks to be excused for his ignorance.

Although some commentators claim *diminutio* was recognized by rhetoricians for its ironic potential, evidence to support such a contention is sparse. Janette Richardson argues that

> . . . Chaucer's peculiar kind of irony really owes little to medieval rhetorical-poetic precept. It is far more accurate to say that Chaucer often *invests* the . . . *diminutio* (disparagement of self) with irony. . . . [T]he very prevasiveness of his irony in all of its various manifestations implies that it stems from an aspect of his peculiar sensibility rather than from literary model.[21]

Richardson, however, has not considered all the possible precedents. Icelandic sagas indicate that the device was common in earlier Germanic culture, and there is no reason to believe that Chaucer himself was not also exposed to this sort of oral behavior in fourteenth-century England.[22]

The type of *diminutio* most often and artfully used in the *Tales* is the deflected apology, although it is little used by the *gentils*. Beginning his tale, the Man of Law uses a standard rhetoric-book excuse. He claims a lack of eloquence, but note how his apology is deflected:

> I kan right now no thrifty tale seyn
> That Chaucer, thogh he kan but lewedly
> On metres and on rymyng craftily,
> Hath seyd hem in swich Englissh as he kan. . . . (2.46–49)

It becomes no more than an excuse to insult Chaucer, who, the speaker feels, is not a very good poet. The lawyer implies that his tale, though a rough piece in prose—which may stand in comparison to Chaucer's work as plain fare to rich food—is nonetheless at least as good as the poet's. This "apology" is a mixture of insult and self-aggrandizement thinly disguised.

The next speaker to employ a deflected apology uses the same excuse as the Man of Law, but this second example is an even more aggressive statement. The Shipman is not going to waste his time on fancy language; he will tell a real tale, for a change[23]:

> . . . it schal not ben of philosophie,
> Ne phislyas, ne termes queinte of lawe.
> Ther is but litel Latyn in my mawe! (2.1188–90)

The Shipman's insulting apology marks a transition between the ironic *diminutio* practiced by the *gentils* and the true deflected apologies of the churls. The churlish variety is much more insulting. The churls never bemoan their lack of skill or talent, but focus on temporary states (such as drunkenness)—

> But first I make a protestacioun
> That I am dronke. . . . (Miller, 1.3137–38)

—or circumstances (such as age or poverty) beyond their control—

> But ik am oold. . . . (Reeve, 1.3867)

> . . . if ye vouche-sauf to heere
> A tale of me, that am a povre man (Cook, 1.4340–41)

The second characteristic shared by these remarks is the speakers' tendency to deflect any possible blame, not merely *from* themselves, but *to* the party most likely to accuse them. When, for example, the Miller is insulted by the Host, he responds by apologizing for his drunkenness, but lets everyone know that it was the Host's ale that got him drunk:

> And therefore if that I mysspeke or seye,
> Wyte it the ale of Southwerk, I you preye. (1.3139–40)

This insinuation is much more biting than it appears on the surface, for the Host has been breaking the law by serving liquor to his guests. According to the London taverners' statutes, this privilege was reserved for the victualing trades. However, the rule was regularly broken in Southwark, and the Host was apparently one of the lawbreakers.[24] This "apology" is not merely a shifting of blame, but a potential threat as well. Robyn does not merely say, "I may be drunk, but *you* made me drunk"; he also implies, "I may be breaking the protocol of the pilgrimage, but you have broken the law—and my drunkenness is palpable proof."

The Reeve later makes a similar apology, deflecting the blame for his ugly language onto the Miller, who has (or so Oswald says) forced him to tell an unsavory tale.

> I pray yow alle that ye nat yow greve,
> Thogh I answere, and somdeel sette his howve;
> For leveful is with force force of-showve. . . .
> Right in his cherles termes wol I speke. (1.3910–12, 3917)

The Reeve is considerably less delicate than the Miller; he can afford to be, because he is deflecting his apology upon a social equal, not a superior. The apology is one verbal ploy that shows class demarcation, being used differently by the two factions. *Gentil* apologies show a connection to the rhetoric books, the churls' to established oral tradition.

2. *Behavioral comparison.* This figure operates by contrasting an ideal picture of an opponent to his less-than-perfect behavior, thus implying that he is unworthy of his title and reputation. A charge of fraud is implicit in such a statement, but as an implication it is socially and legally safe.

The behavioral comparison is a primitive irony that nonetheless proves effective in the mouths of skilled wordsmiths.[25] The oral tradition of this figure is attested in court records, where it is found only in cases of *scandalum magnatum.* The man who delivered this insult would have gotten away with it had he been addressing anyone other than a high civic official; in fact, he was sentenced for abusing not an individual but the "whole estate of aldermanry."

> [An alderman has told a butcher that the latter charges too much for beef. The butcher responds:] It is a good thing for thee and thy fellows, the Aldermen, to be so wise and wary, who make but light of riding on the pavement, as some among ye have been doing.[26]

The pilgrims make copious use of this device, especially when calling others' status into question. When the Canon's Yeoman praises his master, the Host casts doubt by pointing out the Canon's slovenly appearance:

> Why is thy lord so sluttissh, I the preye . . .
> If that his dede accorde with thy speche? (8.636, 638)

Elsewhere, the Host has similar words for the Friar: "ye sholde be hende / And curteys, as a man of youre estaat" (3.1286–87). A more ironic behavioral gibe, with occupational overtones, occurs when the Host upbraids the Clerk. Here Herry Bailly implies that the Clerk's book-learned talents, rich as they may be, are not adequate or appropriate for the purpose of entertainment:

> Youre termes, youre colours, and youre figures,
> Keepe hem in stoor til so be that ye endite
> Heigh style, as whan that men to kynges write.
> Speketh so pleyn at this tyme, we yow preye,
> That we may understonde what ye seye. (4.16–20)

But the Host is, after all, among the most status-conscious of the pilgrims. To such lesser men as the Miller, more general and egalitarian criteria are the bases of ironic comparisons. Mocking the Reeve's fear of cuckoldry, the

Miller states what a *real* husband (himself in particular) would do and slyly insinuates that the Reeve falls short of this ideal:

I have a wyf, pardee, as wel as thow;
Yet nolde I, for the oxen in my plogh,
Take upon me moore than ynogh,
As demen of myself that I were [a cuckold]. (1.3158–61)

Similar behavioral comparisons are delivered by the Reeve (comparing himself to the Miller, 1.3865–66) and Clerk (comparing his heroine Griselde to Alisoun of Bath, 4.1170 ff.).

3. *Simile.* This technique has a long literary history and is particularly famous as an epic figure; it dates back to Homer, and it was analyzed by Aristotle. Yet in Chaucer's time this venerable device had fallen into disfavor. The trend began toward the end of the eleventh century, as the epic genre itself began its decline, and continued into the thirteenth, when two of the most influential rhetoricians—Vinsauf and Matthew de Vendome—spoke of its inferior character. Matthew goes so far as to say that the simile should be avoided, and perhaps someone was listening to him.[27] In their tales such pilgrims as the Knight (quoting Boethius, 1.2987–3089) and the Nun's Priest employ similes, but they avoid the figure in their dialogue. In the churls' indirect insults, however, the simile is a common safety precaution, allowing one to call a spade a spade by saying that he is *like* a spade.

Every pejorative simile implies not merely similarity, but identity. The implication of the insult is clear enough, but as long as "as" or "like" separates the target from the insult, the speaker is safe. This tactic appears often in Icelandic sagas and German romance, where otherwise damning statements are rendered acceptable.[28] Chaucer's folk similes are earthy and show an affinity to those employed in Icelandic saga and German *Schwank:*

[The Host addresses the quarreling Friar and Summoner:]
Ye fare as folk that dronken ben of ale. (3.852)

[When Huberd states that he is free of the jurisdiction of the Summoner, the latter likens Huberd to a whore:]
Peter! so been the wommen of the styves
. . . yput out of oure cure!" (3.1332–33)

That the simile was safe is clear in the legal records. Only two such figures made it to court, and these were exceptional in two senses: 1) both were accompanied by more vulgar and punishable language; and, more important, 2) both were false similes in which the speaker discarded the protective cover of the *as* clause and overstepped his bounds. The following simile, according to the record in which it is found, was accompanied by "moche other more ungodly & inconvenyent langewage moved & spoken":

[The mercer cited for slander said to a fellow tradesman] that he was never his
true brother, but as oon founde & chaunged at the londes ende. . . .[29]

The speaker claims his brother in trade *is* false, a statement punishable in
itself; the charge that his brother is *like* a changeling offers too little, too late
to mitigate the initial insult. Thus, the simile—disparaged by influential
rhetoricians—was nevertheless present in folk rhetoric. The pilgrim's similes are borrowed from this unlettered language.

4. *Conditional insult.* In this figure, the speaker relies upon certain knowledge concerning his antagonist: for example, a character trait possessed by
his foe. The speaker, pretending to be unaware of this trait, states that
anyone with such attributes is a fool, a coward, a criminal. The Miller knows
that the Reeve is capable of marital jealousy; Robyn takes advantage of this
fact by saying that only a lunatic would be jealous of his wife:

Ther been ful goode wyves many oon,
And evere a thousand goode ayeyns oon badde.
That knowestow wel thyself, *but if thou madde.* (1.3154–56)

Conditional insults often serve to goad as well as humiliate, inspiring the
target to live up to certain expectations, or informing him that there is
something wrong with him if he does not. In the *Tales*, this double function
is apparent in the jab directed by Chaucer the Pilgrim toward Herry Bailly.
The Host has just spoken harshly of Chaucer's first tale; Chaucer remarks
slyly that the Host would have to be a snob to criticize the second one:

I wol yow telle a litel thyng in prose
That oghte liken yow, as I suppose,
Or elles, certes, ye been to daungerous. (7.937–39)

Aside from a few lines of dialogue in Icelandic sagas and German romances, I have found no literary parallels for such remarks.[30]

5. *Generalization.* Perhaps the largest category of indirect insult in both
the *Tales* and the sagas, this technique implies guilt through association.
Using proverbs or other general statements, the speaker presents an enthymeme, or truncated syllogism. He vocalizes the first one or two terms,
letting the audience infer the last. The Summoner delivers this fragmentary
syllogism:

1) Freres and feendes been but lyte asonder. (3.1674)
2) [Huberd the pilgrim is a Friar.]
3) [Huberd is very nearly a fiend.]

Had the Summoner stated all three terms, he would have verged on slander. As he speaks only the first, he is safe. In this example, as in many
others, the incomplete syllogism is couched in the form of a proverb-like

statement. Proverbs and *sententiae* were certainly a major part of the elite rhetorical tradition, but they generally served as *topoi*—points of departure for long justificatory arguments, as in the *Radix malorum est cupiditas* which keynotes the Pardoner's parable of greed—or as parts of highly complex and tightly structured debates.[31]

Except when they occur within certain tales (such as the Pardoner's and Manciple's), the pilgrims' proverbs are not set in such formal patterns. The closest parallels to the pilgrims' conversational proverb usage exist not in books, but in present-day oral cultures, where their application without elaboration can make an argument in itself. In Nigeria's tribal legal system, a case can be conducted entirely through an exchange of proverbs. The defendant in one such case, saying that "A single partridge flying through the bush leaves no path" (i.e., one man's opinion counts for nothing when others have already judged against him), was able to "prove" his innocence of the theft with which he had been charged.[32] In folk usage the proverb is often disembodied from any argumentative structures; social context alone makes the speaker's meaning clear.

Chaucer's churls lived in a world somewhere between the two cultural extremes described in the preceding paragraph. These men were members of a basically oral culture that possessed a highly literate superstructure. A case presented before the king's court, no matter how closely it might reflect basic folkloric values, was a matter of special formalized and formulaic pleading more similar in shape to the structure of the rhetoric books than to the more artistic and less "logical" pleadings of African tribal courts. Yet on the streets, Englishmen used tactics similar to those of the tribes, even if Chaucer's contemporaries did so for purposes of persuasion rather than proof. Given the enormous power of speech to influence judgment, the folk system often came very close to proof, and its less rigid system of persuasion often dictated the outcome of the more "sophisticated" trial. For example, a woman's reputation could precede her into the courts; female defendants were sometimes introduced as "common liars" before the charges were read, and were, not surprisingly, found guilty.

The proverb, an acknowledged piece of communal wisdom, allows one to couch negative opinions in socially acceptable language. A man who utters a proverb is merely repeating a phrase he has heard many times before and to which his community has repeatedly given its approval. It is the first term of a folk syllogism, an indisputable term at that, and therefore invulnerable to the abuses which playful rhetoricians often used to create syllogisms that were mockeries of logic:

Mus [mouse] is a syllable;
But a syllable does not nibble cheese;
Therefore *mus* does not nibble cheese.[33]

The great success of the folk syllogism rests in the fact that the proverb, that part of the syllogism which is irrefutable, is usually the only part vocalized. The specific application may be entirely subjective and incorrect, but it is stated only by implication. For example, in *Gísla saga*, Eyjolfr threatens to kill a woman, but Havardr, a member of Eyjolfr's household, criticizes his leader's intent. Eyjolfr responds, "That old saying is true: 'One's worst followers come from home.'"[34] There are a number of parallel statements in the *Tales*. Four of the eight proverbs used for folk rhetorical purposes concern the general human condition. They cite the role of husband—

> [Miller to Reeve]
> An housbonde shal nat been inquisityf
> Of Goddes pryvetee, nor of his wyf   (1.3163–64)

—or acts common to everyone, such as play—

> [Cook to Host]
> "sooth pley, quaad pley," as the Flemyng seith   (1.4357)

—disputes—

> [Reeve, referring to Miller]
> For leveful is with force force of-showve.   (1.3912)

—or storytelling—"Whereas a man may have noon audience / Noght help-eth it to tellen his sentence" (7.2801–2). But the other proverbs and prover-bial adaptations in the *Tales* reveal an obsession with the varied social roles which characterized fourteenth-century England. Fully one half of the proverbs are directed against specific occupational groups. When the Host grows tired of the Reeve's pontifications, he alters a proverb to cast a gen-eral slur on Reevedom: "The devel made a *reve* for to preche, / Or of a *soutere* a *shipman* or a *leche*" (1.3903–4). When the Host ridicules the quiet, aloof Clerk for living up (or down) to his occupational stereotype, he uses a clerical proverb to intensify the mockery: "I trowe ye studie aboute som sophyme; / But Salomon seith 'every thyng hath tyme' [Therefore, you must tell your tale now]" (4.5–6). The Summoner, ridiculing the Friar, adapts proverbs to make his slurs occupational as well as personal in nature: "a frere wol entremette hym everemo" (3.834), "a flye and eek a frere / Wol falle in every dyssh and eek mateere" (3.835–36), "Freres and feendes been but lyte asonder" (3.1674). In addition to the proverbs which focus on occupational rivalry, nearly every general statement used in the folk rhet-oric of the *Tales* is intended to mock or disparage a particular calling:

> [Host, concerning Parson]
> O Jankin, be ye there?   (2.1172)
> I smelle a Lollere in the wynd.   (2.1173)

[Friar, concerning Summoner]
  . . . ye may wel knowe by the name
That of a somonour may no good be sayd (3.1280–81)

As slanderous as these general slurs might seem, they seldom led to social and legal repercussions; only when such words were directed against high officials was punishment likely to ensue.

    6. *Feeling out.* This category is tied to a single situation—encountering a stranger. The tactics outlined here encompass not just one figure, but several, which may be used variously, depending on how the situation evolves. When meeting a stranger, he who speaks well must speak carefully. The speaker should *appear* to praise the stranger, but he must also hold his ground. He shapes his language to show that the newcomer must prove worthy of the praise tentatively extended him. The process of "feeling out" a stranger is documented as early as the eighth century, as it appears in Beowulf's speech with the coast guard, the first man the hero meets after reaching the Danish shore. The coast guard is the first to feel out, hailing Beowulf: "I have never seen a greater earl on earth . . . *unless his appearance is deceiving.*" Beowulf's offer of help shows a similar mixture of deference and doubt; he wants to avoid insulting Hrothgar—and he must do his utmost to keep his offer of help from reflecting badly on the Danish king. Beowulf does so by saying, in effect, "If half of what I've heard is true, Hrothgar *may* want my help"—an example of *deferential criticism.*[35] If in the early stages of the "feeling out" process he senses that the stranger is unworthy of praise, the speaker will begin to make more pointedly negative statements, comparing the idealized phrases of his salutation to what he perceives are the stranger's limitations. The implied insult is obvious.

    Neither the rhetoric books nor the courtesy books mention such strategies, but there is an excellent example in the *Tales.* Except in one case, all the characters are acquainted with each other before the reader meets them, so there is only one opportunity to see this folk figure employed. This occurs when the Canon and his Yeoman ride up to the company and ask to be admitted to their ranks. The Host shows greater civility here than elsewhere, but every word of praise to the stranger is accompanied by a qualification:

Freend, for thy warnyng, God yeve thee good chaunce!
  . . . certein *it woldë seme*
Thy lord were wys, and so *I may wel deme.*
He is ful jocunde also, *dar I leye!* (8.593–96)

The Host's greetings are less threatening than those in *Beowulf;* he could well afford this verbal luxury in a more cosmopolitan place and a less pervasively violent time. Yet, for all its lighter qualities, Herry Bailly's speech is just as aggressive as the Germanic examples. When, through delicate questioning, the Host realizes there may be something shady about the Canon, his language changes. He verges on open insult as he compares the idealized image he first drew to the sorry sight he now sees:

> This thyng is wonder merveillous to me,
> Syn that thy lord is of so heigh prudence,
> By cause of which men sholde hym reverence,
> That of his worshipe rekketh he so lite. . . .
> Why is thy lord so sluttissh, I the preye, . . .
> If that his dede accorde with thy speche? (8.629–38)

The dialogue between the Host and the Canon's Yeoman presents a masterful example of *feeling out:* in fewer than one hundred lines, the Host moves from slightly qualified praise to utter repudiation of the Canon. This he accomplishes through subtle interrogation of the Canon's Yeoman, drawing out the truth by slow turns until the Canon's fraud stands nakedly revealed. Chaucer did not read of such tactics, but Germanic tradition suggests they remained in oral circulation in his time.

7. *Mock praise.* There are other tropes whose folk history is more difficult to trace or which share many folk *and* literary antecedents; mock praise is one. Known as *permutatio* by rhetoricians, the figure is described by Geoffrey de Vinsauf:

> I transfer a name, deriding through antiphrasis, when I call a deformed man "Paris"; or cruel-hearted, "Aeneus"; or weak, "Pyrrhus"; one rude in speech, "Cicero"; or petulant, "Hypolitus."[36]

Chaucer's churls do not, of course, compare each other to classical heroes. Their allusions are much simpler, though they do have the same ironic intent. The Manciple calls the drunken Cook "wel yshape" to joust (9.43), a slur even a drunken man could not mistake; the Wife of Bath ironically identifies Huberd as a "worthy Frere" (3.855) before she insults him; and the Host delivers a long ironic speech to the detestable Physician:

> I pray to God so save thy *gentil cors,*
> And eek thyne urynals and thy jurdones,
> Thyn *hypocras,* and eek thy *galiones* . . .
> . . . thou art a *propre man,*
> And *lyk a prelat, by Seint Ronyan!* (6.304–6, 309–10)

As a man of some social pretension, Herry Bailly draws upon certain classic attributes of the medical profession, but more important for the comic effect of the passage, he also cites the least elevated effects of the doctor's trade. The Host carries *mock praise* beyond the designs of Vinsauf.

8. *Ironic disclaimer.* A color more interesting and artfully employed, this

technique possesses few literary antecedents. Like Brutus's "I come to bury Caesar, not to praise him," this tactic is used to announce an intent exactly opposite that which the speaker is pursuing. The device is most often employed in the "only a game" clause. When a pilgrim has stated, or is preparing to state, something particularly offensive, he simultaneously retracts the remark and rubs it in, saying, "Don't be angry; I was merely joking." The most insulting use of this figure occurs when Herry Bailly, after charging the Cook with all manner of punishable crimes, says he is merely joking: "But yet I pray thee, be nat wroth for game; / A man may seye ful sooth in game and pley" (1.4354–55). The Manciple (9.81), Wife of Bath (3.191–92), and Clerk (4.1175) also use this strategy to preface or cap devastating insults. This trope is particularly appropriate to the earnest games the pilgrims play. Through such repeated disclaimers, the very words *game, pley,* and *bourde* take on serious connotations.

9. *Subjective qualification.* Also called the "seems" clause, this is perhaps the least imaginative of all folk rhetorical devices, but it has a rich oral and literary history. The speaker simply says what he thinks, but adds a cautionary qualification: "it seems to me," or "as I see it." This ploy can be used either to drive home an insult or to temper a negative opinion: the former function is inflammatory, and principally oral, in nature; the second is deferential, elite, and often literary. The oral variety is one of the favorite tropes of the saga authors, who continually offer such phrases as, "It seems to me that little reason for holding my head high could come to me from [an alliance with you]."[37] Some very biting uses of this trope occur in London slander cases. The perpetrator of the following remarks was unfortunate enough to address them to an alderman, though the case would probably not have made it to court if this were all he said. Richard Bole, butcher, was tending shop when an alderman came to buy meat, and complained of the prices. Richard answered, "I *do verily believe* that the meat is too dear for thee, who, *I suppose,* never bought as much meat as that, for thine own use." The double "seems" clause combines a charge of "pauper" with an insinuation of "servant"—both of which would very much anger an alderman.[38]

In elite usage, "it seems"—along with "it is said" and "we are told"—was the phrase of choice for subordinates when telling their kings or lords that something unpleasant was afoot.[39] Chaucer used the device most often in its deferential, refined form. The Knight employs the "seems" clause repeatedly to temper his criticism of the Monk (7.2770–79), and the Host uses it when *feeling out* the Canon's Yeoman (8.594–96, 630–38). The Host occasionally employs this figure in its folk form, to great ironic effect. These remarks to Chaucer the Pilgrim could as easily be classified as examples of *mock deference:*

He *semeth* elvyssh by his contenaunce,
. . . now shul we heere
Som deyntee thyng, *me thynketh* by his cheere.   (7.703, 710−11)

10. *Appeal for consensus.* This is one of the most pervasive figures in the *Tales.* Though found with some frequency in literary disputations, it is essential to oral performance. No matter how much one party may wish to insult another, there is a third party that cannot be offended if the speaker is to succeed: the audience, the community that judges slander, the ultimate determinant of what is insult and what is good speaking. Every effective speaker must cultivate the crowd.

I have counted 53 deferential statements in the links of the *Canterbury Tales,* a figure which seems to indicate that the pilgrims are an exceedingly polite group. When the figures are broken down, however, a distinctly different image emerges. Of the 53, 14 are addressed to the Host, whose position as leader of the pilgrimage requires respect. The majority, 27, are addressed to the crowd, leaving only 12 deferential statements addressed by individual pilgrims to their fellows.

Most deferential statements addressed by individuals to the company are *wedges:* attempts to win the crowd's approval for an attack upon one of their number. With one exception, every pilgrim who feels insulted or injured seeks group support. The Reeve, insulted by the Miller, asks the company to excuse him for the ugly tale he must tell in reply: "I pray yow alle that ye nat yow greve, / Thogh I answere, and somdeel sette his howve" (1.3910−11). The Summoner similarly requites the Friar's tale:

Lordynges . . . but o thyng I desire;
I yow biseke that, of youre curteisye,
Syn ye had herd this false Frere lye,
As suffreth me I may my tale telle. (3.1668−71)

Chaucer the Pilgrim, his first tale cut off by the Host, begs the crowd to allow him to complete a second: "Therefore, lordynges alle, I yow biseche / . . . lat me tellen al my tale, I preye" (7.953, 966). When asked for a tale, the Parson tries to cultivate the support necessary to stave off such criticism as he received when he last spoke to the company (2.1178−83): "And thanne that ye wol yeve me audience, / I wol ful fayn . . . / Do yow plesaunce leefful, as I kan" (10.39−41).

The sole pilgrim who fails to cultivate the crowd merely affirms that the crowd is most important. The sociopathic Pardoner, who takes pleasure in exposing his crimes, is the only character who subjects the group to scorn: "Now hoold youre pees! My tale I wol bigynne" (6.462); "It is an honour to everich that is heer / That ye mowe have a suffisant pardoneer" (6.931−32). Such protestations of superiority are foreign to the standards of oral art, as the pilgrims' disgust illustrates. Wherever employed, the appeal for consensus gives testimony to Chaucer's sensitivity in observing the role of the audience as the ultimate judge of a verbal duel.

THREE FOLK RHETORICAL DUELS

However justly J. M. Manly may have criticized the medieval rhetoricians, he did them no service by analyzing their work merely from an atomistic point of view, listing their figures and commenting on their general lack of inspiration.[40] Robert O. Payne finally gave the rhetoricians, and Chaucer's use of them, a fairer judgment by assessing their styles holistically.[41] The folk rhetoricians in Chaucer's poem also deserve a holistic treatment. The poet presents such a wide range of verbal skills and strategies that the study of isolated figures cannot tell their story.

Before proceeding to an analysis of the three most brilliant verbal duels in the poem, I offer one generalization: the best folk rhetoricians hail from the lowest ranks of the pilgrims, most of whom never saw a rhetoric book and had no need of one. Among the most exalted pilgrims (Knight, Prioress, Squire, Sergeant of Law, and Monk) only the Knight shows any verbal skill in social situations, and the success of his declarations is due only in part to his oral talents. His self-appointed role as benevolent monarch of the pilgrims, underpinned by his very real social superiority, is the major source of his power. His speeches exude deference to his inferiors—an attitude he can well afford, and which his delicacy allows him to exploit successfully, but an attitude significantly absent from the speeches of medieval folk rhetoricians. Among the wealthier members of the commons (Merchant, Gildsmen, Franklin, Host) only the Host uses much folk rhetoric. Herry Bailly is one of the verbal masters among the pilgrims, enormously subtle in his insults of the Canon, resourceful in his mockery of the Physician, and deferential when he has to be—to the Knight, Prioress, Squire, Sergeant of Law, and (when public opinion overrides his view of this cleric) Parson. But the Host is, at least nominally, the head of the pilgrimage, and this position of authority proves too much for a man who is naturally "Boold of his speche" (1.755). His slurs of the Pardoner, Monk, Pilgrim Chaucer, and Nun's Priest overplay the upper hand the pilgrims have granted him. Upper-middle-class pilgrims who engage in insulting word play do so with less subtlety and resourcefulness than their inferiors.

It is among the lower classes (represented by the Clerk, Summoner, Pardoner, Miller, Manciple, Reeve, and Cook) that folk rhetoric blossoms, finding by turns its most skillful and ardent practitioners. Of the eight pilgrims, only the Pardoner refuses to play. The others do almost nothing but play, with varying degrees of skill. The Clerk plays *gentilly*, subtly, but he plays nonetheless. The Reeve sometimes plays poorly. The others are masters of the sport. Nearly every word they speak is drawn from a rich folk rhetorical tradition.

MILLER AND REEVE

The Miller speaks only thirty lines outside the context of his tale, but not one is wasted. Each is a calculated jab at some other pilgrim. Robyn may be drunk, but the Host's liquor has not dulled the edge of his tongue.

He enters the session dramatically, defying the Host and the entire social order set up within the game. Robyn, a lower-class man on holiday with his betters, expects concessions from the upper classes: if they are not forthcoming, he will seize them. He plays his holiday privileges to the hilt, opening the performance with blasphemy:

> . . . By armes, and by blood and bones,
> I kan a noble tale for the nones,
> With which I wol now quite the Knyghtes tale. (1.3125–27)

Feast time is the only time in the calendar during which a miller can pretend equality with a knight, and this Miller immediately declares his festive prerogative to tell a *noble* tale.

The Host understands what the Miller is up to, but wishes to direct a more genteel pastime. He speaks familiarly to the Miller, calling him "my leeve brother," in an attempt to persuade him that "Som bettre man" should tell a tale first. In referring to the Miller's lowly status, the Host has said that thing most certain to make Robyn angry. Like the villeins who seized the holiday meals foolish nobles tried to deny them, the Miller will not be made subservient while on vacation. He replies simply that he will play now or quit the game (1.3133). The Host loses patience, and in a display of verbal excess, calls Robyn a fool.

Robyn does not answer this insult directly; he knows his limits. The Host has given him a victory on the issue most important to him, and the fact that Robyn has irritated a man of higher status is a second victory of some significance. The Miller is too smart to lose his advantage by dealing out verbal abuse to an angry superior. His safest way of avoiding a more direct and potentially unsuccessful clash is to cultivate the crowd and subtly to warn the Host that he is immune to injury at the leader's hands. He does so by offering the *deflected apology* discussed earlier, which puts him in good graces with the company and poses a covert threat to the Host: "I may be drunk, but *you* made me drunk, and did so illegally"—all of this without once specifically mentioning Herry Bailly. (Most of Robyn's subsequent words are reproduced in Figure 3, Chapter 9.)

He now offers the subject of his tale, another well-disguised insult. He is going to tell a story about a carpenter cuckolded by his wife (1.3141–43). The remark is meant to bait a safer foe than the Host: the Reeve, who was a carpenter in his youth. In changing the focus of antagonism from his superior to his peer, the Miller moves to more familiar ground. The switch also allows him to give vent to a stronger antagonism than even the social inequality between the Host and himself: the occupational rivalry between reeves and millers.

Many Chaucerians have argued that the conflict between Reeve and Miller is too intense to be motivated merely by trade competition,[42] but the accounts of intertrade violence summarized in Chapter 6 leave no doubt that occupational disputes among equals superseded every other kind in frequency and intensity. The most abusive and dangerous quarrels occurred between trades that were in direct competition. The quarrel between the Reeve and Miller is based on just such overlapping interests.

Reeves and millers both plied rural trades and were also, perhaps, the two outstanding misfits of the agrarian social order. Both held liminal positions, between the peasantry and the ruling classes, and conducted their business primarily with the lord of the manor, but they also had a certain unpopular control over the lowest classes. It was a major function of the reeve or bailiff (for the functions of both officers are mixed in Chaucer's description of Oswald, as they sometimes were in life) to ensure that the peasants were productive. Oswald, who frightens all his peasants, is clearly an unloved overlord. The miller, who on most manors contracted directly with the peasants to grind their grain and was granted by contract a share of it, also held power over the villeins, a power which, according to almost every folk story and stereotype about millers from the Middle Ages to the present, he constantly abused.[43] Robyn, with his golden thumb, was one of these proverbial thieves.

Within the structure of the demesne, the reeve and miller held extremely privileged positions. They were among the few freeholders on any given estate. At Spelsbury, for instance, there were six freeholders, one of whom was the miller; the reeve there was the richest of the villeins.[44] As this was a relatively common situation, another possible reason for the quarrel between Chaucer's Miller and Reeve becomes apparent: though the reeve had at least nominal power to oversee the works of the miller, he was often in fact a man of lesser wealth and stature than his titular subordinate. Oswald's stark appearance (1.587–92) implies that the rivalry in the *Tales* may be aggravated by such a social imbalance: even if he has enjoyed good fortune in his occupation, he *appears* less successful than Robyn.

As both men were scorned by their superiors and feared by their inferiors, they were in a class by themselves, thrown into direct competition for dominance in the midst of a generally unsympathetic society. It may seem that their mutual marginality would drive the Reeve and Miller into each other's arms for want of other company. But the nature of their trades kept them constantly at odds. As the reeve had surveillance over the mill and based a significant percentage of his returns on the grain that was tallied at the mill, both reeve and miller sought to enlarge their personal wealth by taking the grain and income left untallied in their business exchanges. The gain of one was almost invariably the loss of the other.[45]

Some critics have conceded that a trade fight between a *miller and reeve* would indeed be sufficiently motivated, then hasten to add that the fight in the *Canterbury Tales* is not couched in such terms, but in terms of *miller versus carpenter*. The Reeve was a carpenter as a young man, but he is no longer. There *is* a London carpenter on the pilgrimage, and he should be the one to respond to the taunts of the Miller. Such arguments ignore one important fact. Though there were almost eighty practicing trades in a city the size of London, there were no more than three on most rural manors: miller, blacksmith, and carpenter. In London, a rivalry between a carpenter and a miller was far-fetched, but in the country the idea was easily conceivable. Since millers, carpenters, and reeves were all given exemptions from their rent in return for their services, they were among the rural elite.[46] Furthermore, the mill was one of those fixtures of the country estate where a carpenter's services were most often required, and the reeve was frequently the officer who oversaw the construction work done there—a situation which would bring this antagonistic triad into uncomfortably close proximity. Finally, as reeves were often recruited from among the rich villeins of the manor, the carpenter's craft was one of the few privileged positions from which a villein might ascend to the rank of reeve.[47] Oswald's double career is in no way unusual, and it is not surprising that the Miller would resent that part of the Reeve that was once a carpenter as much as that part which is currently a reeve.

Having established the social base for this conflict, I return to its rhetorical structure. After the Miller has announced the theme of his tale, the Reeve naturally responds with anger: "Do not defame me." Oswald knows that the story to come will not reflect well on carpenters. But in order to win his encounter with Robyn, the Reeve must win the backing of the crowd, so he appeals to them by *generalizing* the Miller's insult: he says, in proverbial terms, that it is a sin to "appeyren *any* man or hym defame." To enlarge his base of support, he adds that it is also a sin "to bryngen *wyves* in swich fame." All good men *and women* should be offended by the Miller's seamy art.

Robyn, a superb verbal duelist, knows how to respond. He redefines the question, making it more specific. Still, his terms are safe. He focuses on the issues just raised by the Reeve: men and women, ruined reputations. "Leve brother Osewold," he says—using the same condescending familiarity the Host has recently used on Robyn (1.3129)—"You can't be a cuckold if you're not married, but to be married doesn't mean that you *are* one. Good wives outnumber bad ones by a thousand to one, and you're crazy if you don't know that. I am married, but *I'm* not foolish enough to think that *I'm* a cuckold" (1.3151–66). In sixteen short lines, Robyn turns Oswald's generalized defense into a fatally specific wound. By asking, in effect, "If you aren't a cuckold, why are you so nervous about my story?" Robyn makes the charge of "cuckold" much more convincingly than he had before. This disclaimer is a vicious attack in disguise, one which humiliates the Reeve in the presence of the entire company.

These are the last words the Miller says outside the context of his tale, but he has said enough to prove his consummate verbal skill. With forceful speech, he has broken up the planned order of the session. With subterfuge, he has turned an apology into a threat against the Host, mocked the entire social order, insulted the Reeve indirectly, and turned a disclaimer into a frontal assault. He accomplishes all this without directly insulting anyone, or so much as admitting that there is an argument in progress. His tale shows that Robyn has yet more verbal tricks to play, but that is a point I leave for a later chapter.

Compared to the Miller, the Reeve is an inept artist, yet he fares no worse against Robyn than anyone else. The Miller has a unique ability to ruffle all his opponents, including the almost irrepressible Host. Oswald is no fool; he never throws a punishable insult at Robyn. He curses, whines, reprimands, but he does not forget the limits of what he can safely say.

In comparison to the Host, the Reeve makes a rather strong showing at first. As we have seen, he has tried to turn the Miller's more personal attack into an attack on all decent human beings. Had his opponent been any other man, he may have succeeded; after all, the essence of folk rhetoric is to gain audience support. But he strives too hard for public approval. The Miller turns the Reeve's appeal on its head: no sane man would take offense at this tale, Robyn cautions, attempting to sever any bond the Reeve may have formed with the crowd. Before Oswald can answer, the Miller has begun his tale.

As Robyn entertains, Oswald has time to structure his rebuttal. His best rejoinder might be to borrow Robyn's tactics and point out slyly that the Miller's story merely reflects the teller's shortcomings: "unhappy, prurient people, people who loathe their moral and social superiors [and Robyn's superiors number very nearly everyone present on the pilgrimage] often tell ugly stories; it's rather sad." But the Reeve has already heard Robyn twist his arguments. A safer, and perhaps equally effective, course of action would be to show no reaction at all—simply to smile, then to begin his tale: "That reminds me of a legend about a Miller. . . ."

But Oswald is hampered by his anger—this and his overzealous appeals for approval undo him. His shortcomings are apparent in the speed and substance of his response to the Miller's Tale. His first words—"So theek . . . ful well koude I thee quite / With bleryng of a proud milleres ye"—put him at a further disadvantage. Once more, the Reeve has openly acknowledged something the Miller will never admit: that the two are really engaged in an argument. The Reeve is constantly on the defensive because he is trying to bring the Miller's insult into the open. Thus, he denies himself a subtle response.

Lacking other recourse—after all, his opponent refuses to fight by his rules—the Reeve again begs the company for support. Like the Miller, Oswald makes an apology. But this protracted speech (1.3867–98)—longer than all of the Miller's speeches combined—is not deflected to the Miller, or to anyone else; it is an exercise in self-pity that gains no sympathy and tends only to reinforce the image of the foolish cuckold that the Miller developed in his tale. Oswald's monologue reveals not only what is most pitiable in him, but also what is most abhorrent: "Avauntyng, liyng, anger, coveitise, / Thise foure . . . longen unto eelde" (1.3884–85). Exposing his own potential for malice and deceit is a serious error that will weaken the effect of his tale: in a sense, Oswald has asked his audience to dismiss his words as the ramblings of a bitter old man. At this point, the Host cuts the Reeve short, and tells him to get on with his tale.

Oswald, his strategy a failure, changes his tone again and launches a full-scale attack on Robyn. Once more he gives away the game, revealing how much the Miller has hurt him, and asks the audience permission to fight ("with force force of-showve"). The only fitting response to this surly soul, says Oswald, is to turn his surly speech against him. Oswald shows the same verbal talent he had shown before his tawdry apology: Robyn "kan wel in myn eye seen a stalke, / But in his owene he kan nat seen a balke" (1.3919–20). But talent is not enough. The Reeve has exposed his feelings; he has construed indirect insult as direct insult and asked the crowd to pity him rather than his opponent. Thus he cannot respond effectively to the subtler challenge of the Miller.

COOK AND HOST

If any pilgrim can match, line for line, the Miller's incisiveness and skill, it is the Cook. Perhaps because only fifty-six lines of his tale were written, this little-recognized figure is known to Chaucerians primarily for the fact that he is the only pilgrim who falls off his horse. Yet there is enough of him in his Prologue to reveal how subtly he can choose his words and to make us wish Chaucer had finished Roger's tale. When we first see Roger he is exulting over the Reeve's Tale. He is perhaps the only pilgrim who enjoys the story—at least he is the only one Chaucer mentions reacting to it. The "joy" with which he demonstrates his approval (1.4326) might arouse suspicions that he has some personal or occupational reason for despising the Miller. He repeatedly insults millers as a class, always being careful to fall short of a direct insult of Robyn, who is no doubt near at hand. Roger mocks the misfortunes of the fictional miller Symkyn:

> I pray to God, . . . / If evere . . .
> Herde I a millere bettre yset a-werk. (1.4335–37)

The Cook's laughter is safe; on the surface, his ridicule is directed at the lower classes. But the Miller is a decoy for the real object of Roger's attack: the Host. Note that the Cook considers the fictional miller a fool in one particular respect: he is a stupid *host.*

> This millere hadde a sharp conclusion
> Upon his argument of *herbergage!*
> Wel seyde Salomon in his langage,
> "*Ne bryng nat every man into thyn hous*";
> For *herberwynge* by nyghte is perilous. (1.4328–32)

These lines may well disgrace the fictional Miller, but they cannot affect the real Robyn, who is not a hosteler. There is a hosteler in the crowd, however: Herry Bailly. Below the surface is a trade rivalry as intense as that between Miller and Reeve, a rivalry aggravated by the particular nature of the Host's hospitality. Just as the Miller had gotten drunk on the Host's ale, the Cook had fed on the Host's food before departing with the company. This must have been a particularly bitter dish for the London Cook, who by law had the right to prepare and be paid for it. The taverners of Southwark regularly defied the law, strongly enforced in London, that hostelers must employ others to prepare and serve food.[48] The Cook's unhappiness at this situation was no doubt intensified by the fact that he had to pay for a meal from which he would normally have profited. Fights over this issue were notorious in Chaucer's time. Thus, the Cook is deflecting onto the Host an insult nominally directed at a fictional miller. But, more than just an insult, the Cook's words pose a threat: "It is dangerous to harbor some people" (1.4333–34)—and the implication is that the Cook is one such dangerous guest.

Roger then introduces his tale, with far greater finesse than the Miller and Reeve have shown:

And therfore, if ye vouche-sauf to heere
A tale of me, that am a povre man,
I wol yow telle, as wel as evere I kan,
A litel jape that fil in oure citee. (1.4340–43)

The Cook calls himself a "poor man," a title that may well have stuck in the Host's ears, for Herry Bailly knows that his own shady business hurts Roger's. Then, like the Reeve, he ignores the Host and goes directly to the company for permission to tell the tale. Also like the Reeve, Roger shows great deference to the group—as well as humility, a trait with which the other churls do not seem to be acquainted. Like the Miller and the Reeve, Roger advances a churl's *apology:* he is a *poor* man, but will tell a tale as well as he can. Yet this apology is stated in very unapologetic language, without the sort of self-derision which characterizes the Miller's sly protestation of drunkenness or the Reeve's self-pitying references to his age and impotence.

Now the Host steps in to speak. He is no doubt angry at the Cook's insinuations against hostelers, and enraged by the fact that the storytelling contest is growing out of control. The last two tales, those of the Miller and Reeve, have been told without his permission. Now the Cook has compounded the insult by following a slur on the Host's trade with another attempt to bypass his authority. The Host decides to take the offensive. First, he reasserts that he is in charge of the festivities: he will *"grant"* the Cook the right to speak (1.4344). Then he adds a threat—"Now telle on, Roger, *looke that it be good"* (1.4345)—and an intense, potentially defamatory charge that tests the Cook to the limits:

For many a pastee hastow laten blood,
And many a Jakke of Dovere hastow soold
That hath been twies hoot and twies coold.
Of many a pilgrym hastow Cristes curs,
For of thy percely yet they fare the wors,
That they han eten with thy stubbel goos;
For in thy shoppe is many a flye loos. (1.4346–52)

Like the three churls, Herry Bailly knows the importance of cultivating the crowd. As the Host can assume that the Cook's Tale will be an attack on him, he wants to make it known that the Cook's profession is an attack on all good pilgrims: many have cursed Roger for preparing rotten food. This is an *implied behavioral comparison:* the company is much better off eating the Host's food than allowing Roger to poison them with his.

But the rest of Herry Bailly's speech is not so subtle. It is a damning statement which could easily have ruined the Cook's reputation and destroyed his livelihood. If the Host's accusations are true, the Cook would suffer both widespread social humiliation and severe legal penalties: he would be taken to court, then to the pillory, accompanied by jeers and mocking music. He might lose even the right to ply his trade. When the Cook, a few lines later, in the context of his tale, refers to a fictional brawler "lad with revel to Newegate" (1.4402), he may well be reflecting on his argument with the leader: for the punishment he describes is the same that he would receive for fraud—or that the Host would face for slander.[49]

If the accusation is false, the fact that the Host is secure in his social superiority would lighten his ultimate penalty. Nevertheless, his impropriety might cost him dearly. Fair court records of the fourteenth century abound with cases in which merchants claimed redress for slanderous words that had hurt their businesses. When the courts upheld such charges, the slanderer paid heavy fines.[50] Thus, Herry feels it prudent to make a disclaimer. But, like the Miller, the Host has a knack for rubbing in an insult at the same moment he is tempering it. After his heavily accusatory speech, he tells Roger not to be mad: "after all, this is only a game." Note the *mock deference* the Host directs to the man he has just labeled a criminal:

Now telle on, *gentil* Roger by thy name,
But yet I praye thee, be nat wroth for game;
A man may seye ful sooth in game and pley. (1.4353–55)

Reaffirming that *he* makes the rules for this game, the Host excuses himself lightly, even as he further fires the quarrel in the name of peace. The Cook is caught in a tight position: if he admits he is guilty of the Host's charges, he merely faces further humiliation from the crowd; if he denies a crime he really did commit, he faces a charge of lying in addition to any other malfeasance. Even if he is innocent, he cannot take too lightly a charge mounted by a man who is so clearly his social superior; simply by protesting innocence, he would be charging Herry Bailly of slander. The Cook has no choice but to change the rules. He responds to Herry Bailly's mocking disclaimer—"A man may seye ful sooth in game and pley"—with a thoroughly ambiguous answer: "Thou seist ful sooth . . . by my fey" (1.4356).

So the Host is telling the truth, but in regard to *what*—the charges against Roger or the fact that one can tell the truth within the context of a game? In his next line the Cook hints that he is guilty: "'*sooth pley, quaad pley,*' as the Flemyng seith" (1.4357). This is a direct warning to Herry Bailly. "A game which is based on truth is no game at all," jibes the Cook, implying, "if you want to play a 'true' game, you had better be prepared to play hard." Roger elaborates on this point, throwing the Host's taunt, "don't be angry," back at him.

And therefore, Herry Bailly, by thy feith,
Be *thou* nat wrooth, er we departen heer,
Though that my tale be of an hostileer.
But nathelees I wol nat telle it yit;
But er we parte, ywis, thou shalt be quit. (1.4358–62)

This is a very unsettling speech: the Cook mimics and mocks the style of Herry Bailly's earlier speech, then promises an unpunishable vengeance, but he is appropriately vague about when the vengeance will be accomplished.

Much later in the poem, the Host finds the Cook almost speechlessly drunk, and demands a tale then, perhaps hoping that the promised vengeance would be dulled by the Cook's incapacity. He mocks the Cook again, but in much more careful language than he had used earlier. The Manciple then steps in and insults Roger in much stronger language, but the Host reproves him for it. "Be careful what you say," Herry Bailly tells the Manciple, "the Cook will remember your strong words and get even with you somehow, maybe by exposing something dishonest you have done" (9.69–75). So speaks the Host to the Manciple, but one wonders if he is not also speaking for himself. This passage near the end of the *Tales* indicates that the Cook has won the earlier verbal duel. Even as the journey nears its end, the Host still feels the effect of Roger's subtle threats.

FRIAR AND SUMMONER

After the clever wordplay of the Miller and Cook—and to a lesser extent that of the Host and the Reeve—the fight between the Friar and the Summoner seems utterly tasteless. When given a chance to perform, the Friar, lauded in the General Prologue for his verbal talents, proves unworthy of his reputation. And the Summoner—who, with the Merchant and Man of Law, is eligible for the dubious honor of being the pilgrim most despised by the poem's narrative persona[51]—lives up to his churlish reputation. Nevertheless, the quarrel between these men does reveal something of the oral artistry of Chaucer's time, if only by delineating the outermost limits of unpunishable speech.

The occupational rivalry between friars and summoners has been well studied since the eighteenth century, and needs little explanation here. The essence of the strife was that friars, as mendicants, were immune to the strictures of the secular clergy. The resulting bitterness between their estates was legendary in Chaucer's time. And, in this particular case, the ongoing quarrel would be aggravated by the fact that both the Summoner and the Friar were extortion artists: both lived by the funds they could wring from the laity, the Friar by begging, and the Summoner by taking bribes from criminals or commissions on the fines of those he arrested unjustly. The occupational antagonism represented by these two pilgrims was so pervasive in Chaucer's time that even critics who see few elements of social drama in the *Canterbury Tales* grant that no further aggravation than "the clash of their professional interests" is necessary to provoke their vehement fight.[52]

There is yet another motivating factor at work in this case. The Summoner has every reason to be jealous of the Friar, for conservative social doctrine and the friars' own charters had ordained that the mendicants follow a simple, ascetic life. But by the late fourteenth century, they had attained enormous wealth as well as academic and political power. According to the older view, even the lowly Summoner—like any member of the church secular—ranked above the Friar, whose calling does not even appear on the protocol lists for noble households.[53]

The Summoner's only hope of besting the Friar lies in ignoring Huberd's real social status and leaning instead on the much-cited theory that has proclaimed friars beggars. Like any smart churl (e.g., Robyn, who leans upon his age-old festive rights to take control of the storytelling contest) the Summoner knows how to invoke the power structure when it will serve him. In his remarks on friars and in his tale, the Summoner—following the lead of the chancellor of Oxford, John Gower, and dozens of contemporary sources, both folk and elite—plays upon two major complaints against friars: they have gone far beyond their allotted place in the social order, and their fancy speech is deceitful. The epithets that the Summoner continually attaches to his foe—"false Frere" and "flatterynge lymytour"—are planted to remind all listeners that Huberd should be considered nothing more than a lying beggar.[54] If the Summoner can strip away Huberd's polite veneer and elicit boorish speech from him, he will have made his case: one's words are oneself, and Huberd is simply a churl in disguise.

The Friar begins with "fair langage," showing himself well versed in the "good speaking" technique of *deferential criticism*. His first words are to a woman, his favorite type of conversational partner. He comments diplomatically on the length of the Wife of Bath's dramatic monologue: "Now dame . . . so have I joye or blis / This is a long preamble of a tale!" (3.830–31) But the Friar's "ladykiller" reputation is far stronger than his performance. Like Mozart's Don Giovanni, Huberd never makes a conquest while on stage. Alisoun has only scorn for his coy remarks. She responds first with mock deference—"[I will tell my tale] if I have licence of this worthy Frere" (3.855)—then goes on to present within her tale a scathing characterization of friars. The Wife's remarks are not lost on the Friar, who responds with a biting, but eloquent, critique of her tale. He begins with a delicate blessing, and goes on to praise Alisoun's narrative, but soon makes it clear that he is offering strictly *qualified praise*. The subject of her speech was difficult, and she has acquitted herself well, but she has gone beyond her depth:

> Dame, . . . God yeve yow right good lyf!
> Ye han heer touched, also moot I thee,
> In scole-matere greet difficultee.
> Ye han seyd muche thyng right wel, I seye;
> But, dame, heere as we ryde by the weye,
> Us nedeth nat to speken but of game,
> And lete auctoritees, on Goddes name,
> To prechyng and to scole eek of clergye. (3.1270–77)

Huberd's *gentil* speech is worthy of the Knight's. In deference it surpasses even the Knight's critique of the Monk's Tale. In circumlocutory ambiguity, it outshines the forthright language of the Knight. Here Huberd appears to be a truly *gentil* practitioner of the precepts of good speaking. But it soon becomes apparent that these deferential remarks are merely setting the stage for a full-scale attack on the Summoner. As soon as Huberd begins his disclaimer ("Us nedeth nat to speken but of game") his adroitness in folk rhetoric is apparent. "Only a game": this phrase has been heard before in the Host's speech to the Cook—and will be heard several more times before the journey ends. It is a sure sign that an insult will follow. The Friar soon clarifies what kind of game he will play: "I wol yow of a somonour telle a *game*" (3.1279). At this point, all gentility ends. The Friar has deflected his criticism of the Wife onto the Summoner. This is a neat rhetorical diversion, but it proves to be his last attempt at subtlety. Henceforth the Friar and the Summoner do nothing to conceal their mutual animosity.

The first blows were actually exchanged earlier, just after the Friar first opened his mouth. After Huberd tells Alisoun to get on with her tale, the Summoner charges Huberd with meddling: "Lo, goode men, a flye and eek a frere / Wol falle in every dyssh and eek mateere" (3.835–36). This well-crafted insult combines *generalization* with *appeal for consensus* ("Lo, goode men"). But the Summoner does not want a subtle debate, for two reasons: because he is no match for the Friar in book rhetoric (Chaucer the pilgrim has already told us that the Summoner's Latin is pitiful), and because he wants more than anything else to expose the churl lurking beneath the Friar's double-worsted semycope. After all, the Summoner is unable to support any illusions about his own status, and *his* reputation will not suffer from a coarse verbal duel. So he sets forth the rules of his game with ugly invective: "amble, or trotte, or pees, or go sit doun" (3.838). The Friar remains cool, at least for the moment, but lets it be known that he is all too eager to play at the Summoner's level:

Now, by my feith, I shal, er that I go,
Telle of a somonour swich a tale or two,
That alle the folk shal laughen in this place. (3.841–43)

These are not direct insults. The indefinite article is kept before the noun, as it will be throughout the developing quarrel. This type of generalization is the least imaginative insult, but it is adequate to avert a charge of slander.

Unlike the Cook and the Miller, the Friar makes no attempt to disguise his attack. Giving vent to the pervasive animosity the middle class felt toward its inferiors, Huberd employs the same insulting familiarity Herry Bailly used on the Miller. But in so doing, the Friar invites similar speech from the Summoner—speech which would affirm that the two are social equals. The Host instantly recognizes the Friar's error. When Huberd proclaims "A somonour is a rennere up and doun / With mandementz for fornicacioun" (3.1283–84), Bailly notes the disjunction between the Friar's speech and his *apparent* gentility: "sire, ye sholde be hende / And curteys, as a man of youre estaat; / . . . lat the Somonour be." But the Summoner sees that Huberd has fallen into a self-destructive language pattern and insists on the foul tale: "Nay, . . . lat hym seye to me / What so hym list. . . ." In the ensuing insult match, the two men will show themselves equals in abusive speech. But this equality will make the Summoner the victor, for Huberd's *gentil* bearing will be forgotten by himself and his audience, and he will appear as churlish as the Summoner.

The Summoner can now be as vicious as he pleases: he throws out a few curses before he announces his intention of attacking friars. The intensity of competition is made concrete in the "numbers game" the two clerics play: the Friar will tell "a tale or two" of summoners; the Summoner retorts that he will tell "two or three" about friars. This interchange aptly characterizes the spirit of the ensuing argument, wherein the two match each other nearly word-for-word and abuse-for-abuse as the tale progresses, to "quite" each other "every grote."

From this point forward, the fight does not merit detailed analysis. I will simply outline the parallel nature of the argument, which resembles the modern urban pastime of "playing the dozens" in its symmetrical escalation.[55]

1) Generalization traded for generalization
   Friar:
   A1. Of a somonour may no good be sayd (3.1281)
   A2. A somonour is a rennere up and doun
       With mandementz for fornicacioun (3.1283–84)
   Summoner:
   B1. I shal hym tellen which a greet honour
       It is to be a flaterynge lymytour (3.1293–94)

    B2.   His office I shal hym telle. (3.1297)
2)   Simile traded for simile
    Friar:
    A.   For thogh this Somonour *wood* were *as an hare*,
        To telle his harlotrye I wol nat spare (3.1327–28)
    [He mentions that friars are not under summoners' jurisdiction; to which
    the Summoner responds]
    B.   *Peter! So been the wommen of the styves*
    . . . yput out of oure cure!* (3.1332–33)
3)   Charges of falsehood exchanged
    Friar (within tale):
    A. This *false* theef, this somonour (3.1338)
    Summoner (after Friar's Tale):
    B. Ye han herd this *false* Frere lye (3.1670)
4)   Charges of lying exchanged
    Summoner:
    A. Ye han herd this false Frere *lye*
    Friar:
    B. Ther thou *lixt,* thou Somonour! (3.1761)

The Summoner shows wit as well as a knack for alliteration in his "Friar proverbs" ("A flye and eek a frere," "freres and feends"). Both narrators show considerable skill in telling their tales. But the only delicacy shown by either rests in their hairline avoidance of verbal suicide. Their wordplay resembles the modern game of chicken: each sees how close he can come to the brink of disaster, and each tries to taunt the other into crossing that line. The most telling example of their goading game is the dialogue surrounding Huberd's charge of "thief."

The Friar, telling a tale of a thieving summoner, begins to treat his fictional summoner as if he were a real person. "Even if the crook were as crazy as a hare, I will say anything that I please about him. Everyone knows that summoners have no jurisdiction over friars; therefore I am safe." As explained in Chapter 5, confusing the boundaries of fantasy and reality is a common oral narrative tactic. But the real-life Summoner responds by jumping into the fantasy to return the insult: "we have no jurisdiction over whores either!"—one of the Summoner's more clever insults. Herry Bailly now speaks, telling the Summoner to shut up and insisting that the Friar resume his tale. The Friar does so:

"This false theef, this somonour," quod the Frere,
"Hadde alwey bawdes redy to his hond. . . ." (3.1338–39)

Until the reader (or listener) arrives at the word "hadde," there is no indication that the Friar has indeed returned to his past-tense narrative. Chaucer underscores the ambiguous nature of the slur by placing the phrase, "quod the Frere," between the insult and any evidence that the narrative has resumed. Three discrete insults in this passage go to the brink of verbal violence: the Friar's charge of madness (saved by fiction), the Summoner's charge of whore (saved by simile), and the Friar's very serious counter-charge of thief (saved by fiction). The quarrel of these two unsavory churchmen proves, as does no other exchange, the importance of the literal in medieval slander. Only the thinnest of lines divides their dialogue from the slander cases received in the dockets of medieval courts. But that line was so clearly etched in the minds of the pilgrims that not even the angriest or surliest of them crossed it once.

EIGHT

License to Lie

The Churls' Rhetoric of Fiction

Chaucer's churls, his model practitioners of folk rhetoric, are also the most expert, most frequent tellers of a particular type of tale—the *Schwank*. Five of the seven *Schwänke* in the *Canterbury Tales*—those of the Miller, Reeve, Cook, Friar, and Summoner—are told by lower-class pilgrims.[1] Past readers of Chaucer have long seen a certain aptness in this pairing of base tales with base men. The obscenity, irreverence, and contentiousness of the churls' narratives reinforce the standard view of the lower classes as set forth in estates satires throughout the Middle Ages. But to view such tales simply through the eyes of those *gentils* who did not tell them is to neglect the fact that the churls manipulate narrative in much the same way, and for much the same reasons, that they structure their potentially dangerous dialogue. The connection between *Schwänke* and verbal abuse is no coincidence, for each of the churls' tales is a figurative slap, dealt out in the context of a verbal duel and directed to the purpose of settling the score with a rival pilgrim. The *Schwank*, as fashioned by the churls, is the ultimate indirect insult, the finest figure of folk rhetoric.

Before examining the *Schwank* as a weapon in the pilgrims' discourse, I review its place in medieval and modern folklore, as well as its uses in medieval literary tradition. Then, citing modern parallels, I outline the folk techniques for using tales as indirect insults. Finally, I take a close look at the specific tactics used by certain churls to shape their tales into derisive commentaries on other pilgrims in the crowd.

SCHWANK AND FABLIAU

In Chapter 2 I explained how the folktale has been characterized as a lie by clerics and taletellers alike from classical times to the present. On the other hand, the rival force of realism is also at work in such narratives: the teller gives his story a setting which conforms with that of his listeners, presents a hero who pursues their activities and ideals, and offers himself to the audience as a real-life emissary from the fictional world. Of all the types of the folktale, none is more realistic than the *Schwank;* thus none is more easily adapted to its social context. The *Schwank* is defined by Linda Dégh as a humorous story, "a relatively long, well-structured realistic narrative without fantastic or miraculous motifs," unfolding a plot whose action "is obvious and easy to comprehend."[2] According to Hermann Bausinger and Klaus Roth, the content of the *Schwank* involves the most basic human drives—"eating, drinking, sex"—and the most fundamental social conflicts—peasant versus landlord, trade versus trade, husband versus wife, clergy versus laity.[3] The *Schwank* is "rooted in social reality"—it "concerns the everyday."[4]

Though the most obvious function of this form is to amuse, "the *Schwank* is not concerned only with humor"—it has a more serious side as well.[5] The telling of such tales satisfies "the inclination of the common man to mock what is most esteemed."[6] More specifically, the *Schwank* mocks the social order, and the foibles and pretensions of certain types and professions of men, stripping away their polite veneer and exposing their vulnerabilities— just as the Summoner strips away the *gentil* cloak of the Friar. Thus, the *Schwank* engages in social criticism of the most competitive sort.[7]

This characterization is based primarily on twentieth-century European folk narratives, but it is equally applicable to a huge corpus of tales recovered in written form from the entire Indo-European culture area from classical times to the present. Indeed, some critics have asserted that the *Schwank* as defined here is the oral realization of a primal expressive need common to all societies.[8] But, more important for the present purpose, the modern folkloric concept of the genre conforms ideally with the content and functions of the tales told by the pilgrim churls. All five of the churls' tales are classified as *Schwänke* by folklorists, all five have been collected orally within the last century, and there is no reason to believe that they were not also told orally in Chaucer's time, in much the same ways and for the same reasons that Chaucer's churls tell them.[9]

I have employed the term *Schwank* and presented this brief description for the purpose of overriding a debate that has clouded Chaucer studies for a century. Chaucerians have long identified the churls' tales as *fabliaux,* in specific reference to a body of French poems which began to appear in the second half of the twelfth century and thrived for little over a hundred years before falling into relative obscurity. From the beginning, scholars have battled with particular vehemence over the provenance of the *fabliaux.* Joseph Bédier claimed they were bourgeois in origin.[10] Per Nykrog, however, insisted that these poems are "so profoundly penetrated by the way of thinking of [the nobility] that it is necessary to view them as a courtly genre just to understand them."[11] Charles Muscatine has attempted to turn the argument back in favor of Bédier's point of view. Muscatine contends that Chaucer's *fabliaux* developed from a French bourgeois tradition which reflected the artistry and point of view of the rising middle class.[12] The debate, then, embraces two smaller questions: the ultimate social sources of the French *fabliaux* and the degree to which Chaucer is indebted to the French poems. It is reasonable to ask if the resolution of either question would reveal much about the special purposes to which Chaucer put his *Schwänke*.

Why should the intent and artistry of the churls' tales be tied so irrevocably to these French poems? The identifiable sources of Chaucer's poetry and the social disposition of the English court argue against any strong influence from the *fabliau*, a form which was "effectively dead" in France before Chaucer was born, and which, as far as can be determined, never achieved popularity in English courtly circles.[13] Of all Chaucer's poems, only one (the Reeve's Tale) has an indisputable analogue among the *fabliaux*. The other churls' tales could have come from many other sources: the Summoner's (though it has a distant *fabliau* analogue) may have had an oral source, the Friar's is most strongly documented in exemplum literature, the Miller's finds parallels in every humorous medieval genre.[14]

Moreover, the stylistic connections between Chaucer's tales and the *fabliaux* are rather tenuous. Few critics would fault Muscatine's finding that Chaucer's *Schwänke* and the French form share some perspectives: a sense of realism, a joyful cynicism, a celebration of animal appetites. But such general similarities could easily have issued from a shared source broader than literary convention: a cultural style of the times, or, more likely, the generic nature of the *Schwank*. When the churls' tales and the French poems are subjected to closer stylistic comparison, few common traits emerge. The "impersonality, lack of rhetorical adornment and of characterization, and rapidity of narration" which Nykrog identifies as hallmarks of the *fabliaux* may surface in the Shipman's Tale, but are not marked in the narratives of the Miller, Reeve, Friar, and Summoner.[15] Some scholars find closer stylistic parallels to Chaucer's *Schwank* style in Vinsauf's rhetorical treatises or in English popular romances; and some judge the churls' tales as unique in the literature of Chaucer's age.[16]

Finally, the *Schwank* was omnipresent in the Middle Ages, and everywhere it took the form best suited to the intent of the teller. Though the *fabliau* was a relatively isolated development that exerted little influence on subsequent literature, its parent form, the oral *Schwank*, found its way into writing through many media. *Schwänke* surfaced in *exempla* long before the *fabliau* came into being,[17] and by the late Middle Ages, such stories were appearing in many generic and social contexts. To give one example: among the eleven medieval analogues to the Miller's Tale cited in two prominent studies are two (very distantly related) French *fabliaux* and one (relatively close) *fabliau* from Flanders. But there are also two Italian *novellas*, a German mock epic, a Latin *exemplum*, a German *Fastnachtspiel*, an English ballad, a German *Meisterlied*, a German prose tale, and a Latin "fable" (more accurately designated a *Schwank-exemplum*).[18] There is no evidence that any of the authors who drew upon this plot cared particularly about its social or generic origin. What did matter to them was that a given plot was adaptable to their diverse purposes, and each writer freely worked the story to meet his special expressive needs.

Chaucer, too, had a special purpose in telling the churls' tales, a purpose which had little to do with whether others had told similar tales about the nobility or the *bourgeoisie*. The poet gives us in his text all the evidence we need to determine why his *Schwänke* are fashioned as they are. Chaucer was presenting tales *told by churls, about other churls*, specifically for argumentative purposes. An examination of these poems in their proper context as oral tales has been too long waiting.

Medieval sources, silent on the subject of storytelling contexts, also withhold direct documentation of the uses of *Schwänke* as social criticism. I must turn to recent folklore research to shed light on the matter. Only in the last few years has it become clear that *Schwänke* play a particularly strong role in expressing social grievances.[19] Certain types of *Schwänke* have been defined as contests between two stereotypic characters, each representing a different status or calling. The teller identifies one of the characters—the villain, or dupe—with a rival class or trade. The villain begins the story in a position of dominance, but is tricked into an ignominious reversal at the tale's end.[20] Thus, the *Schwank*, like the Feast of Fools, offers an inversion of the normal order, allowing the teller and his partisans in the audience to experience in play a momentary victory over the opponent. This is certainly the tactic at work in the Reeve's, Friar's, and Summoner's tales.

The general shape of the *Schwank* remains relatively constant wherever it is told, but the specific roles of the dupe and the trickster are filled by characters relevant to the immediate situation. When the poor agrarian workers of Mecklenburg tell *Schwänke*, the rich landowner is the most common villain, followed by the clergy, who heavily taxed the faithful. Similarly, in rural French Canada, where a semi-feudal system persisted until World War II, the conflict between peasant *(habitant)* and lord *(seigneur)* is the single most popular *Schwank* theme. Consider "The Bargain Not to Become Angry" (AT 1000), in which the hero is given commands by an ogre, but feigns stupidity and takes the commands literally: for example, when told to "put the sheep to pasture," the hero pretends to bury them. He cuts off their tails and sets them in the field (so the ogre will think they've been slaughtered and buried there), then sells them at market for a handsome sum, which he keeps for himself. Through a series of similar sleights, the hero destroys the ogre's property, rapes the ogre's wife, and mutilates the ogre himself. This tale appears worldwide with various characters filling the roles of the two protagonists, but it is always told in French Canada with the *habitant* as hero and the *seigneur* as ogre.[21]

It is safe to assume that a similar situation applied in the Middle Ages. Though no oral texts survive, literary contexts affirm that, as *Schwank* plots remained stable, the role of the dupe was constantly changing. Literature, as I have stated, must incorporate a context to be understood, because the author's work must survive on paper, outside the situation in which it was created. Many medieval literary *Schwänke* supply *internal social contexts;* when they do, it is clear that the villains are given roles corresponding to the objects of satire. Among the eleven analogues to the Miller's Tale, for example, five different occupations—noble, peasant, merchant, shoe-maker, and smith—representing two of the three estates, figure variously as dupes. One German analogue, Heinrich Wittenweiler's *Ring,* is an express and vicious satire on peasants written for the upper classes—a fact apparent from the poem's first lines.[22] The Miller's Tale analogue is just one of several episodes; another scene depicts peasants in a mock tournament, riding farm animals into the lists. Neidhard von Reuenthal, a real-life murderer of peasants, makes a fictional appearance at the tournament to humiliate the farmers. Not surprisingly, the dupe of Wittenweiler's analogue is a peasant. There is no earlier literary source in which a peasant plays that role, and no particular reason to believe there was one. Because Wittenweiler understood the dynamics of the *Schwank,* he would have changed the personnel of his oral or written source to accord with the aim of his satire.

Oral and aural artists do not have to incorporate such an obvious context, because their audience is present during the work's rendition. Nevertheless, the teller of tales and the popular playwright adapt their works to their audiences, who leave traces of their presence in the text, creating an *allusive* context. Such works exhibit the social concerns of the audience. Hans Folz's *Vast spotisch Paurnspil* is just such an aural work, written for Shrove-Tide, a festival similar to the mixed-class entertainments described in Chapter 4.[23] This play was presented in late medieval Nürnberg, one of the richest urban centers of the Holy Roman Empire. The entire social structure of the city would be represented in the audience, which was similar in range to the crowds that witnessed the English Corpus Christi dramas. Therefore, the play had to appeal to a broadly based urban population. Folz, a surgeon, lived rather far up the social scale, and his play was presented to mock the types of social inversions which normally occur at holiday time. His target

was the lower classes in general—but with the urban churls well represented in the audience, his safest mark was the rural churl, the peasant—a
figure against whom his entire audience could unite in derisive laughter. In
the play, twelve peasants tell self-ridiculing stories. One of them is an analogue to the Miller's tale. Folz may have read Wittenweiler's *Ring*, but he
certainly did not have to. The story would have been about a peasant, no
matter who had played the role of dupe in the tale first heard by the author.

Chaucer's *Schwänke*, of course, have a double context: the *internal social
context* which presents the storytellers along with their tales, and the *allusive
context* of each text, wherein the narrator's message shows traces of influence by the fictional audience. The churls use *Schwänke* as modern folk
narrators do, and (to judge from the aural texts of surviving *Fastnacht-
spielen*) as they were often told aloud in the Middle Ages.

This explains, in part, why no verifiable source has ever been found for
any of Chaucer's seven *Schwänke*. The more "approved" literary genres—
saints' lives, *exempla*, and moral romances—possessed authority. They were
supposed to be retold in basically the same form in which they had first
been written; hence, the tales of the Clerk, Man of Law, and Physician, as
well as the Melibee of Chaucer the Pilgrim, follow identifiable sources quite
closely. But the *Schwänke*, even in their literary forms, were malleable by
tradition, and changed to fit each situation. Consequently, the literary history of the *Schwank* is dauntingly difficult to trace, and its oral forms—
probably better known to Chaucer than the written ones—even more so.

Social criticism plays an important role in Chaucer's *Schwänke*, but their
real rhetorical brilliance lies in their individuality. Many of the *Tales* are
renowned for the way in which they reflect the teller's personality, but the
Schwänke are also notable, conversely, for the way in which the fictional
dupe reflects the personality of the teller's foe. Though literary critics tend
to view these individualized insults as Chaucer's idiosyncratic creations,
such tactics were part of the folkloric processes at work in his time. He did
not invent this type of story; he was simply the most brilliant translator of a
long-established oral tradition.

I use the term "churl's tale" to identify narratives crafted specifically to
serve as indirect insults. All churls' tales are *Schwänke*, but not all *Schwänke*
are churls' tales. Dégh has noted two distinct functions of *Schwänke*: to
reform people by magnifying their bad habits and to "express disapproval
by scoffing at persons of bad conduct."[24] Both functions were recognized in
the Middle Ages. For example, Caspar Cropacius's *Fabula de sacerdote et
simplici rustico* was written for the milder functions of warning and reform-
ing.[25] This *exemplum*, which shares the plot of the Miller's Tale, draws upon
the techniques of allusive context used in oral sermons. The author pre-

sents the type of the simple farmer to illustrate the errors that even the good-hearted can make. In Cropacius's version, a friar (playing the same role as Chaucer's Nicholas) attempts to deceive a farmer (Chaucer's John the Carpenter) in order to gain the favors of the farmer's wife. He preaches about an impending flood, the simple farmer believes him, and as the husband prepares for the End the friar sleeps with the cuckold's wife. In proper clerical fashion, the *exemplum* ends with a moralizing proverb: "He who believes readily is readily deceived." Cropacius's tale is chiding, but not vicious. Unlike Wittenweiler and Folz, he intends not to ridicule peasants, but to persuade his listeners that blind faith is no virtue when extended to the promises of treacherous men. The Miller's version of the same story is put to a radically different purpose. It is not, then, the content of the story, but rather *the intent of the teller,* that makes a *Schwank* a churl's tale. In the folk tradition Chaucer imitated, the intent is to deliver a safe but scathing blow at an opponent by means of a tale in which a fictional villain resembling the real-life opponent is humiliated. The skillful teller consolidates his victory by adding the laughter of the audience to his insult.

A close look at one modern churl's tale in its social context clarifies the techniques employed by expert oral artists. In the late 1930s, when the *seigneurial* system still flourished in French Canada, folklorist Luc Lacourcière asked the lord of a certain *seigneurie* for permission to attend a *veillée* (or evening storytelling session) held by the *habitants* of the estate. The request was granted, but the *seigneur's* wife, having heard of Lacourcière's reputation as a man of letters, sent her son to witness the event, normally off-limits to the highborn. The *veillée* was about to begin when the *seigneur's* son joined the *habitants*. His entry provoked a sullen silence. Lacourcière tried to get the *habitants* to ignore the intrusion, to tell their tales and sing their songs. No one was willing to do so. After some time, a man stood up and announced he had a story to tell. It was a tale that Lacourcière—the foremost authority on the French-Canadian folktale—had never heard before, and has not heard of since. For this reason, we can assume that the teller invented it—or, more accurately, shaped it from traditional motifs— just before the telling:

> A long time ago, it's good tell you, there was a son of an *habitant* and a son of a *seigneur*. The *habitant's* son had a magnificent horse. It won all the races and earned some reputation for the owner. The *Seigneur's* son heard about this famous horse and tried to race his own handsome, well-bred colt against it. Every time they ran, the horse of the *habitant* left the *seigneur's* son far behind. Nothing the rich boy tried could help him win the race. One day the *seigneur's* son came to visit the *habitant* boy. "You know, you have such a magnificent horse. How would you like to give it to me?"
>
> "I would not do that, *seigneur*."
>
> "Perhaps I could buy it from you? I could make you very comfortable."

"It may seem strange to you, *seigneur,* but my horse has made me feel very comfortable already."

"Then why don't you loan him to me for a while? I would like that very much."

The *habitant's* son thought: This may be a good idea. When he rides my horse himself, he will only know all the better it is far finer than his own. "You have a bargain. You may borrow the horse."

The next morning, the son of the *habitant* was at work in the fields when the *seigneur's* son rode close by on the great horse, kicking up great clouds of dust. Again, the next morning, the same thing. Every morning for days, weeks, months, the *seigneur's* son rode by, and said nothing to the *habitant,* made no gesture to return the colt. Finally, the *habitant* thought it was time to do something about it. He walked up to the big *chateau,* told the maid at the door he would like to see the son of the *seigneur.* The maid got a butler, who found another butler, who found the boy way back in the castle—and finally the boy was at the door.

"You know," said the *habitant's* son, "this is a magnificent *seigneurie.* Would you give it to me?"

"What a ridiculous question. I'd never do that."

"Then why don't you loan it to me for a while?"[26]

At this abrupt ending, the *habitants* broke into loud laughter and the *veillée* began in earnest. This *Schwank,* a masterful example of the churl's tale, incorporates the most common traits of the pilgrims' stories: anonymity, situational aptness, testing the opposition, and ridicule by association.

Anonymity. Bearing their "un-wyse tales," the pilgrims described by Langland in *Piers Plowman* had "*leve* to lye al hur lyf-time." If the tale was a lie in the Middle Ages, it was also a safe lie: clerics inveighed against taletellers, but did not imprison them. The great rhetorical strength of the churl's tale is that it provides license to tell a lie which conceals a factual antagonism. The narrator can insult his antagonist to his heart's content, as long as he does not name him; otherwise, the tale is merely another form of slander.

The narrator of the French-Canadian story follows this rule. He makes no mention of the lord's son who is also in the room. In fact, he does not address a single word directly to his antagonist. The audience knows that the story is about the lord's son—and the lord's son must know as well; yet no one can *prove* it. Buried within fiction, the insult is anonymous, and safe.

The same rule seems to have applied in the Middle Ages. London's ecclesiastical slander records—missing for the fourteenth century—state the same restrictions in extant cases from the fifteenth century onward. In W. H. Hale's collection of precedents, no singer or taleteller is brought into court simply for singing a song—even an obscene one—unless he has singled out people *by name* in the verses.[27] The same stricture applied for singers outside London, as attested in this sixteenth-century record from Oxfordshire:

Anna Wrigglesworth of Islipp appears and denies the charge that ever she made any ryme, but she said a certeyne ryme, and for goodwill she told the same to goodwife Willyams and her daughter because she thought it was made to their discreditt. . . . :

If I had as faire a face as John Williams his daughter Elizabeth hass
Then wold I were a tudrie lace as goodman Boltes daughter Marie dosse
And if I had as mutche money in my pursse as Cadman's daughter Margaret
  hass
Then wold I have a bastard less then Butler's mayde Helen hasse.[28]

Like the *habitants*, Chaucer's churls avoid Anna Wrigglesworth's error. The more clever and subtle pilgrims, such as the Miller, do not even acknowledge the possibility that their tales might be construed as insults. The more choleric of them—Reeve, Summoner, and Friar—make it clear that they mean to offend their antagonists, but they too remain within the boundaries of safety.

Situational Aptness is the second tactic of the churl's tale: the tale's theme and content should reflect the real-life situation which has triggered the narrative insult. The *habitant's* tale retold above is a perfect example. As the great majority of French-Canadian *Schwänke* concern the conflict between lord and peasant, the *habitant* who performed the tale had an almost unlimited variety of materials from which to choose. But such *Schwänke* as the "Bargain Not To Become Angry" (summarized earlier in this chapter) present the hostility in different terms. Though the lord is by no means depicted as an ideal personality in these tales, it is the *peasant* who initiates most of the cruel actions: he steals the *seigneur's* bounty, rapes the man's wife, rips flesh from his back. Such a story would ill suit the purposes of an *habitant* responding to a noble's intrusion at a *veillée:* the tale would not only misrepresent the role of the innocent peasants, but would also put the lord's son in the role of relatively innocent dupe. This is the most probable reason why the *habitant* had to create a new tale: as compensation fantasies told invariably when no noble was present, the existing body of *Schwänke* about *seigneurs* would present the peasants at the *veillée* in a far more aggressive role than they were in fact playing.

The tale told by the *habitant*, however, presents an apt reflection of the situation which inspired it. The real-life *seigneur's* son had done exactly what his fictional counterpart did: envying something that belonged not to him but to the peasants, he simply seized it. Just as the fictional noble took away the peasant's horse, the real-life *seigneur* had taken the *veillée* from the peasants.

Testing. The *habitant's* tale is also a message to the peasants in his audience, reminding them that they—like the fictional hero—could act defiantly, could tell their tales and demand their rights, with or without the lord's approval. The performance seems to have been successful on this didactic level, first by allowing the peasants to chastise the lord, second by inspiring them to proceed with the *veillée* in spite of him. The story served not only to ridicule the opponent, but also to challenge him and nullify his threats.

In other modern contexts, the aspect of challenge is equally apparent. French Canadian lumberjacks used to sing derisive songs aimed at foremen who pressured their workers unnecessarily. A song sung under such conditions would feature a cruel or stupid foreman, and though it did not mention any names, all present knew at whom the barb was aimed. And the foremen "had to take it. They were obligated to laugh."[29] Interviews with the lumberjacks revealed two important functions for their mocking stories and sung diatribes. First, and most obviously, the performances were sanctioned activities, safety valves granting expression to otherwise unutterable feelings of anger. Like many *Schwänke*, the lumberjacks' songs were warnings that the foreman had gone too far in bossing his men and that he had to mend his ways. Second, they provided means by which the men could test the foreman. Though he could hear the derisive songs and infer readily enough that he was the butt of them, the foreman was not supposed to appear angry—it was very important that he should keep his composure. Throughout the day, in other contexts, the foreman had been giving the workers orders and testing their ability to cope with stress. By singing mocking songs, the workmen administered a compensatory test, one which the foreman had to pass to maintain their respect.

Medieval oral performances often involved such tests. At the *Festi Stultorum,* songs and mock sermons humiliated the clergy by naming their titles, but not their names. We may assume that, when the vicars of Viviers were forced to listen to the parody songs of the Abbot of Fools, and when the real-life bishop had to wait upon the choirboy named Bishop for a Day, these churchmen, like the foremen, had to "take it." Extant records testify to the troubles that ensued when "betters" could not endure such barbs. Chaucer's churls, like medieval revelers and present-day peasants, use fiction to challenge opponents and, in more playful contexts, to test their good humor as well.

Within the tale the principal tactic is *ridicule by association*. The speaker draws as strong a parallel as possible between his real-life antagonist and the tale's dupe. The link can be made in many ways, through reference to the occupation, status, physical appearance, excesses, or personality of the foe. The ultimate test of the storyteller's art is how well and how subtly he can transfer his feelings about his real-life antagonist into his tale. In the *habitant's* tale, the villain takes on traits of the real-life villain: he is not simply a noble, but the *son* of a noble. The result is a narrative enthymeme:

   1) Lords' sons are selfish
   2) [You are a lord's son]
   3) [You are selfish]

As the last two parts of his message are merely implied, the peasant's tale effectively generalizes the real-life situation, and the insult is safe.

Stereotyping helps direct and sharpen the insult. The *habitant's* tale exploits two well-known stereotypes concerning nobles. First, they are incredibly greedy: no matter how much they have, they will still covet what they do not own. Second, they are blithely insensitive to the needs of others. The narrator thus seized upon the perceivable actions of the real-life boy who, though much better off than the peasants, still insisted they share their *veillée* with him, and who seemed utterly insensitive to the fact that his presence was ruining the *veillée*.

Parallel instances of generalization occurred in the coarse parody of the Feast of Fools, wherein songs addressed by the congregation to the mock potentate say in effect:

   1) Beau Sire Asne
   2) Evesque Notre
   3) [Notre evesque est un asne]

The fool's performance also played upon the stereotypic traits most often assigned the Church elite: pomposity, disdain for the poor, a penchant for delivering interminable, irrelevant sermons.

Despite such festive analogues, it is Chaucer himself who presents the most persuasive evidence that the churl's tale was common in the Middle Ages. His churls' narrative techniques so closely resemble the *habitant's* that it would indeed be coincidence if these two performance styles—separated by over five centuries—did not share a continuous folkloric tradition. A close look at some successful and some failed churls' tales shows the poet's mastery of the esthetic of the oral *Schwank*.

THE MILLER

In the Middle Ages, as today, when two strangers meet, each tends to use his knowledge of the other *as a type* in order to assess that person's character, interests, and intent.[30] Chaucer's knowledge of this phenomenon is recorded in the General Prologue, where—from a wealth of specific information that might lead his audience to view each pilgrim as an individual—the poet's pilgrim persona selects traits that invite us to label his subject a type. Thus, the Prioress, whom modern readers may see as a failed nun, is viewed by the narrator as a perfect lady. The narrator uses like exaggerations to present the Franklin as a symbol of amenity, the Knight as a model of nobility, and the Parson as the emblem of piety.[31]

A similar process of stereotyping takes place when two relative strangers engage in a dispute: each uses his knowledge of the other as a *type* in order to size up and attack his opponent. Chaucerians tend to assume that the poet designed the portraits and actions of his pilgrims according to some elite system of stereotyping: the estates satires, the medieval sciences of physiology and physiognomy, the theological doctrine of the Seven Deadly Sins. The *Canterbury Tales* does contain elements of each of these elite views. But it also contains a great deal of folk stereotyping, a fact which has been recognized in only the most general way.

Stereotyping begins as soon as the Miller refers to the Reeve. Robyn's succinct plot summary—

> . . . I wol telle a legende and a lyf
> Bothe of a carpenter and of his wyf,
> How that a clerk hath set the wrightes cappe (1.3141–43)

—introduces an occupational slur and leaves no doubt that what follows is to be a *Schwank,* and an obscene one at that. Robyn's synopsis is similar to the "arguments" which graced the tops of manuscript and broadside versions of bawdy ballads from the late Middle Ages to the nineteenth century: "Being an account of . . . The Biter Bitten, or, the Broken Well filled by the Joyner and the Joyner's Wife."[32] Both titles, though formulaic introductions to fictional works, imply that the events soon to be detailed may actually have happened. The Miller speaks of "a legende and a lyf," the broadside proclaims an "account"—and other early fictional broadsides speak of "events that lately fell," a "case that happened then," and so on.

If the Reeve needs further evidence that Robyn's tale will concern cuckoldry, he need only recall the songs and stories told about millers. From the Middle Ages to the nineteenth century, millers were portrayed in folklore as freehanded adulterers.[33] One reason for this stereotype was purely imagematic: "grinding grain" is one of the commonest euphemisms for sexual intercourse in British *Schwank* tradition, and for the purposes of metaphor, it was fitting that a miller be given the opportunity to grind it with some cuckold's wife.[34] And there were other, less metaphorical reasons for the popular conception of the miller as lecher. When the *villeins*—often in the company of their overseer, the reeve—left their homes in the pre-dawn hours to walk to work, the miller was still in bed. This German folksong is one of many that dwell enviously on that fact:

> And when the farmer gets up early
> And goes down to his field. . . .
> The old miller lies easy
> By his lovely wife and sleeps. . . . [35]

It was enough to make any farmer unhappy. Even more distressing was the idea of what the miller might do to the *farmers'* wives when the men were working. The slur on carpenters, and the suggestion that the Miller is living up to his stereotypical reputation as the village adulterer, inspire Oswald's angry response. Robyn has already gone too far, as far as Oswald is concerned.

Nevertheless, much of the Reeve's anger seems inherent in his personality: he is a joyless and bitter man, and his words are far angrier, far less subtle than Robyn's. Critics say we should expect the Reeve to behave so meanly; Chaucer has described him, physiologically, as a slender, *colerik* man (1.587). Yet the Reeve is mean-spirited not only because he is *colerik*, but also because he hails from Norfolk. Estates satires do not deal with such regional stereotypes, but Chaucer's fictional Miller and his real-life audience were well aware of this folk device. We know from the General Prologue (1.619) that the Reeve is a Norfolk man; but even if Chaucer had not told us, the Reeve would have given it away. His accent faithfully imitates Norfolk dialect. As Chaucer has made an obvious link between Norfolk and the Reeve, it is surprising that Chaucerians have not made the connection between the Reeve and the Norfolk stereotype. The documentary evidence is irrefutable.[36] The *Descriptio Norfolciensium*, a twelfth-century work in Latin by a Peterborough monk, is—to my knowledge—the earliest extended regional satire to have been recovered from medieval England.[37] The manuscript consists of twelve short *Schwänke* (many of which are still in oral circulation today) embedded, like the *Canterbury Tales,* in a fictive frame: Caesar has sent out messengers to evaluate the nature of each of his provinces. A *nuncio* returns to say:

> I have traversed the seas. I have examined the territories of the entire world, but nowhere, I must confess, is there a province as completely abominable as Norfolk. The land is barren, the people most worthless, full of guile, deceitful, and envious—and different from all other people. This report makes public their customs and works. . . . (lines 10–17)

Two of the longer narratives in the *nuncio's* "report" convey the flavor of this vicious satire:

> One summer a man of Norfolk diligently collects his honey, placing it in a jar, unguarded, then attends to other business. But the rustic's dog, half dead from hunger, spies the storage place from afar and leaps to the spot. While the farmer is gone, the dog eats all the honey. Then, the rustic calls the dog in a sad, anxious voice, full of distress: "Don't you gulp down two—or more— pickled fishheads almost every day? You will return that honey, by daylights! From now on you will certainly eat worse." He pins down the dog with two sticks, and . . . the dog vomits up the swallowed honey. The farmer once more collects the honey in an earthen pot, and proceeds to carry it to the nearest

market. When he comes to the market wishing to sell this stuff, he is approached by someone looking to buy honey; that man sees this junk and says, "Hey, rube, your honey is all rancid." The peasant, filled with great anguish, swears by broad daylight, "The honey is of excellent quality; yet it is true that, a short while back, it was in a dirty container." (147–72)

A certain nobleman of the said province, constantly sitting and counting his money, began to take coins from his purse; a single coin happened to fall from his side. A tame crow which had been standing nearby leaped up all of a sudden and swallowed it. When the lord saw this, he wept and wailed in grief and distress. Seizing the crow, he held it by a foot; then he squeezed [its neck] hard with a spiked switch [to force the bird to vomit up the coin], never thinking that it would sooner or later have to shit. Nothing availed. The crow caws from excessive torment; finally the learned man thinks up a wonderful plan. He firmly fixes a stake in the ground, and ties the crow to the stake by means of a small cord. He gives special orders that it not eat anything. This fast is enforced for two days straight. After forcing the crow to eat small pills, he dug through all the droppings left by the bird—thus he found the coin. After he had found it, never in his life had he been so happy, and the entire country danced with him because he had discovered a drachma he had once lost. (199–224)

The chain of tales is brought to an end with further insults from the fictional *nuncio:*

I do not wish to tell you more of such trifles: I shall now attend to only the most glaringly true of the matters remaining. These people stand out in all countries because they infect others with their evils. After leaving their homeland, they never come back thereafter, if they are able. Although at first they present themselves in their new homes as simpleminded, later they are shown to do evil. A crow flying across the sea would not leave its tail behind; neither would evil abandon the Norfolker, for as the limb carries the vices of the head, so a man carries the evil of his country. . . . I have related in part, but not fully, the customs and works of Norfolkers, for I have neither the inclination nor the paper sufficient for the task—even if both were more abundant than Norfolk itself. So let us pray, most devoutly, that the God of us all, with His power, may correct the vices of these aforementioned men—or else destroy them all, together with their country. (225–36, 249–55)

It is nearly certain that Chaucer did not know the *Descriptio Norfolciensium,* but it is nearly inconceivable that he did not know the oral tradition on which the poem was based. The Norfolk stereotype was conveyed in *Schwank* form from the tselfth to the nineteenth centuries; I have found over forty post-*Descriptio* tales that present a similar portrait of the Norfolker. Several of these date from Chaucer's time. Throughout its eight-hundred-year history, the stereotype has retained a remarkable stability.

How closely does this regional portrait accord with that of Chaucer's Reeve? In *Schwank* tradition, the adjectives most often applied, implicitly or explicitly, to Norfolkers are *stupid, cruel, irascible, guileful, greedy,* and *antiso-cial.* Only the label *stupid* fails to fit Oswald. However, stupidity is the most common Norfolk trait in the *Descriptio* narratives, which are in fact classified by folklorists as "numskull tales." Aside from this one important attribute, the traits most common in oral tradition well suit those assigned the Reeve.

Like his numskull alter egos, who sift through bird droppings for missing coins and try to sell once-eaten honey, Oswald practices cheapness, hoard-ing, and acquisitiveness—all forms of all-consuming *greed:* "Ful riche he was astored pryvely" (1.609). As one fictional Norfolker finds nothing more pleasant than to pass the time counting and recounting his money, the Reeve shows a compulsive talent for tallying his master's goods (1.597–600). These stores the Reeve cherishes and—not without reason—con-siders his own. Through sleight, he "gives" and "loans" his master what was already his master's to begin with (1.611). Indeed, Oswald's greed is so great that he seems to practice it not merely for personal gain, but so that there will be a little less wealth in the world for others to share. His true wealth "pryvely"—and uselessly—hidden, Oswald displays none of its outward benefits. Rather, he carries a "rusty blade" against his naked legs, as if his greed were so great that he must deny himself to feed it.

Like the plight of the rich Norfolkers (of another *Descriptio* tale, 39–51) who let their bread rot rather than eat it, Oswald's *underfed* frame is less the result of need than greed. In the *Descriptio* Norfolk is described as the "barren" home of scrawny men who chew on weeds (18–21). Though W. C. Curry and others have claimed that Oswald's thinness is emblematic of his *colerik* character,[38] one could as easily maintain, following the argument of the *Descriptio,* that the impoverished land of Norfolk is responsible for this Norfolker's emaciated frame: "if you sow choice wheat there, you reap darnel" (19–20). Oswald's Norfolk roots ensure his starved appearance, which he further cultivates by closely shaving his beard and hair (1.588–90) to present a figure as unpromising as the thistle-filled Norfolk farmlands, "bare of all good things" (24).

"An impious land produces impious men," states the *Descriptio* (51–52). More than greedy, Oswald is *cruel.* Usually, greed is the cause of Norfolk cruelty, as when, for small monetary gains, the *Schwank* characters torture food and coins from the bodies of hapless animals. The Reeve's cruelty is similarly motivated by greed. Those who fear him most, "adrad of hym as of the deeth" (1.605), are those whose job it is to audit the Reeve's tallies and the workers who produce the goods he hoards.

The Norfolk numskulls are called *devious* and earn that epithet in many of their actions. They practice clever falsehoods: a father who does not want to spend money on a cake for his son claims the food is unhealthy (34–38); caught by a customer, the man who sold honey vomited up by his dog states obliquely that the stuff was recently in a dirty container. Norfolkers are described as similar to "the silly dog [that] wags its tail and in your presence shows a face full of joy, [but] bites and brings wounds if you turn your back" (241–44). This description also fits Oswald, who shows a benign face to his lord, but steals from him secretly.

The Norfolk stereotype also embraces *antisocial* tendencies. The farmers of the *Descriptio* are "different from all other peoples," and their unwholesome characteristics make them stand apart from a crowd. They refuse to open their doors to strangers (143–46), delight in cheating the men who help them earn their bread, and viciously strike out at others for no apparent reason. Similarly, the Reeve keeps his distance from his fellows: "Evere he rood the hyndreste of oure route" (1.622)—perhaps to spy upon them, but certainly to avoid their company.

Finally, like the Reeve, the stereotypical Norfolkers are *colerik:* they fly into unprovoked rages—attacking blades of wheat (26–33), yelling at their horses (130–33), cursing strangers (117–21), fiercely beating the animals that have swallowed their winnings. The Reeve's quickness to anger will become his ruling trait as Chaucer's poem progresses. Yet Curry, in saying that the Reeve is so tempered because he is *colerik*, has told, at most, half the story. As any Englishman of Chaucer's time would readily attest, the Reeve is coleric *because he hails from Norfolk*. In depicting Oswald as a *colerik* man from Norfolk, Chaucer has set up a double referent: his audience could use elite physiognomy or folk prejudice to arrive at the same conclusion.

This helps explain why the Miller is so mild in his attack on the Reeve. Of all Chaucer's verbal duelists, Robyn is the least openly offensive. Of all Chaucer's *Schwänke*, the Miller's is easily the most evenhanded and good-natured, leading most readers to extend a certain sympathy to all the characters in his tale, which is not the normal audience reaction to a *Schwank*. In his exchange with Herry Bailly Robyn has shown he can be curt and obscene. But the Miller knows—first from his stereotypical knowledge of Norfolkers, and second from Oswald's paranoid reaction to Robyn's plot summary—that he does not have to push the Reeve too far to obtain an angry response. By conducting his insult campaign in the mildest possible manner, the Miller will win the respect of the crowd. He knows as well as they do that it was considered a mark of superior breeding to refrain from such angry diatribes as the Reeve's.

Not long after Robyn begins his story, it is clear to all that he is a master narrator; he tells the finest of Chaucer's *Schwänke*—indeed, arguably the finest *Schwank* to survive the Middle Ages. This feature is often judged unrealistic: if Chaucer is striving for verisimilitude, how can he put such a brilliant tale in the mouth of the crude Miller? Yet there is evidence from ancient, medieval, and modern sources to indicate that the level of art in the

Miller's tale is, in a fictional sense, well suited to its teller. Chaucer aptly identifies the Miller as an expert exponent of lower-class artistic traditions current in the Middle Ages. Chaucer has prepared his audience for the Miller's verbal acumen, and for the subject of his tale, by describing him as a "janglere and a goliardeys" who sings "of synne and harlotries" (1.560–61). But popular conception had already labeled the Miller a master artist. The connection between millers and oral entertainment—especially the telling of *Schwänke*—is documented in medieval proverbs. Le Roy Ladurie notes the importance of the mill as a center of storytelling; this association is at least as old as Apuleius, whose fictional rogues tell their bawdy tales at the millhouse. Because people congregate there and idle as grain is ground, the mill makes a natural stage for tales—and the miller, who hears them all, is the leading artist in his native milieu.[39]

It is not only what Chaucer says about the Miller, but what he has the Miller say, that testifies to Robyn's oral artistry. E. Talbot Donaldson's study of "The Idiom of Popular Poetry in the Miller's Tale" shows how Robyn constantly borrows and improves the shopworn phrases of lower-class romances and lyrics.[40] It is a critical commonplace to note that the Miller's is the only one of the *Tales* that employs the stock epithets of alehouse poetry: "hende Nicholas," "joly Absolon," "sely John." But Donaldson further shows that the Miller transforms other well-known figures found in the lyrics and romances performed by real-life goliards. "Geynest under gore" ("prettiest under a skirt"—a title popular poets award their finest ladies) is translated by Robyn to "Upon her lendes, ful of many a goore" (1.3237). Popular romance merely suggests sexuality, identifying the woman through her clothes. But the Miller calls our direct attention to what his lady's skirts conceal. The Miller's verse, then, suits his status and purpose. He has announced his intention to tell a noble tale to "quite" the Knight's— and that is exactly what he does, in language appropriate to the two men's relative status. Robyn employs the speech with which yeoman minstrels typically described lords and ladies, but he "lowers" his diction to show, ironically, how the assumed delicacy of the *gentils* is simply a mask for the baser impulses shared by all people. His tale mimics the styles Robyn would be expected to employ: a poetry of stock figures and phrases, but verse more cleverly and contentiously wrought than that of other amateurs.

But to return to Robyn's attack on the Reeve: it is the subtlest indirect insult in Chaucer. At first, there seems to be little obvious relationship between the *colerik* Reeve and the tale's rather likable dupe, John the Carpenter. In light of this fact, Frederick Tupper asserts that Chaucer did not mold the tale to suit a professional rivalry, but rather invented a secondary rivalry (Miller vs. Carpenter, rather than Miller vs. Reeve) to suit a preexisting tale. Yet, if this is likely, why is it that none of the medieval analogues names the cuckolded husband as a carpenter?[41] Moreover, as I have shown, the role of the *Schwank* dupe was subject to change at each oral or written telling.

A more pertinent question is whether the Miller's tale is an appropriate description, not of reeves or of carpenters, but of Oswald. The narrative threads linking John the Carpenter to the Reeve are few in number, yet the connection is secure. All would agree that the dupe of Robyn's well-told joke resembles Oswald in three particulars: both are carpenters, advanced in age, and (at least according to the implications raised in Robyn's disclaimer) afraid they may be cuckolded. The Reeve is sensitive about all three matters, and he cannot feel anything but anger as Robyn proceeds to make a cuckold of Oswald's fictional alter ego.

Yet a fourth trait links John indirectly to Oswald. John, like the Norfolkers portrayed in folktales, is an idiot. Though the Miller's tale would break the mold of any generic category to which it were assigned, it is as much a numskull tale as a *fabliau*. John, the dupe, a man of "rude" wit (1.3227), is identified five times by the telltale epithet "sely." His actions demonstrate that he merits his title. When John feels Nicholas is behaving idiotically, he tells a numskull tale of his own.

> So ferde another clerk with astromye:
> He walked in the feeldes for to prye
> Upon the sterres, what there sholde bifalle,
> Til he was in a marle-pit yfalle—
> He saugh nat that. . . . (1.3457–61)

But the carpenter's jibe is better suited to himself than to Nicholas: it will be John, eyes fixed on a heavenly reward, who will take a fall by failing to recognize the adulterous situation under his own nose. Thus John is a numskull, and the record of his misadventures could be easily strung together with the Norfolker jokes found in the *Descriptio*.

How can such a tale ridicule the Reeve, who is not an idiot? Though idiocy is one of the few negative traits Oswald does not possess, idiocy constitutes the generic essence of the numskull joke and the prevailing element of the Norfolk stereotype. By exploiting the popular image of the Reeve's Norfolk background, the Miller makes Oswald guilty of "stupidity by association." This is a cleverly calculated insult: disguising all but the few barbs most likely to enrage Oswald—the slander of carpenters, the slur on age, the specter of cuckoldry, and the stigma of idiocy—Robyn unfolds a tale whose seeming innocence wins the approval of the crowd and works Oswald into a fury.

The Miller's ploy would be too subtle to succeed if Oswald were not so easily angered. But Robyn, having sampled Oswald's rage, can bank on the probability that his opponent will not fail him now. Indeed, the Reeve is so upset by the Miller's Tale that he grows to resemble the foolish John rather closely. In the prologue to his own tale, Oswald tries to win the crowd's sympathy by harping on his old age and loss of virility (1.3867–99). But in so doing, he manages only to reinforce the sly insinuation of cuckoldry planted earlier by the Miller—and to strengthen the audience's impression that the silly old cuckold described in the Miller's Tale indeed bears more than a passing resemblance to Oswald. In the end, the Reeve's fabled anger causes him to lose the fictional slander match and to adopt the role of numskull. As the Miller perseveres unperturbedly (in the fashion of the finest folk orators, with gentle protestations of innocence and good faith), the Reeve boils over and ruins his rebuttal (1.3913–15). While other verbal duelists use ridicule by association to create fictional creatures in the likeness of their opponents, Robyn forces the Reeve into the Norfolker's stereotypical role using Oswald's very real anger to make him appear an idiot.

Thus, the Miller's Tale is the natural extension of the folk rhetorical style which the Miller has used in the exchange preceding the story. Robyn's story, like his indirect insult technique, is an extended *feeling out* procedure, a very successful tease, in which the Miller proves not merely that the Reeve can't take a dirty joke, but that he can't take a good-humored one. Robyn reveals to the entire company that Oswald cannot laugh.

THE REEVE

Oswald may be a poor debater, but he is a master of the churl's tale. In many respects, the Reeve's Tale is the exact opposite of the Miller's, yet it is an equally competent, and more characteristic, example of narrative insult. Unlike the surviving analogues to the Miller's Tale, the antecedents of the Reeve's may have already featured a miller fixed in the dupe's role.[42] In any case, a medieval reeve would have no trouble finding a ready-made story about a cuckold miller. If Robyn has made one rhetorical error in his encounter with the Reeve, it is in bringing up the question of adultery. From the fourteenth century onwards, for every *Schwank* ballad featuring a miller as adulterer, there are three referring to millers who lose their wives or pretty daughters to the advances of strangers.[43] The image of miller as cuckold is apparently based on the deep-seated envy which the peasants felt toward him, an envy which the greedy, competitive Reeve would share. As the dandies of village society, millers possessed wealth and privilege that others did not. The use of adultery to level such social differences is one of the major strategies of the *Schwank*. A fictional conquest of an enemy's wife provides a vicarious satisfaction for the narrator and his allies in the audience. The Reeve's Tale is appropriate not only to the stereotype of millers, but also to the specific context in which it is told, for it answers one fictional charge of cuckoldry with another. The Reeve has much in common with the French-Canadian *habitant* who countered a noble's real-life entry into his *veillée* with a fictional invasion of the *seigneur's* chateau.

But the Reeve lacks the feigned casualness of the best folk rhetoricians; true to his nasty nature, this Norfolk man makes no apologies. "This is a tale about a miller, and it is meant for you," he so much as tells Robyn at the beginning and again at the end of the story (1.3916, 4324). Within the tale, the Reeve makes the dupe's identity transparent. Using *insult by association*, he links Robyn to the tale's dupe on four levels: occupation, physical appearance, dress, and personality. Oswald's *Schwank* portrait is a carnival mirror image of Robyn, magnifying all the Miller's ugliest traits.

Most of the details of Oswald's brilliant caricature are discussed by George Fenwick Jones in "Chaucer and the Medieval Miller."[44] Therefore, I am brief in my comparison. The fictional Symkyn, like his alter ego, is large. Both are accomplished wrestlers (1.548; 1.3928). Both have large nostrils (1.554–57; 1.3934), but the fictional Miller also has a skull like an ape's (1.3935). Both are pipers (1.565–66; 1.3927)—but the Reeve implies through humorous juxtaposition that the fictional miller plays the pipes like a true churl, much as a fisherman beats nets (1.3927). Both are thieves (1.562–63; 1.3939–40) and both carry swords (1.558; 1.3930–32). But while Robyn carries his blade for show, Symkyn carries his to threaten others ("Ther was no man, for peril, dorste hym touche"; 1.3932, cf. 1.3957–60). Robyn dresses ostentatiously, in a blue hood; Symkyn wears red hose. Both colors are worn illegally: medieval legislation forbade churls such dress. In the best style of the stereotyper, the Reeve has created a close copy of his enemy—and, by adding one particularly ugly fictional trait for every two or three true ones, Oswald makes Robyn seem uglier than he is.

To enhance the grotesquery, the Reeve sketches a wife and daughter as coarse as Symkyn. The daughter, like many romance ladies, has "eyen greye as glas" (1.3974), but also the telltale squashed ("camus") nose of the peasant: this touch is a neat reversal of the *Schwank* stereotype of the *schöne Müllerin,* the predominant popular image. Oswald's crowning slur is the mention that Symkyn's wife is the parson's bastard daughter—a blow augmented by the comment that Symkyn has married the choicest bride possible to "saven his estaat of yomanrye" (1.3949). If one hates a miller, no match could be more appropriate for that socially marginal soul than the illegitimate daughter of a priest. Both millers and bastard children of clergy were classed officially as "disreputable persons" in late medieval Germany, where they were denied certain freedoms by law.[45] Such an insult would be taken very poorly by Robyn. His pretensions are strongly implied in his clothes and bearing, and he cannot feel flattered as Oswald takes them, refashions them in fiction, then destroys them with their bearer.

The style in which Oswald tells his tale is stark and relentless; even the "seductions" are brutal, and the savage beating of Symkyn is described with obvious relish. No indirect insult could be more devastating than this—and that is its failing. The tale reinforces the stereotype of the cruel Norfolk man. Oswald's flaw lies not in his taletelling talents, which are considerable, but in his bitterness. The story of Symkyn is a disproportionately cruel response to the Miller's Tale. Indeed, the pilgrim audience may see in Symkyn more of the Reeve than of the Miller. No matter how vicious Robyn is, he is too subtle ever to *appear* as vicious as Symkyn. The fictional miller, the creation of the Reeve's most angry moment, embodies the proverbial *choler* of the Norfolk man: Oswald and his dupe are both "emblems of perverse irascibility."[46] Robyn may hate Oswald, but he has presented him a likable, if pitiable, alter ego; the audience has laughed at John the Carpenter, but not too savagely. The Reeve delivers a safe response, but it is not situationally apt: it reveals too much anger to earn the backing of the crowd.

FRIAR AND SUMMONER

The negative narrative portraits of the Friar and Summoner are based on stereotypes promoted by all levels of medieval society. This was especially true in the case of friars, who were insulted in the learned tracts of the chancellor of Oxford as well as in the obscenely vicious songs of illiterate folk. Ridiculing clerics was both a popular art and an elite science. Chaucer could have based his caricatures on any source: estates satire, sermon, song, *Schwank*.[47]

One of the best measures of the unpopularity of friars is the Summoner's "proverbial" attack: "A frere wol entremette hym evermo" (3.834), "Freres and feendes been but lyte asonder" (3.1674). These slurs have all the earmarks of a well-established enmity. The set phrases are memorized and close at hand, ready for use at the slightest provocation. Among modern parallels to this proverb-ridden antagonism are the serf–clergy rivalries of Mecklenburg. The priest is such a common fixture of abuse in the peasants' tales that narrators pepper their stories with proverbs: "priests take too much," "priests always meddle," the tellers say in beginning their *Schwänke* of duped clerics. In Chaucer's world a similar, venerable antipathy toward the cloth gave rise to similarly negative generalizations.[48] Suitably, the Friar's and the Summoner's tales concentrate on the central fixture of the medieval clerical stereotype: impious greed.

The Friar's Tale is a perfect example of a well-worn jest adapted to the special purpose of indirect insult. Robert D. French makes essentially the same statement about this story that I have made about all the churls' *Schwänke:* "The tale with which the Friar provokes the ire of the Summoner is merely an adroit application of a familiar story, which could be fastened upon nearly any unpopular functionary."[49] It is the simplest of stories: a devilishly cruel official falls, appropriately, into the company of the Devil. Satan states it is his purpose on earth to collect all that is sincerely offered him. The two pass a farmer cursing his livestock and a woman cursing her child; both say, "Devil take you!" But the Devil takes neither because the curse "did not come from the heart." Finally, they come upon a woman who vehemently curses the official. The Devil takes his companion off to hell: "that curse came from the heart."

Archer Taylor has studied the variants exhaustively.[50] His analysis centers on details of plot (e.g., how many and what kinds of animals and people are cursed before the villain is finally carried off) and concludes that the variation is so marked that the tale must have oral currency. Taylor is surely correct, but his search for an *Urform* clouds the central function of the tale: to choose a dupe appropriate to the social function of each tale. Taylor's list of villains is a long one: judge, lawyer, knight, bailiff, peasant have all played the role that Huberd assigns the Summoner. And, again, as the contexts are missing for most of these tales, only assumptions can guide us in determining their aptness.

Exemplum material provides the only certain *allusive context:* here, the tale is directed to an aural audience and is clearly cautionary, rather than directly insulting. The *rusticus,* or farmer, plays the dupe. Medieval clerics used *rusticus* in the same way as we use "yokel"; to designate a man who does not know enough to know what is good for him.[51] The moral posed in one fourteenth-century *exemplum* is that to cheat others is to risk damnation, a principle far removed from the Friar's Tale and most of its secular variants. The *rusticus's* punishment results not from extreme cruelty, but from a relatively minor sin. In the sermon analogues the poor woman who delivers the fatal curse shows anger, but far less motivation than the outraged Rebekke of the Friar's Tale: "O may the devil take you, body and soul, for your wishes to afflict my soul at the market, when you traded with me and did not pay me." This *exemplum* does not make the dupe an evil soul, but rather warns all to beware of any lapse of charity.

Default on payment is one thing; extortion committed for the sheer joy of it is another. Huberd's tale examines that second phenomenon. His fictional summoner has cruelly afflicted an old woman, charging her more money than she owns to expiate sins she never committed. When the old woman's curse falls upon the summoner, he is given a chance to repent. But even with the devil standing next to him, he cannot soften his stand, but simply redoubles his greed: "I would rather have all your clothes than repent of my charges" (3.1633), he tells the widow. No one hearing this tale could feel its dupe is unjustly sent to hell.

The fictional summoner is another creation of insult by association: a "slye boye" who caricatures the Summoner's outstanding traits as presented in the General Prologue. Both men are harlots (1.647, 3.1328), extortionists (1.649–51, 3.1350–68), taverners (1.635–37, 3.1349), pimplike companions to bawds (1.663–65, 3.1339). But Huberd, like Oswald, further abuses his antagonist by associating the fictional summoner with more crimes than his real-life counterpart can be charged with: the storial church lackey is a madman (3.1327) and a torturer of old women (3.1377–78), a monster so enamored of the evil nature of his work that he enjoys the losses of his victims more than his own gains.

The villain protagonist holds the center of every scene. The Friar brilliantly contrives to make the summoner's co-star, the Devil, seem noble by comparison. As Satan talks with old Rebekke, he even gives the summoner a second chance, reminding the extortionist of the deal the two have drawn (3.1626–27). The implication is clear: not merely through his evil acts, but principally through his perverse pleasure in them, the pilgrim Summoner is damned beyond all hope.

In his fictional rebuttal, the pilgrim Summoner also relies principally on insult by association: his dupe possesses Huberd's unsavory gentility. He is a lady's man, a sweet-talking thief as opposed to a more forthright one. The story is fashioned to express the philosophy that "dainty" theft is even more reprehensible than the fictional summoner's coarse cruelty. In the Summoner's tale, the oily friar carps sanctimoniously on a child's death and flirts with a woman as he tries to milk money from her ailing husband. The mock gentility of the real Friar is subjected to the worst sort of ridicule when his alter ego's efforts at extortion are rewarded by nothing more than a massive fart. The Summoner's Tale almost begs us to think back to the Friar's, and conclude that, whatever his faults, the fictional summoner is more honest than the fictional friar: by implication, the same relationship applies to the two pilgrims.

There are not sufficient analogues available in medieval or modern tradition to indicate the extent to which the Summoner altered his tale to fit the specific insult situation in which he was engaged. If Chaucer used *Li Dis de le vescie à prestre*—the closest medieval analogue—he failed to develop the character of the sick man who ultimately duped the friar:

> [The] excellences of *Li Dis* . . . might well lead one to think that Chaucer had never seen it: had he encountered the character of the Priest, had his attention

been called to the possibilities for irony in speech and situation, he surely would have developed them in the Summoner's Tale.[52]

"But," Walter M. Hart continues, "the Summoner must tell a tale at the expense of the Friar; the character of the friar must then be the important matter, not the plot, not the character of the sick man." If *Li Dis* was Chaucer's source, the poet altered it to suit the rhetorical needs of the churl's tale. The Summoner's subtlety—which is, in any case, hardly his strong point—may have suffered from such changes, as might the "absolute" value of the tale as art, but the narrative remains a masterpiece of the use to which Chaucer put it.

In the Reeve's and Friar's tales, the rudest characteristics of the tellers' antagonists are listed, exaggerated, added to. The Summoner would have difficulty fitting his tale to the same mold because, at least superficially, Huberd is too refined to suffer greatly from such a caricature. The Summoner, therefore, concentrates on the one trait—hypocritical gentility—which he finds most abhorrent in Huberd. The real strength of the Summoner's tale is that he constructs similar fates for his real-life enemy and his fictional dupe. In Chapter 7 I explained how the Summoner exposed the churl hidden in Huberd. In his tale, the Summoner consolidates this victory by turning the sweet talking Frere John into a "wilde boor" grinding his teeth in rage (3.2160–62). The man who had preached so eloquently against anger (3.1981–2120) is now himself the emblem of fury.

As the lowly Summoner conquers the "gentil" Friar, he ends his tale—as so many *Schwänke* end—with a pair of class reversals. First, the "lewed, burel" Thomas, despised by Friar John, levels his foe's pretensions with a fart. (It is interesting to note that Chaucer's most successful practitioners of class warfare, the Miller and Summoner, both use that ultimate expression of man's animal nature to dispel the feigned gentility of would-be nobles.) Then, when Friar John's patron, the lord of the village, is unable to say how the fart can be divided among the brothers in John's convent, a lowly squire comes forth with a solution. The Summoner's Tale gives Fortune's Wheel one half turn, reversing the social order that has made the teller an object of scorn.

ON THE BORDERS OF THE NARRATIVE WAR: THE TALES OF THE CLERK AND THE MERCHANT

The early sections of Chapter 7 explained how Chaucer plays upon a "discourse gap" apparent among the pilgrims. The Host's inept attempt to mimic the Knight's criticism of the Monk demonstrates this division, as well as the fact that the two warring philosophies of rhetoric are often brought into uncomfortable proximity on the pilgrims' road. Herry Bailly cannot succeed in a "higher" form of discourse, but—as will be shown in a look at the Merchant's Tale—*gentilmen* who stoop to tell churls' tales experience similar unsuccess. Chaucer shows us failure on both sides; churls cannot speak *gentilly*, nor *gentils* churlishly, to full effect. Such instances of poor speaking suggest not only the depth of social division among the pilgrims, but also the poet's philosophy of an equality of artistry marking the two forms of discourse: neither is easily mastered, for both have been developed in response to specific social needs.

To explain: as has been noted, the plots of the upper-class tales carry a clear authority. The moral romances of the Clerk and Man of Law and the saints' lives of the Physician and Prioress are all told by Chaucer in much the same way they had been told for centuries. Formalistically, the plots are inflexible, and the poet must rely on nuance, the smallest detail, if he is to make them diverge in any way from their tradition of sameness. But, more to the point, the *gentil* tales are *socially* inflexible: along with their authority, they carry a clear authoritarianism. All depict a static and hierarchical society, in which the power structure will not waver. Theseus in the Knight's Tale, Alla in the Man of Law's—both represent positions of uncompromising power. Even if we read into these tales (as so many have into the Knight's) evidence of a higher order which transcends temporal power, the divine is *interpreted* by those who possess the highest earthly status: in the Knight's Tale, it is Theseus, not Palomon or Arcite or Emily, who delivers the lesson of his lessers' misfortunes.

Furthermore, the *gentil* tales teach not only the permanence of the social order, but subservience to it. Custance and Virginia are not supposed to question their fates. If they are virtuous, they will accept the injustices done them. Only under such conditions can they expect redemption in this world or the next. The behavior of these heroines parallels the behavior of the *gentils* who tell their stories: like Custance and Dorigen, the Man of Law and Franklin are humbly obedient. When the Host asks them for their tales, they respond submissively: "Biheste is dette" (2.41), says the Man of Law; "I wole obeye / Unto your wyl" (5.703–4), echoes the Franklin.

Yet, on both the narrative and interactive levels of discourse, the *gentils'* submissiveness is merely a mask. As Chapter 4 explained, the *gentils*, through their obedience on holiday, are simply underscoring the fact that they are in control. If they bow to the churls on festive occasions, the churls must bow to them on all others. Similarly, if listeners accept the world view presented in the *gentils'* tales, the order of things remains static, and the *gentils* remain ahead, retaining their privileges. It is no great sacrifice for the *gentils* to defer to a system that places them on top. The Man of Law does not identify himself with his heroine Custance, nor does the Physician see himself reflected in Virginia: rather, both identify themselves with the social order that decrees those females' fates.[53] The explicit morals the *gentils* attach to their tales attest to this fact: from the tale of Custance's suffering, the Man of Law can deduce no more appropriate lesson than that it is better to die than to live poor (2.114). To the Physician, Virginia's story means only "Forsaketh synne, er synne yow forsake" (6.286), a moral which consoles only the powerful: Virginia, the weak one, is sinless, but is murdered nonetheless. So the *gentil* and churl narratives represent antithetical impulses: the former, rigid in form, is equally rigid in its depiction of society; the latter, adaptive and contentious by nature, performs within its fictive frame the same social inversions enacted during festivals. These are two self-contained realms of discourse, difficult to bridge, as an examination of two pilgrims' attempts to bridge them affirms.

Of all the non-*gentil* pilgrims, only the Clerk tells a *gentil* narrative, a tale which, like the Physician's and the Man of Law's, features a passive heroine and a rigid social order. Like the *gentils'* tales, the Clerk's has specific antecedents which Chaucer has altered only slightly (though these minimal changes are, as will be shown, of great importance). The fact that the Clerk can tell such a tale at all is directly attributable to his marginal position in the social order. Chaucer's Clerk has studied the *gentil* arts long and hard, as the General Prologue states (1.303), Herry Bailly echoes (4.1–20), and the Clerk's own demonstration of his knowledge of Petrarch confirms (4.31–38). He is thus conversant in the language of the *gentils*.

But the Clerk's status as a student denies him *gentil* privileges. He remains one of the lessers in his academic environment, where he has the opportunity to hear and practice churlish diction. Just as the churls of the Church hierarchy rose to power on the Feast of Fools, university students had their feast, during which it was their custom to "hurtle enthymemes": the boys apparently used folk speech ("the old wit of the cross-roads") to "lacerate their comrades outspokenly, though mentioning no names"—and to ridicule their elders.[54] In short, late medieval schoolboys observed many of the folk rhetorical techniques earlier discussed: name avoidance, generalization, ridicule by association, and the couching of insults in artistic forms.

The Clerk, then, knows two rhetorical dialects, and he will use them both in his tale. He accepts some tenets from the *gentils'* philosophers, but in the end he rejects their philosophy and adopts the ethos of the churls. Though the Clerk plays the *gentils'* game—beginning his tale with the characteristically *gentil* obsequy, "I am under youre yerde" (4.22)—he and his fictional heroine, Griselde, play hard, with an almost inconceivable fierceness of patience.

Set against the religious and secular stories of the *gentils,* the Clerk's Tale presents an anomaly. It might be expected that the Clerk, like the other religious professionals, would present a narrative world in which the corruption of secular power is outweighed and eventually overwhelmed by a conception of heavenly justice. St. Cecilia's sweatless survival of the boiling water torture contrived for her (in the Second Nun's Tale), the miraculous song that pours from the slit throat of the little clergeoun (in the Prioress's): these offer the listener proof that the meek will eventually gain their reward. But there is no supernatural compensation for the tortures suffered by Griselde, no supernatural punishment for her torturer. In the Clerk's Tale, power remains in the hands of one mortal, almost mythically under-motivated villain, the Marquis Walter, beyond whose earthly rule the Clerk does not invite us to look. All the tale's religious imagery is invested in the description of powerless Griselde, several times compared to Christ—and, though it is implicit that Griselde's faith helps her endure her adversity, true Christianity is associated only with the oppressed, and offers them no deliverance.

Furthermore, the Clerk's Tale contains no benign secular powers. Walter, the agent of an inhuman evil, remains unpunished at the story's end. In the *gentils'* tales there are both evil mortal leaders and virtuous ones. The Physician presents the diabolical Apius and the good Virginius; the Man of Law serves up the same opposition, with the sinister Sultaness and Donegild set against the virtuous Hermengild and Alla. As is common in such stories, the moral characters are close relatives of the heroines: Alla is husband to one leading lady, Virginius father to another. These men represent the best of leadership on both familial and governmental levels, and eventually bring nation and family into accord, to demonstrate the idea that a good leader is like a good parent or husband, and both should be obeyed implicitly by the lower orders, be they women, children, or peasants.

But here too the Clerk has tampered with the moral framework of the *gentil* tale, presenting in Walter a monstrous figure who is neither a good husband nor a good leader. When he decrees that Griselde shall be sent all but naked back to her father's house, the Marquis abuses simultaneously his wife and his lower-class subjects. The clerk, then, questions the morality of the *gentils:* rulers, like parents and husbands, *should* be benevolent monarchs, but is it not possible that they be evil? Nearly all of Chaucer's subtle additions to Petrarch's narrative exploit the failure of the *gentil's* tale to provide solutions to the problem of social injustice. Most of these contributions either intensify the descriptions of Walter's cruelty (4.459—62, 620—23) or heighten the audience's sympathy for Griselde (4.215—17, 260—94). At times the Clerk intrudes directly to voice abhorrence of Walter:

> But as for me, I seye that yvele it sit
> To assaye a wyf whan that it is no nede,
> And putten hire in angwyssh and in drede. (4.460–62)

In another Chaucerian interpolation, the Clerk upbraids his own profession for failing to find virtue in such women as Griselde:

> Though clerkes preise wommen but a lite,
> Ther kan no man in humblesse hym acquite
> As womman kan. . . . (4.935–37)

These few additions undercut any positive value that may be ascribed to the behavior of the powerful. The oppressed Griselde remains a heroine, but the world in which she suffers holds no hint of virtue.

In closing his tale, the Clerk expresses the churls' philosophy more openly. He relativizes his moral: in an unjust world, no one could or should resemble Griselde. Patience is a virtue, but to submit unquestioningly to unjust power is not. Griselde's sufferings can instruct the oppressed, but offer no solution. The Clerk's Tale is a romance penetrated (first in Chaucer's interpolations, then more explicitly in the humorous coda) by the philosophy of the *Schwank*. It questions the very authority it seems at first to advertise—and, like the *Schwank*, the story of Griselde ends with an inversion of the principles of the power structure. The hybrid tale succeeds because the teller has mastered both the *gentil* and the churl narrative codes. Through his characterizations of Walter and Griselde—the former falling far short of the hero's role, the latter exceeding our expectations of the victim—the Clerk has turned the morality of the romance against itself.

Just as we might label the Clerk's romance a *Schwank* in disguise, we may consider the Merchant's Tale, clearly a *Schwank* in origin, a failed romance. The Clerk uses a "higher" artistic form to question higher temporal authority. The Merchant, correspondingly, uses the low humor of the *Schwank* in an effort to show the base nature of the wife he detests. Just as Herry Bailly fails in the discourse of gentility, the Merchant—denied by his superior status the chance to use the genre for the social purposes which gave rise to it—proves embarrassingly inept as a teller of *Schwänke*.

The Merchant's prologue makes clear the purpose of his tale. He has, he says, a cruel wife. This overbearing woman continually abuses him—although how, exactly, he never clarifies. Because he can no longer bear to recount his own sorrows (4.1243–44), the Merchant undertakes to translate his wife's evils into fiction. His *Schwank*, then, as the teller hints (4.1222–25), is meant to illustrate the antitype of Griselde, to expose a woman lacking all *gentil* virtue.

But this strategy is flawed. It is true that no true romance heroine could match the character of his wife, but had the Merchant set the lady May within a romance setting, he could have played upon the incongruity of the situation—just as the Clerk had exaggerated Walter's failings by miscasting him as romance hero. Instead the Merchant saddles himself to the *Schwank*, thus creating a narrative configuration that will ultimately ruin his ploy. As

I have discussed, the central object of criticism in the *Schwank* is the tale's dupe. The Merchant sees himself as an innocent victim and therefore casts the dupe, January, in his own image. But, flexible as the *Schwank* is, the genre will not suffer the possibility of an *innocent* victim. The Miller has done the near-impossible in creating a rather likable dupe, John the Carpenter, but even John must lie in his own, empty bed, for he has married a young woman in spite of the fact that he is an aging, jealous man. At the end of the Miller's Tale, even John's redeeming qualities cannot save him from ridicule—both within and without his tale, the carpenter's fall is the occasion for wild laughter, as witnesses turn all his pain into a joke (1.3842). So the Merchant will fail: he lacks the Miller's skills in folk rhetoric, and once he has cast himself as dupe, there is nothing he can do to soften the process of fictional self-abuse.

As his tale unfolds, the Merchant shows certain skill in negative portraiture. In May he creates an opportunist whose hands are on January's estate already on her wedding day, whose fidelity does not survive her first four days of marriage, whose sense of romance is best illustrated in the fact that she reads and secretes Damian's love letter in the privy. She is a character who, if misplaced in romance, would win no love from the reader—and thus accomplish the Merchant's purpose of creating an ugly likeness of his wife.

But the dynamics of the *Schwank* are such that if the victor is ugly, the victim must be uglier. The *Schwank* does not dwell on moral judgments, but simply declares winners and points mockingly at losers. May's dupe ultimately appears less savory than May herself. The Merchant's alter ego, January, is the worst of fools. I agree with the general critical contention that much of this negative portrayal is intentional on the teller's part. Though the Merchant identifies himself with January's plight, he tries to distance himself from the old fool. By the Merchant's reasoning, if *he* can point out January's flaws, he can prove himself superior to his fictional other. But in recognizing only half of January's shortcomings, the narrator reveals his own. "Love is blynd," moans the Merchant (4.1598), and, though few would be so deluded as to mistake January's lechery for love, the Merchant is one of those few. He seeks, through analogy to January, an excuse for his own failed marriage. The Merchant, after all, can see January's *folye*, and January cannot.

But from what moral perch does the Merchant look down upon January? It is through the person of Justinus—January's brother, "soothly called" (4.1477) the "Just One"—that the Merchant claims his higher reason. And what is Justinus's world view? First, that marriage is a serious business and one should scrutinize the woman he intends to marry. Second, that even the most careful man may eventually find his seeming virtuous wife to be a shrew. (Justinus himself has a wife praised widely by his neighbors, but *he* knows the woman is a bane.) Finally, that, as all women are evil, the best Justinus can wish for January is that the new-found wife will put him through purgatory on earth, so that upon death he may ascend directly to heaven.

Here, the Merchant's narrative blindness is further complicated by the fact that there is no room in the *Schwank* for superior moral judgments. Though Justinus's speeches convey a sense of cynicism appropriate to the *Schwank,* they carry a sense of righteousness foreign to the genre and lack the lightheartedness which tempers the *Schwank*'s low assessment of humanity. Though the Merchant claims that Justinus occasionally uses joking words (4.1656), their effect, like the whole of the tale, is far too cynical to inspire healthy laughter. The use of Justinus as the poem's moral backbone finally fails. Given the logic of Justinus's message ("women are no damned good"), May's sorry behavior is inevitable, almost excusable, but January's—and, by extension, the Merchant's own—is not. If men are so superior to women, an enlightened man should know better than to marry—or, even if blinded by love, a newly enlightened man should be able to place himself above the pains occasioned by his wife. But neither January nor his creator can take that step. May remains in control, and the old lovers' obsession with her pettiness renders them pettier. When in the final scene May masters her husband through deceit, January emerges as the absolute master of self-deceit, a trait which has allowed, even sanctioned, May's sin.

In his tale the Merchant is able to alter neither the *Schwank*'s basic nature nor his own. May's flaws serve only to magnify his. The Merchant may understand that the *Schwank* audience does not necessarily identify with the winner, but he fails to understand how inevitably the audience's scorn turns upon the loser. To the two types of symbolic blindness embedded in the tale—January's blindness to May, and the Merchant's blindness to the flaws in Justinus's reasoning—the churls in the audience would add a third: the narrator's failure to sense the essence of the *Schwank.*

THE MANCIPLE'S TALE

Properly speaking, this is the last of the *Canterbury Tales;* the Parson's non-narrative sermon is the only performance to follow. The tale of the crow is not in its strictest sense a *Schwank.* More fable than *fabliau,* it works by rules different from those outlined above, a system that allows the audience to sympathize with the victim and to perceive the victor as villain. But the Manciple's Tale is also Chaucer's final foray into folk rhetoric, and constitutes a sort of handbook and explanation of the art.

To put the tale in context: the Manciple has just insulted the Cook, plainly and dangerously—"Fy, stynkyng swyn!" (9.40). Perhaps for the first time on the journey, a man has crossed the barrier of punishable insult. Roger has gone into a rage, but drunkenness has prevented him from avenging the slur. Herry Bailly speaks for the Cook, however: "But yet, Manciple, in feith thou art to nyce / Thus openly repreve hym of his vice" (9.69–70). Note that it is not the Manciple's negative opinion of the Cook which the Host considers foolish, but rather the fact that the insult is delivered "openly." The Manciple perceives the Host's meaning, and attempts to extricate himself from the problem: "I would rather buy the Cook's horse than have him fight me. I was only joking, really" (9.76–80). He offers the Cook a peace offering of wine, then proceeds to tell his tale.

The themes of the Manciple's Tale are the very themes I have discussed in the past three chapters: the boundaries of safe speech and the necessity of concealing negative thoughts within a framework of lies. The Manciple identifies himself with the crow: the bird, once white and sweet of song, that informs Phoebus Apollo that the god's wife is an adulteress. Under a reasonable system of justice, the bird would be rewarded. But Phoebus, enraged, kills his wife, then falls into anguished guilt and projects it on the crow: "My wife is guiltless. You are a traitor and a false thief." With the same language the Reeve and the Summoner have used in their verbal duels, Phoebus says, "I wol thee *quite* anon thy false tale" (9.293), then pulls the crow's feathers, turns them all black, ruins the bird's beautiful song, and sends him screaming to hell.

Phoebus is the real villain of the tale. The god represents the upper classes, the Host, the Cook, and all others who would rather hear nothing than hear the truth. The Manciple reasons covertly: if a man is a fool for calling a swine a swine, he had best obey the hypocrites who feel they are better served with lies or silence. Midway through his tale, the teller makes an ironic aside which is not included in any of Chaucer's assumed sources. After calling the lover of Phoebus' wife a "lemman," the narrator adds a deflected apology:

> Her lemman? Certes, this is a knavyssh speche!
> Foryeveth it me, and that I yow biseche.
> The wise Plato seith, as ye may rede,
> The word moot nede accorde with the dede. (9.205–8)

The Manciple goes on to say that he is a rude man: he cannot see the difference between a *gentil* mistress, properly called a *lady*, and a poor woman—who, in the same role, would be known as *wenche* or *lemman:* "And, God it woot, myn owene deere brother, / Men leyn that oon as lowe as lith that oother" (9.221–22). His intent, of course, is to say that proper speech—the language of decorum and indirection described in Chapter

7—is a lie; perhaps a necessary lie cultivated for survival's sake, but a lie nonetheless. It may be best to be quiet. The close of the tale underscores this lesson:

> . . . be war, and be noon auctour newe
> Of tidynges, wheither they been false or trewe.
> Whereso thou come, amonges hye or lowe,
> Kepe wel thy tonge, and thenk upon the crowe. (9.359–62)

Thus ends the tale which Chaucer intends us to perceive as his last exercise in fiction. One of his finest demonstrations of the hidden language of insult, it is also a retraction of sorts. Chaucer, who daily spoke the language of diplomacy before his betters in civil and royal service, must have shared the Manciple's disgust at the deceitful rules which helped him hold his jobs, the same rules that survive in his poetry. In the Manciple's Tale, the poet reaffirms the necessity for those rules, but he also abjures them with more than a hint of weariness. There is always the option of silence. It is time, says Chaucer, for the taletelling to end.

PART THREE

Gentil Folk

NINE

Back to Court

Throughout this study I have focused on Chaucer the ethnographic artist, the poet who drew upon folklore for description and artistic effect. He was an acute observer of the general shapes and detailed interactions which characterized oral performance in his time. Furthermore, he extended the territory of literature by converting to writing some of the most imaginative aspects of verbal art. But can Chaucer be considered a *folk poet* as well as an observer and translator of folk culture? Did he not only witness and imitate, but also participate in, the folk artistry of medieval London? I address the question in three steps. First, I consider an *aural* Chaucer, who performed his work aloud before a certain community of listeners. Second, I attempt to define that community and determine the extent of its influence on the poet. Finally, I examine Chaucer's words to Richard's court for evidence of folkloric style: signs of the shaping influence of an aural audience, and signs that the poet responds to this influence by adopting folk rhetorical techniques addressing his *gentil* listeners.

Did Chaucer write his works for reading aloud? Ruth Crosby answers in the affirmative, citing many of his poetic passages which refer to a listening audience.[1] Drawing upon many of the same examples, Dieter Mehl argues the opposite, that the poet employed references to live audiences merely for the purpose of holding the attention of silent readers.[2] The evidence cited by both is almost exclusively internal, and consists of such directions as "whoso list it nat *yheere*" (1.3176) or "*Turne over the leef* and chese another tale" (1.3177). The fact that these two phrases are juxtaposed in the *Canterbury Tales* gives some idea of the problems such evidence presents. The arguments are rendered doubly futile by recent research on verbs of address in Middle English; Chaucer's contemporaries used the verbs "say" and "write" interchangeably in literary discourse.[3]

It should prove more fruitful to examine some of the criticisms and evidence which go beyond the question of authorial address. One often repeated argument against Chaucer's "aurality" is the supposition that the *Canterbury Tales* is so complex and rich in its internal allusions that no listener could derive the fullness of the poet's intent. Complexity, of course, is a relative concept. On the surface, the thought content of the *Tales* is not as difficult as the doctrinal treatises of Ockham and Aquinas, nor even as such poetic entertainments as Jean de Meun's continuation of the *Roman de la Rose*. Chaucer's poem is most complex on the levels of personal and textual interrelationships: the conflicts among the pilgrims, the relationships between the pilgrims and their tales, the ironical relationships between what the poet—or one of his characters—says and what he means.

The charge that Chaucer's poetry is too complex for aural presentation implies a deficiency in either the understanding or the memory of the listener. Concerning understanding: the interrelationships of the pilgrims—which are based on traditional systems of stereotyping and oral disputation—would be most easily understood when rendered in their native medium. To accept the arguments of the previous three chapters is to accept their logical corollary: that the art of the *Canterbury Tales* rests largely in its brilliant application to writing of a rhetorical system which was principally oral in the first place. Chaucer's contemporaries would be able to follow the poem more easily if it were read aloud than if it were read silently. The *Tales* is as much an assault on literary convention as it is a literary masterpiece. This basic dialogic aspect of the poem has been largely ignored by most interpreters: modern critics, trained in techniques of silent reading, do not *hear* the nuances that were developed in an oral environment, in response to conversational needs. In comparison to the *Canterbury Tales*, even such revolutionary poems as the *Roman de la Rose* come relatively easily off the page. Aspects of dialogue, character relationships, and dramatic irony are so much more set and less subtle in the French poem that oral inflection would make little difference in the interpretation or understanding of it.

But what of a listener's capacity to remember the many details that give Chaucer his artistic depth and ironic effect? Consider first that Chaucer is all-inclusive in his system of reference, describing his characters redundantly, and in both elite and folk terms. If the word *colerik* is not sufficient to convey the nature of the Reeve, the persistent references (both direct and in the form of dialect) to his Norfolk background would be more than enough. Chaucer's intratextual references work by the same principle of multiplicity. How could the average listener, hearing the Reeve's description of the sword-wielding Symkyn, recollect that Robyn the Miller—introduced in the General Prologue, which may have been read days or weeks before—also carried a long blade? Again, the *Tales'* rich, often redundant network of allusion functions well: in describing Symkyn, the Reeve describes not only Robyn's sword, but also the man's occupation, size, voice, clothing, greed, pretensions, and talents as an athlete and musician. One reading presents a dozen referents; and, as surely as repeated silent readings, repeated listenings would bring more and more of the picture into focus.

Furthermore, anthropological data leaves no doubt that the memory of a man brought up in a primarily oral culture is far better than the oral memory of twentieth-century Chaucerians.[4] Fourteenth-century England was a predominantly oral culture, particularly insofar as poetry in English was concerned. Even among the highest classes, the art of memory was carefully cultivated. Vinsauf speaks of the various mnemonic systems developed by orators, and of the necessity for refined men to retain such skills. The same applied for listeners. Primary education was based on aural presentation and memorization. Courtesy books were read aloud, repeated, memorized. Teachers were advised to inculcate good memory. The manuals are replete with commands that students store in mind words, thoughts, systems of behavior: "if there be any words that yee kenne nouhte, spyrre whils yee yt ken; What yee yt knowe, yee mowe holde yt in horde."[5]

Good listening was cultivated in poetic performance as well as in moral instruction. A timeworn image depicts Chaucer's audience as rowdy and inattentive—constantly chattering, fighting over food, laughing and not listening, like a group of school children exulting in the presence of a substitute teacher. But, again, evidence does not support such a view. In 1388, when Froissart read his ponderous romance *Meliador* before the court of Foix, the hall was silent: "While I was reading no one presumed to speak a word for [Count Gaston] insisted that I should be heard distinctly."[6] There is more than a hint of forced silence here, but none in the following. Le Mareschal de Boucicaut, a supremely literate noble and contemporary of Chaucer, spent whole days listening: "he filled the time in hearing read such fine books as saints' lives, or stories of ancient heroes."[7] These examples not only affirm the importance of listening; they show that oral performances were enjoyed by Chaucer's acquaintances.

More immediate evidence has been presented by Mary Hallmundsson, who finds that Chaucer was a member of two literary circles: one at court, where he had a noble audience, the other at Chancery, where middle-class public servants entertained each other.[8] Chaucer's friend Hoccleve "was a member of a literary dining club called the 'Court of Good Company,' which met at the Temple on the first Thursday of every month, and it was probably for these occasions that he wrote *La Male Regle* and *The Letter of Cupid*." The "Ballade of the Court of Good Company," addressed to Henry Somer—another associate of Chaucer—was almost certainly read at the "Court." There also survives "A Moral Ballad of Henry Scogan, Squyer" (yet another of Chaucer's friends), composed "for my lord the Prince, my lord of Clarence, my lord of Bedford, and my lord of Gloucestre, the King's sonnes," for presentation at a dinner hosted by "[worthy] merchants in the

Vyntre in London, at the hous of Lowys Johan." Such documents, all involving Chaucer's associates, establish Chaucer's place in an aural milieu—
and, further, give some indication of his audience: nobility, bourgeois, civil
servants—all occasionally in the same crowd.

There are many other arguments for Chaucer's status as an aural poet.
Bertrand Bronson mentions that the *Canterbury Tales,* like all Chaucer's
longer works, is divided into segments that could be read aloud comfortably
in an hour to an hour and one quarter.[9] Several critics speak of the rarity of
books in merchant and even royal households; if upper-class Londoners
craved narrative entertainment, it would have to be supplied largely by
word of mouth.[10] Finally, though many doubt that the *Tales* was intended
for an aural audience, fewer dispute D. S. Brewer's claim that such earlier
works as *The Parliament of Fowls* were written for recitation at court festivals.[11] Given this assumption, it would be natural to consider the possibility that Chaucer's early experience as an aural poet may have influenced his style throughout his life.

Yet it cannot be established that Chaucer read aloud from the *Canterbury
Tales.* And one wonders about the importance of aurality as a measure of
medieval folklore. Even Vinsauf, that most sophisticated practitioner of
official artistic doctrine, gives young poets instructions on oral performance, describing the tone of voice, projections, and the gestures and poses
an orator should adopt.[12] Chaucer could easily be an aural poet without
being a folk poet. So I ask two questions more pertinent to folkloric inquiry:
does the poem, like all folk art, reflect a community background; and does
the poet, as distinguished from his churlish characters, employ folk diction?

The poet's artistic and public circles were the same: the people he worked
for were identical to those he entertained. Gervase Mathew has estimated
that this elite company of nobles and bourgeois numbered no more than
two hundred fifty men and women.[13] Chaucer, of course, knew every one.
His relationship to them was traditionally set, and though it was an elite one
in its professional sense, it reflected folk processes in its entertainment
aspect. There is no evidence that Chaucer was a paid performer: even if he
were occasionally rewarded with a stipend or a prize, King Richard had not
institutionalized poetry. The English court lacked the official system of
sinecures and offices for bourgeois poets that prevailed in fourteenth-century France.[14] Settings for artistic expression were most often informal—
and it is in precisely such settings that folklore thrives. As Froissart notes of
his youth in an earlier English court, conversation on love and the practice
of sung and spoken art were omnipresent at table, in hallway, and in chamber.[15]

The poems exchanged in such circles were certainly not all folkloric in
content; often, artists presented the literary forms developed and refined

through two centuries of French tradition—*ballade, virelai,* delicate romance. Nevertheless, the size of the group and the close relationship among its members, added to the fact that so many of its entertainments were demonstrably aural in nature, should make critics re-evaluate certain ideas about the "manuscript histories" of many of the poems of the time. Hallmundsson has taken a first step toward doing so. Commenting on the fact that Hoccleve's *Male Regle* and Henry Scogan's *Moral Ballade* are strikingly similar, she dismisses the standard critical opinion that their resemblance derives solely from the fact that they contain common "conventional subject matter."[16] Hallmundsson has shown that these men were members of the same literary club. It is likely that similarities in their poems owe much to conversations, to ideas borrowed and shared and—I add—to their *listening* to one another's poems.

Though the artistic forms and styles of Chaucer's community were part of an elite international literary culture, the interpersonal relationships of these French and English poets were effectively those of a folk community. Unlike the elite author of today, the medieval poet could not choose his audience, could not address only that cross section of the public that shared his convictions and interests. The process by which poetic works were shaped centered on a relatively small and stable audience, which imposed its expectations on the performers. The poet of Chaucer's court community has many traits in common with the traditional taleteller.[17] Both can be creative only within a framework of values determined by listeners. Artistry is a matter of working within the shell of *their* constraints, performing when and where they expect performance, and treating a topic appropriate to the setting.

Chaucer's poetry often implies the influence of such an aural audience. "The Complainte of Mars" and *The Parliament of Fowls* were occasional poems probably presented to the court on St. Valentine's Day. A third poem, the *Legend of Good Women,* was apparently composed on command. Chaucer tells us—perhaps playfully, but perhaps not—that the *Legend* was written as a penance for an earlier work that cast doubt on the virtue of ladies. As surviving charters of medieval poetic societies mention punishments for those who impugn ladies, we have some reason to take Chaucer at his word—and, further, to assume that community pressures indeed influenced his productions.

In a folk community, as in Chaucer's, "ownership" of many tales is shared. Alterations made by one good narrator may affect the ways in which others tell the same tale. Traditional plots are reshaped in a continuous process of dialogue between teller and audience, teller and teller. If these facts are considered, the manuscript histories of the poems of Chaucer's community must be read in terms of the oral and intragroup relation-

ships. Two examples: Chaucer was not the only man to compose St. Valentine's Day poems. Othon de Graunson, the French knight, wrote several,
including *Le Songe St. Valentin,* similar in its general outline to the *Parliament,* but lacking close linguistic parallels to Chaucer's poem and containing
differences in several major details. Critics have long speculated about
which man *read and imitated* the work of the other, but the question is more
easily answered in terms of community. Graunson, a frequent visitor to
England and protégé of John of Gaunt, was a member of Chaucer's community. There is no verbal link between the poems, and no resemblance so
striking that it could not have issued from Graunson's once hearing Chaucer's poem, or vice versa.[18]

The correspondence between Chaucer's Man of Law's Tale and Gower's
tale of Custance is closer than in the previous case, but so was the relationship between Chaucer and Gower. Critics have debated which man saw the
manuscript of the other. But the perceived connection between the two
texts has been distorted by our habit of silent reading. Edward A. Block has
shown that the *verbatim* resemblances between the two tales amount to only
forty words (nine passages altogether).[19] A well cultivated memory, such as
Chaucer and Gower both possessed, could easily retain such information
after one hearing; and, as Chaucer and Gower moved continually in the
same circles, the "original" author may have performed the first poem for
the other man many times before the second tale of Custance was composed.

An observation on the extra-literary life of this elite group, a point to
which I will return: this was a troubled community, divided against itself,
and Chaucer's place in it was precarious. Though his reputation as a poet
was firm well before his death, his public life was one of constant peril. As a
commoner, Chaucer had to rely on the good graces of the king and nobles
to retain patronage positions. He held many: Controller at the London
Customs House, Clerk of the Works, Justice of the Peace, Deputy Forester.
These jobs were not easily procured or held. "Desire noon office," states a
contemporary courtesy book:

> For than . . .
> Thou muste thi neigboris displese & dere
> Or ellis tho myste thi self forswere
> And do not as thin office wolde,
> And gete these mawgre heere & theere
> More than thank, an hundrid folde.[20]

At no time and place was this injunction more true than in London in the
1380s. A mortal struggle was in progress between London's royalist and
antiroyalist factions as Chaucer was serving at the Customs House, and

Customs was the center of it. Evidence suggests that Chaucer quit his lucrative post in December of 1386 to avoid danger or death. It would not have helped the poet to have been a favorite of Richard II: the King himself was a virtual prisoner in the Tower of London when the trouble came to a head in 1387. Nicolas Brembre, another favorite of Richard's who paid Chaucer's salary at Customs, was executed by the antiroyalist faction little over a year after Chaucer quit his post and left London. The spring after the execution, three warrants were issued for Chaucer's arrest, but he did not answer them. The charge as published was personal debt, but there were rumors running through London that summer that John Chirchman, the man who filed suit, was engaged in a life-and-death struggle with the king.[21] Even three years after Brembre's execution, the bitter fights continued. A municipal proclamation ordered that no one so much as voice an opinion concerning the dead man; the penalty was a year's imprisonment.[22] Within eight years of that proclamation, the king himself had been deposed, then, in questionable circumstances, he died.

During the period in which the *Canterbury Tales* was composed, the balance of governmental power shifted three times with such violence that neither the King's protégés nor his opponents were safe more than half the time. A man of Chaucer's position had to do some elaborate sidestepping to stay alive. His status as artist would not have been enough to save him. Thomas Usk, a fellow poet, was executed along with Brembre in the fury that Chaucer escaped. Usk's fatal flaw was conspicuous partisanship. He worked for, then against, Brembre's greatest enemy—John Northampton—and he made his opinions known. Had Usk followed the Manciple's advice—to tell no tales, true or false—he might have kept his head. Chaucer, however, survived all the violence.

In sum, Chaucer's literary and occupational communities were nearly identical. His literary community was not a folk community in the strictest sense, but its channels of communication were so similar to those of a folk group that medievalists would gain from applying the concept of community to studies of textual relationships. Chaucer's course in his community was upwardly mobile, but perilous—he was, so to speak, a churl to the royalty and nobility he served, a fact to which I will return, as it has some bearing on his art.

Chaucer was certainly not trained as a folk poet, but in a sense he became one. His earliest poems show his indebtedness to established literary tradition, and all his works received the most orthodox praise, but Chaucer's last poem came from many traditions. Prior to Chaucer's time nobles recognized only two types of poet born beneath their station: the amusing minstrel, "janglere and goliardeys"; and the classically and clerically educated

teacher. But in the fourteenth century, the status of the minstrel was changing, as members of the middle class came more and more to fill that role.
Chaucer was one of these rising *bourgeois*. His business, presumably, was to
amuse.

Yet an examination of the first ninety years of Chaucer "criticism" (1385–
1475) reveals that the poet is regarded not as an entertainer, but as a
teacher.[23] His name is attached to 120 epithets, and all but a handful reveal
an elite cultural view. He is evoked most often (23 times) as *master*—by
Lydgate, Hoccleve, James IV of Scotland, and others. He is also known as a
rhetor (14), *eloquent* (8) and *noble*(6); an *excellent* (3), *gentil* (3) *translator* (3) of
great *sentence* (3); a *notable philosopher* (2) possessing *science* (2) and *wisdom*
(2); a veritable *Geoffrey of Vinsauf* (2), a second *Petrarch, Cicero, Socrates,
Januens the Grammarian* (1 mention each). Only four epithets suggest that
Chaucer may be delightful as well as instructive. One of these (*glade*) comes,
significantly, from Gower, who knew him personally. Lydgate calls him *gay*.
Two others say he is *fresh*.

By all accounts, this is an impressive critical portrait, but of whom?
Gower? The Chaucer of the Monk's Tale and the Retraction perhaps, but
what of the folk rhetorician of the Canterbury pilgrimage? This composite
critical sketch reveals more than a little uneasiness concerning Chaucer's
place in the literary scheme of things. The eulogizers fail to note those
aspects of his poetry which are now generally recognized as his greatest
achievements.

Just as Chaucer the poet could not be suitably typed according to prevailing literary standards, the *Canterbury Tales* violated all pre-existing generic
standards. The earlier frame tales known in England were all *exemplum*
collections. All had expressly moral intent and content. The *Tales* has no
such express purpose—at the end, the author himself asks forgiveness for
having written the better part of it. Chaucer was treading on slippery
ground. He was never officially recognized for his most pronounced
qualities as a poet, and he chose to express himself in a literary form which
had no built-in protection. If the *Tales* had been a dream vision, the poet
could safely have said many things: the dream being regarded as a form of
divine truth, the dream poem gave the author an accepted excuse for
communicating controversial material.[24] Similarly, the estates satires and
other clerical tracts were safe, for they operated principally by generalization: the moralist damned everyone as a class, thereby communicating otherwise punishable opinions.

Both the dream vision and the estates satires sanctioned language that
was taboo in conversation. In the *Roman de la Rose,* the subtlest of the
French dream poems, the refined fictional characters address their fellows
with more open abuse than Chaucer's churlish pilgrims use.[25] The same is

true of the romances on Chaucer's writing table—*Gamelyn* and the poems of the Auchinleck manuscript abound with expletives that never appear in the links of the *Tales*.[26] Romance writers had a well established prerogative to use vicious speech: indeed, one of the major functions of romance is to allow authors and audiences to do, say, and feel vicariously what is not possible for them to experience in real life. Chaucer was aware that the established genres allowed overt expression. His Man of Law's Tale (a good if unremarkable romance) fully exploits its generic license to convey direct insult: the narrator labels one villainess the "roote of iniquitee," "Virago," "Semyrame the secounde," "serpent under femynynytee," "scorpioun," "wikked goost" (2.358–60, 404).

The generic nature of the *Canterbury Tales*, however, did not allow many such freedoms. Not only did Chaucer's frame tale, with its clear lack of moralistic tone, violate accepted literary dicta; many of the tales told within the frame were also off-bounds. All but one of the obscene *Schwänke* in Middle English appear in the *Tales*. The one exception, *Dame Sirith*, is clearly not an upper-class creation. In the churls' tales, Chaucer presented his noble and bourgeois audience with fictions they had never before conceived of as literature.

The English court expected people of refinement to speak in refined tones. Chaucer's pilgrims follow this rule faithfully. The Merchant, for example, plays upon the term "strong hore"—a frequently punished oral epithet—but he paraphrases it in a refined way, "stronge lady stoore" (4.2367)—a ploy which allows him to make his point safely.[27] Delicacy was required of Chaucer as well as of his fictional *gentils*, but in the *Canterbury Tales* the audience witnesses decorum no more that half the time. Chaucer, of course, invented churlish characters who bore the brunt of his foul language. Yet would the creation of lowborn fictional foulmouths be an adequate defense for their creator?

Probably not. Just as the setting, cast, and use of language in the tales were very realistic, so were the portraits. At least some of them were modeled after real people. Manly and his followers have made an airtight case for Herry Bailly, as well as plausible identifications of the Man of Law and the Cook. Some of the pilgrims were almost undoubtedly social types, but others were thinly disguised portrayals of actual people.

Even if Chaucer had not wished to be a realist, the creation of such a daring and dramatically new literary form would have required him to become one. To allow himself the liberties necessary to explode literary tradition, he fell back on accepted nonliterary traditions—folk rhetoric and the oral *Schwank*—which he knew would help him avoid censure in the volatile milieu in which he worked. Thus, Chaucer became at once the most brilliantly innovative and the most folkloric of poets, and the peculiarly mixed vision of his *Tales* becomes one of our most illuminating windows into the folk culture of the Middle Ages.

In delicate situations, Chaucer uses folk rhetoric on his own courtly audience. He leans upon the precept of his churls' tales: folk rhetoric is not indispensable because it is attractive, but vice versa. A relatively early example of folk rhetorical technique is found in the *Legend of Good Women* (F 378–79). Chaucer almost never made a political statement. His most detailed criticism of the ruling class appears in this more-or-less conventional dream vision.[28] Margaret Galway believes that it is based on a real speech, the reproof delivered by Joan of Kent to Richard II after the latter had quarreled with John of Gaunt.[29] Joan told Richard that the tyrannies he practiced, and the flatterers who misled him, would bear witness to his downfall. This would be a particularly difficult speech for Chaucer to repeat or state his opinion on, as both John and Richard had been his patrons. Understandably, Chaucer disguises the criticism he voices in the passage. His speech compares, by implication, Richard's behavior to that of the lords of Lombardy, who were then engaged in very cruel actions. Whether or not Galway has correctly established the political context of this passage, the political content of Chaucer's verse is unmistakable.

The lines from the *Legend* are of special interest because they invite comparison to another author's handling of the same material. John Gower, Chaucer's friend, writes in *Mirour de l'omme:*

> They say that in Lombardy
> there are tyrannous lords
> who live without restraint,
> without law to hold their lives in check;
> instead pride and lechery
> and envy are more celebrated.
> In their pride they hate the church,
> since they prefer not to heed at all
> the teaching or decree of God;
> and through lechery they
> violate both wives / and virgins. . . .
> No one may escape them
> who is close to their power.[30]

Gower's treatment of the lords is straightforward. His only attempt to avoid blame for his speech is his introductory remark, "they say," often used by royal servants to tell their kings unwelcome news. Such a qualification, however, was not safe: English law dictated that if a report proved to be merely a rumor, the man who repeated it would be punished—unless he were to produce the name of the person from whom he first heard it.[31] After this one insufficient qualification, Gower's speech proceeds to pure invective, listing a number of charges (lawlessness, anticlericism, rape,

plunder) and assuming a number of evil motivations (pride, hate, covetous-
ness, lechery, avarice—a nearly complete catalogue of the seven deadly
sins).

But Gower did not have to be subtle. A court poet, but no servant of the
king, he was not dependent on Richard for survival. Equally to the point,
Gower wrote his criticisms within the context of two acceptable clerical
genres: the moral complaint and the estates satire. Gower's extra-court
status and his chosen literary form lent him license to deliver such *general*
invective against the ruling classes.

For Chaucer, however, indignation was a dangerous luxury. A public
servant could not be so open in stating his mind, as the case of Thomas Usk
confirms. Chaucer's "political statement" therefore hides behind folk rhetorical conventions. His parallel to Gower's passage shows considerable
subtlety. The poet guards himself in four ways: First by putting the critical
remarks within the dream vision form; next by assigning the speech to a
fictional character—in fact, an abstraction, the allegorical Queen of Love,
who uses it to upbraid an equally fictional King. Third, although Chaucer
makes the same charge that had been leveled by Joan of Kent against
Richard's court and by Gower against nobles in general, this public servant
directs it against the allegorical court of Love. Finally, Chaucer couches the
charge in folk rhetorical diction. Here the Queen of Love defends Chaucer,
saying that the King may be accusing him falsely:

This shoolde a ryghtwis lord have in his thoght,	(behavioral comparison)
And nat be lyk tirauntz of Lumbardye,	(negative simile)
That han no reward but at tyrannye.	
For he that kynge or lord ys naturel,	(behavioral comparison)
Hym oghte nat be tiraunt ne crewel,	(general statement)
As is a fermour, to doon the harm he kan.	(simile) (F 373–78)

Chaucer uses two similes, a general statement, a proverb, and two behavioral comparisons—the stock in trade of oral rhetoric, but relatively rare
items in courtly poems. Unlike Gower, he does not make a long list of
damning charges against the lords, but lets a brief allusion serve. If this
message was made for King Richard, Chaucer was not about to say so. The
king did not take kindly to certain kinds of criticism: when Richard thought
Thomas of Arundel had insulted the memory of Queen Anne, he beat the
Earl to the ground.

In the more playful context of the *Tales*, Chaucer addresses touchy situations with the same adroitness used by his most verbally skilled churls.
When he comes to the first ticklish passage in the tales proper—the presentation, for the first time, of an English *Schwank* to the English court—
Chaucer uses a folk rhetorical pattern that parallels the speech of the crafty

FIGURE 3

1) Deflected Apology, casting blame indirectly on another.
2) Indirect Insult—often employing A) proverbs or B) general statements, which make the speech sufficiently abstract to ensure the speaker's immunity from a charge of slander.
3) An Elaborate Disclaimer—which often serves more to intensify than to soften the insult; it also employs proverbs and general statements.
4) Repetition of the Insult on a Higher Level of Abstraction.

The Miller

[1) - 1.3137–3140]
But first I make a protestacioun
That I am dronke, I knowe it by my
    soun;
And therfore if that I mysspeke or seye,
Wyte it the ale of Southwerk, I you
    preye.
[2) - 1.3141–3143]
For I wol telle a legende and a lyf
Bothe of a carpenter and of his wyf,
How that a clerk hath set the wrightes
    cappe.
[3) - 1.3151–3166]
. . . Leve brother Osewold,
Who hath no wyf, he is no cokewold.
(A)
But I sey nat therfore that thou art
    oon;
Ther been ful goode wyves many oon,
And evere a thousand goode ayeyns
    oon badde. (B)
That knowestow wel thyself, but if thou
    madde.
Why artow angry with my tale now?
I have a wyf, pardee, as wel as thow;
Yet nolde I, for the oxen in my plogh,
Take upon me moore than ynogh,
As demen of myself that I were oon;
I wol bileve wel that I am noon.
An housbonde shal nat been inquisityf
Of Goddes pryvetee, nor of his wyf. (A)
So he may fynde Goddes foyson there,
Of the remenant nedeth nat enquere.
[4) - 1.3187–3854]
The *Miller's Tale*
    Indirect insult of the Reeve

Chaucer

[1) - 1.3167–3175]
What sholde I moore seyn, but this
    Millere
He nolde his wordes for no man
    forbere,
But tolde his cherles tale in his manere.
M'athynketh that I shal reherce it
    heere.
And therfore every gentil wight I
    preye,
For Goddes love, demeth nat that I
    seye
Of yvel entente, but for I moot reherce
Hir tales alle, be they bettre or werse,
Or elles falsen som of my mateere.
[1) *and* 2) - 1.3176–81]
And therfore, whoso list it nat yheere,
Turne over the leef and chese another
    tale;
For he shal fynde ynowe, grete and
    smale,
Of storial thyng that toucheth
    gentillesse,
And eek moralitee and hoolynesse.
Blameth nat me if that ye chese amys.
[3) - 1.3182–3184]
The Millere is a cherl, ye knowe wel
    this;
So was the Reve eek and othere mo,
And harlotrie they tolden bothe two.
[2) - 1.3185–3186]
Avyseth yow, and put me out of blame;
And eek men shal nat maken ernest of
    game. (A)
[4) - 1.3187–3854]
The *Miller's Tale*
    A potential insult to the court

Miller (Figure 3). Both statements, of course, are apologies. But both are deflected apologies, embedding a series of insults. Chaucer first says, "don't blame me, blame the Miller." But then he turns on his audience: "It is your problem, not mine, if you don't like my story. It will be your fault if you do not like it but choose to listen anyway." There are dozens of authorial apologies in Middle English letters[32]—all but Chaucer's follow elite rhetorical strategies. Chaucer's "apology" is something new in literature, but old in the language of the streets.

Scores of books and articles have celebrated Chaucer's irony. Critics have searched for its sources in rhetorical tracts, Middle English romances, and Old French satires, but few parallels have been found. The conclusion commonly drawn is that Chaucer himself was the father of this language. I have maintained, however, that much of his irony was fostered by necessity. This is not to say that such subtlety is solely a product of folklore. His literary background, the reactions of his audience, and—most important— his personality were powerful contributing factors. Irony pervades not only the *Tales,* but also the early poems modeled after conservative literary conventions.

Yet Chaucer grew tired of the constraints of conventional literary expression. *The Parliament of Fowls* carries occasional poetry past its apotheosis: when the birds abandon the indecisive tercel in the midst of the courting ritual, the poem deconstructs the occasion it was written to celebrate. Similarly, *Troilus* is an anti-romance, which in its conclusion destroys the very premises of the genre. These are the only complete works of Chaucer's maturity, and both defy their generic constraints. He broke off writing two of his finest middle-period works—*The House of Fame* and *The Legend of Good Women*—in midstream. By the middle of the 1380s, Chaucer seems to have been ready for an even more dramatic change, ready to embrace forms and styles more closely suited to his expressive needs and personality. These techniques had been developed orally to fill much the same needs that Chaucer felt. Therefore, he turned to folktale and folk rhetoric at the end of his career.

It was as Chaucer began the *Canterbury Tales* that his experience with courtly intrigue and public office became most dangerous, and it was also then that folk rhetoric exerted the strongest impact on his poetry. The poet had learned that if life itself is valuable, virtue is relative: truth, loyalty, and goodness must be considered in light of the fact that each of his patrons and leaders defined them differently. He surrendered the unified truth of the dream vision and created a poem in which every person could tell a story reflecting an individual truth. He turned from the absolute diction of fantasy literature to the relative diction used by commoners to express their opinions as forcefully but as safely as they could. And when he turned to his audience, at court or at Chancery, he brought the language of indirection with him to enable him to say as much as he safely could about the rich, if relative, truths he had learned. Read against the plan laid out in the General Prologue, the *Canterbury Tales* is simply another of Chaucer's unfinished poems. But much of what is finished within it is finished in so many ways: the tales, tellers, and narrative contexts are interwoven in a manner as multivocal as the city in which he plied the arts of survival.

Critical imagery often depicts Chaucer as a lighthearted joker: a man of "mirth," a "libertine," a "joking Bard," creator of "darling things" and "foolish stories," a soul both "simple" and "naive" who loved play above all other pursuits.[33] I have no doubt that Chaucer delighted in his use of language, but I am also convinced that he mastered many of his ironies not because he wanted to, but because he had to. I wish to question only those who claim that Chaucer's playfulness is solely the product of a jovial spirit, that the poet has no *ernest* in his *game.* Chaucer's game encompasses all his poetic reality, a reality that carries with it, as I have shown, a dangerous measure of truth. As Roger of Ware says, "Sooth pley, quaad pley." When game imitates reality, it is no longer simply game. Chaucer knew his playful moves too well for us safely to assume that he went through them only for the fun of it. He wouldn't have known so well how to parry if he'd never faced a sword.

Notes

The following abbreviations are used in the notes:

BA   *The Literary Context of Chaucer's Fabliaux,* ed. Larry D. Benson and Theodore M. Andersson. Indianapolis: Bobbs-Merrill, 1971.

BB   *The Babees Book,* ed. Frederick Furnivall. EETS, original series, no. 32. London: Trübner, 1868.

BD   *Sources and Analogues of Chaucer's Canterbury Tales,* ed. W. F. Bryan and Germaine Dempster. Chicago: University of Chicago Press, 1941.

CCR   *Calendar of Coroner's Rolls of the City of London,* ed. R. R. Sharpe. London: Richard Clay, 1913.

CPMR   *Calendar of Pleas and Memoranda Rolls of the City of London,* ed. A. H. Thomas. Cambridge: Cambridge University Press, 1929.

ChauR   *Chaucer Review*

ChauS   Publications of the Chaucer Society

CS   *Five Hundred Years of Chaucer Criticism and Allusion,* ed. Caroline F. E. Spurgeon. ChauS, 2nd series, nos. 48–50, 52–56. London: Trübner, 1914–1935.

DB   *Writers and Their Backgrounds: Geoffrey Chaucer,* ed. Derek Brewer. Athens, Ohio: Ohio University Press, 1975.

EETS   Early English Text Society

EKC   *The Mediaeval Stage,* ed. E. K. Chambers. 2 vols. London: Oxford University Press, 1903.

IF   *Íslenzk Fornrit*

JAF   *Journal of American Folklore*

JFI   *Journal of the Folklore Institute*

ML   *Memorials of London and London Life in the XIIIth, XIVth, and XVth Centuries,* ed. Thomas Henry Riley. London: Longmans, 1868.

MLN   *Modern Language Notes*

MLR   *Modern Language Review*

MP   *Modern Philology*

MS   *Mediaeval Studies*

PMLA   *Publications of the Modern Language Association*

RV   *Le Folklore de la Guerre de Cent Ans, d'après les lettres de rémission du Trésor des Chartes,* ed. Roger Vaultier. Paris: Guénégaud, 1965.

SATF   Société des Anciens Textes Français

Spec   *Speculum*

TS   *English Gilds,* ed. Toulmin Smith, Lucy Toulmin Smith, and Lujo Brentano. EETS, o.s., 1870.

All citations of Chaucer's work and references to "Robinson" are from *The Works of Geoffrey Chaucer,* 2nd ed., F. N. Robinson. Boston: Houghton Mifflin, 1957.

1. CHAUCER THE STORYTELLER

1. These quotes, from William Godwin's *Life of Geoffrey Chaucer* (1803) and Richard Wharton's *Fables* (1805), are in CS 2:7,22.

2. Anonymous, from "The Book of Curtesye" (c. 1477), CS 1:57.

3. John Lydgate, "The Life of Our Lady" (c. 1409–1411), quoted in CS 1:19.

4. For a description and interpretation of this illumination, see Alfred David, *The Strumpet Muse: Art and Morals in Chaucer's Poetry* (Bloomington: Indiana University Press 1976), pp. 9–11.

5. M. H. Spielmann, *The Portraits of Geoffrey Chaucer*, ChauS, 2nd series, no. 31, 11–12.

6. These quotes are found, respectively, in *The Legend of Good Women* (1554) and *Troilus and Criseyde* (1.52, 54). Ruth Crosby analyzes these oral references in "Chaucer and the Custom of Oral Delivery," *Spec* 13 (1938): 413–22.

7. For a study of the probable performing situation of the *Parliament of Fowls*, see D. S. Brewer's introduction to his edition of *The Parlement of Foulys* (London: Nelson, 1960), pp. 3–7.

8. *Troilus* 2.80–84; Wife of Bath's Prologue 3.711–93.

9. *Canterbury Tales* 1.3177; *Troilus* 1.7.

10. The age of the portraits, as well as the stylistic conventions incorporated in them, are discussed in David, *Strumpet Muse*, pp. 9–11; Aage Brusendorff, *The Chaucer Tradition* (1925; reprinted in Oxford: Clarendon, 1967), pp. 19–22; Margaret Galway, "The *Troilus and Crisey-de* Frontispiece Again," *MLR* 57 (1962): 173–78.

11. Dieter Mehl, "The Audience of Chaucer's *Troilus and Criseyde*," in *Chaucer and Middle English Studies in Honour of Rossell Hope Robbins*, ed. Beryl Rowland (London: George Allen, 1974), pp. 173–89; Derek Pearsall, "The *Troilus* Frontispiece and Chaucer's Audience," *Yearbook of English Studies* 7 (1977): 68–74.

12. Representative works by these men: Kittredge, *Chaucer and His Poetry* (Cambridge, MA: Harvard University Press, 1915); Donaldson, *Speaking of Chaucer* (New York: Norton, 1972); and David's *Strumpet Muse*.

13. Robertson has made this point often, but nowhere more explicitly than in *Chaucer's London* (New York: Wiley, 1968), pp. vii–viii.

14. Representative compilations include *ML;* F. W. Maitland, *The Court Baron*, Selden Society Pubs. no. 4 (London: Quaritch, 1891); *BB.* Representative works of "humanist" historians include G. G. Coulton, *Chaucer and His England* (London: Methuen, 1908); and Charles Pendrill, *London Life in the Fourteenth Century* (New York: Adelphi, [1925]).

15. See M. M. Postan, *Essays on Medieval Agriculture and General Problems of the Medieval Economy* (Cambridge: Cambridge University Press, 1973); George C. Homans, *English Villagers of the Thirteenth Century* (New York: Russell, 1941); James A. Raftis, *Warboys: Two Hundred Years in the Life of an English Mediaeval Village* (Toronto: Pontifical Institute, 1974); Barbara A. Hanawalt, *Crime and Conflict in English Communities, 1300–1348* (Cambridge, MA: Harvard University Press, 1979).

16. The most popular attempts to place Chaucer in historical context are all *potpourris:* D. S. Brewer's *Chaucer in His Time*, Maurice Hussey's *Chaucer's World*, Edith Rickert's book of the same title, Ian Serrailler's *Chaucer and His World*. For a brief commentary and bibliography, see L. D. Benson, "A Reader's Guide to Writings on Chaucer," in DB, pp. 338, 366–67.

17. Derek Brewer, "Gothic Chaucer," in DB, 24n.

18. *Funk & Wagnalls Standard Dictionary of Folklore, Mythology, and Legend* (New York, 1949), s.v. "folklore." The entry contains twenty-one different definitions of folklore; Taylor's and Thompson's remarks are taken from their separate contributions. Thompson makes a list similar to that quoted from Taylor.

19. Francis Lee Utley, "Some Implications of Chaucer's Folktales," *Laographia* 22 (1965): 598–99.

20. Taylor, in *Funk & Wagnalls Standard Dictionary of Folklore*, p. 402; Thompson, in *ibid.*, p. 403.

21. Emmanuel Le Roy Ladurie, *Montaillou: The Promised Land of Error*, trans. Barbara Bray (New York: Braziller, 1978); the book contains folktales collected by inquisitors from the peasants of Foix; these are, to my knowledge, the only verifiable full-length oral folklore texts from the fourteenth century.

22. Albert Wesselski, *Versuch einer Theorie des Märchens* (Leipzig: Kraus, 1931); and *Märchen des Mittelalters* (Berlin: Stubenrauch, 1925).

23. Elfriede Möser-Rath, "Literature and Folk Tradition: Sources for Folk Narrative of the Seventeenth and Eighteenth Centuries," *JFI* 5 (1968): 175–86.

24. *The Confessions of Saint Augustine,* trans. John K. Ryan (Garden City: Doubleday, 1960), pp. 135–37.

25. Sylvia Thrupp, *The Merchant Class of Medieval London* (Ann Arbor: University of Michigan Press, 1948), pp. 156–58, presents figures demonstrating that the gildsmen of late fifteenth-century London were largely illiterate (sixty percent of her sample population could not read); there is every reason to believe that illiteracy was even more widespread one hundred years earlier, when Chaucer wrote. Recent evidence suggests Chaucer's courtly audience was more literate than once supposed, but that, even at court, there seems to have been a distinct preference for oral performance; Richard Firth Green, *Poets and Princepleasers: Literature and the English Court in the Late Middle Ages* (Toronto: University of Toronto Press, 1981), pp. 58–59, 97–100.

26. Thrupp, pp. 161–62. Although Thrupp states that all of the richer merchants read some English, her inventories of their books reveal that entertainment literature constituted only the smallest fraction. The same seems also to have been true of the nobility in Chaucer's time: Green, *Poets and Princepleasers,* pp. 128–30.

27. Jean Froissart, *Chronicles,* trans. Geoffrey Brereton (New York: Penguin, [1968]), pp. 374–78, 404–408. The episode at the court of Foix is well known, the instance of Richard II reading aloud to Froissart less so. When Froissart presented his *Chroniques* to Richard, the king read some of it, "for he could both read and speak French well."

28. Ilhan Başgöz, "The Tale-Singer and His Audience," in *Folklore: Performance and Communication,* ed. Dan Ben-Amos and Kenneth S. Goldstein (The Hague: Mouton, 1975), pp. 143–203; Albert B. Lord, *The Singer of Tales* (Cambridge, MA: Harvard University Press, 1960); idem., comments in *Oral Literature and the Formula,* ed. Benjamin A. Stolz and Richard S. Shannon (Ann Arbor: Center for the Coordination of Ancient and Modern Studies, 1976), p. 175.

29. *The Complaynt of Scotlande,* ed. James A. H. Murray, EETS, e.s., nos. 17–18 (1872) 1:61.

30. Utley sums up the evidence for this statement in "Some Problems," pp. 598–99; Taylor and Walter Morris Hart present arguments for the oral origins, respectively, of the Friar's and the Summoner's tales; BD, pp. 269–74, 275–77.

31. "Folk Literature: An Operational Definition," *JAF* 74 (1961): 193–206.

32. Linda Dégh, *Folktales and Society: Storytelling in a Hungarian Peasant Community* (Bloomington: Indiana University Press, 1969) 95; Lord, *Singer of Tales,* pp. 16–17.

33. Phillips Barry was the earliest exponent of this view, now considered fundamental to folklore studies. D. K. Wilgus reviews Barry's work and theories in *Anglo-American Folksong Scholarship since 1898* (New Brunswick: Rutgers University Press, 1959), pp. 69–78.

34. Alan Macfarlane, *Reconstructing Historical Communities* (Cambridge: Cambridge University Press, 1977), p. 9.

35. An unusually detailed account of the mumming with which Richard II (then still a prince) was regaled in 1377 is quoted in EKC 1:394–95. For accounts of British folk mummings and their functions, see EKC 1:205–27; Henry Glassie, *All Silver and No Brass: An Irish Christmas Mumming* (Bloomington: Indiana University Press, 1975); *Christmas Mumming in Newfoundland: Essays in Anthropology, Folklore, and History,* ed. Herbert Halpert and G. M. Story (Toronto: University of Toronto Press, 1969).

36. Utley certainly understood the importance of the community in the creation of folklore; in his posthumously published "Boccaccio, Chaucer, and the International Popular Tale," he brilliantly described Chaucer's own oral culture; *Western Folklore* 33 (1974): 181–201. Nevertheless, Utley never incorporated the idea of community into his working methodology.

37. George A. Plimpton, *The Education of Chaucer: Illustrated from the School-Books in Use in His Time* (Oxford: Oxford University Press, 1935); Robert A. Pratt, "The Importance of Manuscripts for the Study of Medieval Education as Revealed by the Learning of Chaucer," *Progress of Medieval and Renaissance Studies* 20 (1949): 509–30.

38. Traugott Naunin, *Der Einfluss der mittelalterlichen Rhetorik auf Chaucers Dichtung* (Dissertation, Bonn, 1929); John M. Manly, "Chaucer and the Rhetoricians," *Proceedings of the British Academy* 12 (1926): 95–113; Robert O. Payne, *The Key of Remembrance: A Study of Chaucer's Poetics* (New Haven: Yale University Press, 1963).

39. One of the hundreds of expressions of this point of view is found in Robert A. Pratt and Karl Young, "The Literary Framework of the *Canterbury Tales*," BD, p. 33.

40. Francis Lee Utley, "The Last of the Miller's Head?" *MLN* 56 (1941): 534–36; B. J. Whiting, "The Miller's Head," *MLN* 52 (1937): 417–19; A. N. Wiley, "The Miller's Head Again," *MLN* 53 (1938): 505–7.

41. "Chaucer as a Philologist: The Reeve's Tale," *Transactions of the Philological Society* 81 (1934): 1–70.

42. Of the ten phonetic markers used by Fernand Mossé to divide Middle English into dialect regions, 6 are common to Norwich (the Reeve's region), Ipswich (Chaucer's ancestral home), and London (the seat of the "standard" Middle English in which Chaucer wrote); the remaining 4 are shared by Norwich and Ipswich, but marginal to London. Therefore, the dialect spoken in the Chaucers' native region was distinctly closer to Norwich speech than was London speech; *Handbook of Middle English*, trans. James A. Walker, 5th ed. (Baltimore: Johns Hopkins University Press, 1968), pp. 21, 24, 38, 57, 77.

43. Rossell Hope Robbins, "Geoffroi Chaucier, Poète Français, Father of English Poetry," *ChauR* 13 (1978): 93–115, disputes the notion that Chaucer composed solely in English, but there is no hard evidence to support Robbins's view.

44. Chaucer's use of native English colloquialisms has not yet been explored in the detail it deserves. As Norman Davis states, "the appearance of so many colloquial or informal words first in Chaucer is no doubt largely to be explained by the comparatively few works before his time in which his kind of realistic dialogue found a place" ("Chaucer and Fourteenth-Century English," in DB, p. 83). The fullest exploration of Chaucer's debt to oral speech is found in Ralph W. V. Elliot, *Chaucer's English* (London: Deutsch, 1974), pp. 181–239.

45. B. J. Whiting has demonstrated that Chaucer used proverbs to a far greater extent than did any other well-known medieval author; furthermore, he states, Chaucer's proverbs are particularly "folkloric" in form and function; *Chaucer's Use of Proverbs* (Cambridge: Harvard University Press, 1934), pp. 18–20 *et passim*.

46. John M. Manly, *Some New Light on Chaucer* (New York: Holt, 1926).

47. H. Marshall Leicester, Jr., "The Art of Impersonation: A General Prologue to the *Canterbury Tales*," *PMLA* 95 (1980): 218.

2. THE COMMUNITY OF PLAYERS

1. John M. Manly, *Some New Light on Chaucer* (New York: Holt, 1926).

2. "Chaucer and the Seven Deadly Sins," *PMLA* 29 (1914): 93–128.

3. For the vital role played by the audience in folk oral art, see Chapter 1, note 28; also Roger D. Abrahams, "Personal Power and Social Restraint in the Definition of Folklore," in *Toward New Perspectives in Folklore*, ed. Américo Paredes and Richard Bauman (Austin: University of Texas Press, 1972), pp. 16–30.

4. From *Fables Ancient and Modern* (1700); CS 1:278.

5. This tripartite division was employed in Chaucer's time by authors as diverse as Gower (*Vox Clamantis*, book 3, chapter 2) and Wycliffe ("Schort Reule of Life"). For the general currency of this division, see *Chaucer: Sources and Backgrounds*, ed. Robert P. Miller (New York: Oxford University Press, 1977), pp. 155–234; Ruth

Mohl, *The Three Estates in Medieval and Renaissance Literature* (New York: Columbia University Press, 1933), pp. 98–110 *et passim.*

6. I assume here that there are thirty-three pilgrims, including the Canon's Yeoman (who joins the pilgrimage as it is in progress), Chaucer the Pilgrim, and Host Herry Bailly. Unlike some commentators, I count all three of the nun's priests mentioned in the General Prologue (1.164), though only one appears later in the poem.

7. TS, p. 178. The editors comment on the uniqueness of this expression, which reads in full, *Quilibet affectans in dictam fraternitatem recipi, qui est ejusdem status fratrum et sororum qui dictam fraternitatem primo inchoaverunt, videlicet, de statu communum et mediocrum virorum.*

8. This line has many possible meanings. John H. Fisher assumes that Chaucer is referring to the order of the tales within the poem, not to the ranking of the pilgrims: *The Complete Poetry and Prose of Geoffrey Chaucer* (New York: Holt, 1977), p. 23. Of the four Chaucerians I asked to interpret the line, all considered my reading viable, and two considered it the preferred reading.

9. These protocol lists are found in *BB*, pp. 186–90, 284–86, 381.

10. Homans, p. 232; Du Boulay, in DB, pp. 36–37.

11. That is, if the Shipman were, as Manly asserts, a shipowner; *Some New Light on Chaucer.*

12. The Wife of Bath's social and economic status has been the subject of prolonged debate. Some recent critics, including Mary Carruthers, hold that the Wife is a wealthy merchant woman; see Carruthers's excellent essay, "The Wife of Bath and the Painting of Lions," *PMLA* 94 (1979): 209–22. There are several possible interpretations of the Wife's standing, but her behavior could place her in the churl's category, and her occupation is not defined with sufficient clarity to allow us to place her among the *haute bourgeoisie;* cf. Manly, *Some New Light,* pp. 228–31.

13. *BB*, p. 186.

14. Homans, pp. 245–46.

15. *Ibid.,* pp. 260–61.

16. Victor Turner, "Pilgrimage and Communitas," *Studia Missionalia* 23 (1974): 305–27.

17. Victor Turner and Edith Turner, *Image and Pilgrimage in Christian Culture: Anthropological Perspectives* (New York: Columbia University Press, 1978), pp. 131–33.

18. RV, p. 128.

19. Quoted as translated in TS, p. 128.

20. *Ibid.,* pp. xxiv–xxvi. The precise reason for the legislation is a subject of some speculation; May McKisack describes the act as "the outcome of a nervous dread of secret fraternities": *The Fourteenth Century, 1307–1399,* vol. 4 of *The Oxford History of England* (Oxford: Clarendon, 1959), p. 374. As the same Parliamentary sitting that ordered the gild returns also passed the repressive Statute of Laborers and purged England of some of Richard's most powerful supporters, it seems reasonable to assume that Parliament was indeed worried that the gilds might become either centers of support for the king or vehicles of a more general resistance to the legislature.

21. In surviving records, parish gild returns handily outnumber those of the trade gilds, but it is clear that many returns have been lost.

22. George Unwin, *The Gilds and Companies of London,* 4th ed. (New York: Frank Cass, 1963), 110–15.

23. The entire membership list is printed in TS, pp. 452–60. St. George's was not, strictly speaking, a parish gild, but a corporate ceremonial organization that included members from several Norwich parishes. Though grander in scale than parish gilds, St. George's mirrors the parish groups in structure and function. Its unusually detailed enrollment list is invaluable.

24. EKC 1:223.

25. These were St. Katharine in St. Mary Colechurch; St. Fabian and St. Sebastian; and St. James Garlickhithe. See Unwin 122; TS, Part 1, records #1 and #3; Sylvia Thrupp, *The Merchant Class of Medieval London* (Ann Arbor: University of Michigan Press, 1948), p. 34.

26. TS, part 1, record #14.

27. For example, see TS, part 1, records #1, #3, #17, and #22, all of which are select-membership gilds, and all of which are from the urban centers of London and Norwich.

28. *Ibid.*, part 1, records #6, #8; Unwin, p. 122.

29. Ten of the first twenty-two charters in TS require the assent of gild members for a new member's entry; likewise, ten mention no membership dues.

30. Unwin, p. 115.

31. TS, p. 179.

32. According to my sample from part 1 of TS, 41 of the 49 gilds (about 84 percent) had mixed-trade membership.

33. Unwin, p. 111.

34. Records of these three gilds are found in *ibid.*, p. 115; Thrupp, pp. 34–35.

35. Seventeen of the first 22 records in TS mention female membership, usually with the formulaic phrase, "brethren and sistren"; for examples of the (at least nominal) equality of men and women in gild workings, see TS, pp. 179, 264.

36. *Ibid.*, pp. lxxxviii–xc.

37. Thrupp, pp. 36–37.

38. *Ibid.*, pp. 34–37; TS, p. lxxxvi; Unwin, pp. 116, 119; H. F. Westlake, *The Parish Gilds of Mediaeval England* (London: Society for Promoting Christian Knowledge, 1919), pp. 72–76.

39. See, for example, TS, part 1, records #1, #7, #15, #20.

40. Westlake, pp. 70, 79, 87.

41. Unwin, p. 122; TS, p. 60.

42. TS, record #20.

43. Westlake, p. 87; cf. TS, pp. lxxxviii–lxxxix.

44. J. J. Jusserand, *English Wayfaring Life in the Middle Ages*, trans. Lucy Toulmin Smith (London: Benn, 1884), p. 222.

45. Unwin, p. 111.

46. Westlake, p. 28. Twenty-six of the 49 gild returns catalogued in TS list their year of origin; of these, 22 (or 85 percent) were founded after Chaucer's birth (assuming 1340 to be the date) and 20 (or 77 percent) after he reached manhood (1360).

3. THE ROLE OF THE PILGRIM

1. Johan Huizinga, *Homo Ludens: A Study of the Play Element in Culture* (London: Routledge, 1949).

2. RV, p. 127.

3. Gregory's directive is quoted in Bede's *Ecclesiastical History of the English Nation*, book 1, chapter 30; trans. D. D. Knowles (New York: Dutton, 1910), pp. 52–53.

4. RV, pp. 125–65, 166–73; for the cited examples, see pp. 120, 122, 134, 167, 170.

5. Turner and Turner, *Image and Pilgrimage*, pp. 35–37, 146–49.

6. Boucicaut's pilgrimages are described in *Le Livre des faicts du Mareshal de Boucicaut*, in *Nouvelle collection des mémoires pour servir à l'histoire de France*, ed. J. M. Michaux (Paris, 1836) 2:326; the Countess of Clare's pilgrimage is recounted in Henry Littlehales, *Some Notes on the Road from London to Canterbury in the Middle Ages*, ChauS, 2nd series, no. 30 (1898), p. 52.

7. RV, pp. 166, 129, 169–70.

8. Littlehales, p. 52; RV, pp. 167–68.

9. E. Talbot Donaldson notes that the Retraction appears as an addendum to the Parson's Tale, neatly dovetailed into the sermon of Chaucer's most sincerely religious pilgrim: *Chaucer's Poetry: An Anthology for the Modern Reader*, 2nd ed. (New York: Wiley, 1975), pp. 1143–44.

10. There is more than a little uncertainty concerning the identity of the character who delivers the speech I here attribute to the Shipman. Various manuscripts assign the speech to the Shipman, Squire, and Summoner; Donaldson assigns it to the Wife of Bath. See Robinson, p. 696; Donaldson, *Chaucer's Poetry*, p. 1074.

11. Emmanuel Le Roy Ladurie, *Montaillou: Promised Land of Error* (New York: Braziller, 1978), p. 259.

12. I examined the pilgrims' stories to arrive at a behavioral assessment of their various attitudes toward play. Fourteen of the twenty-three tales are told more or less expressly for nonreligious, often impious purposes. Among the remaining eleven, at least two (the Pardoner's and the Nun's Priest's) in some way ridicule religious precepts and practices.

13. Glending Olson, *Literature as Recreation in the Later Middle Ages* (Ithaca: Cornell University Press, 1982).

14. Littlehales, p. 52; cf. Jusserand, p. 207.

15. *Piers Plowman*, ed. W. W. Skeat (London: Oxford University Press, 1886), C Text, Passus I, ll. 47–50.

16. Jusserand, pp. 220, 232–33; Christian K. Zacher, *Curiosity and Pilgrimage: The Literature of Discovery in Fourteenth-Century England* (Baltimore: Johns Hopkins University Press, 1976), p. 54.

17. Dégh, *Folktales and Society*, pp. 65, 354.

18. Johannes Bolte and Georg Polívka, *Anmerkungen zu den Kinder- und Hausmärchen der Brüder Grimm*, 5 vols. (Leipzig: Dieterich'sche, 1913–1931) 4:2. The term *fabula* did not always designate an oral folktale, but could be applied more generally to any fiction. However, in all of the cited quotes, context ensures that folktales are the subject of discussion.

19. For Anglo-Saxon correspondences between the word "tale" and the idea of lying, see *Anglo-Saxon Dictionary*, ed. Joseph Bosworth (Oxford, 1882), s.v. *tael, tæl, taelen, taelend, tal, tal-lic, talu-*. In Middle English the confusion between "story" and "lie" is equally pronounced. In the *Oxford English Dictionary* (s.v. "tale"), definitions 4 and 5 indicate that the designation of "tale" as "story" dates back at least to A.D. 1200 and that of "tale" as "lie" at least to 1250. The uncertain division between these two shades of meaning is still evident today: the second edition of F. H. Strathman's *Middle-English Dictionary* (Oxford: Clarendon, 1891) assigns the meaning "tale, speech, narration" to this passage from Exodus: "[The devil] Wente into a wirme, and tolde ever a *tale*." Yet the *Oxford English Dictionary* uses the same quote to illustrate the meaning, "A mere story, as opposed to a narrative of fact; a fiction, an idle tale; a falsehood."

20. Karoly Gaál, "Some Problems of *Märchen* Research from Burgenland, Austria," in *Folklore on Two Continents*, ed. Nikolai Burlakoff and Carl Lindahl (Bloomington: Trickster, 1980), pp. 363–71.

21. Dégh, *Folktales and Society*, p. 86.

22. *Ibid.*, pp. 63–81; see especially p. 67.

23. "The Historical Chaucer," in DB, pp. 34–35. Although Du Boulay states that thirteen of the pilgrims are travelers, he specifies only twelve: Knight, Squire, Monk, Friar, Merchant, Man of Law, Franklin, Shipman, Reeve, Summoner, Pardoner, and Manciple. In addition, the Wife of Bath and Clerk are considered travelers by the narrator of the poem. Among the tales generally judged to be Chaucer's best, only the Miller's and Nun's Priest's are told by men who are not necessarily travelers (and Robyn's artistry is due to the fact that he is an accomplished minstrel).

24. Francis Lee Utley, "Some Implications of Chaucer's Folktales," *Laographia* 22 (1965): 588–99.

25. Dégh, *Folktales and Society,* pp. 99–100, 105, 111, 113.

26. See, for example, *Folktales of Hungary,* ed. Linda Dégh (Chicago: University of Chicago Press, 1965), pp. 46–57, 142–47.

27. This motif is intimately connected with "Cinderella" (AT 510, episode a[1]), but also appears in many other tales, including AT 301, 325, 326, 403, 409, 425, 450, 480, 500, 501, 511, 513, 550, 551, 554, 706, and 707.

28. *Folktales from French Louisiana,* ed. Corinne L. Saucier (New York: Exposition, 1962), p. 103. Such endings blur the distinction between the narrator's presence at the events related in the tale and his presence at the tale's telling; the effect of this ambiguity is to suggest that, in distant places, stories and their subjects are equally and interchangeably real. This device appears throughout Europe; cf. Bolte and Polívka 4:26–29.

29. *A Dictionary of British Folktales,* ed. Katharine M. Briggs (Bloomington: Indiana University Press, 1970), Part B, vol. 2, pp. 446–47.

30. The three stories outlined here are found in *The German Legends of the Brothers Grimm,* ed. and trans. Donald Ward (Philadelphia: ISHI, 1981) 1:157–58, 2:164–65. The parenthetical DS (*Deutsche Sagen*) refers to the numbers in Ward.

31. Briggs, Part B, 2:427–28.

4. CHAUCER AND THE SHAPE OF PERFORMANCE

1. A much more detailed version of this argument appears in Carl Lindahl, "The Festive Form of the *Canterbury Tales,*" *ELH* 52 (1985): 531–74. I thank Johns Hopkins University Press for allowing me to use material from that article.

2. See, for example, Frederick Tupper, "Chaucer and the Seven Deadly Sins," *PMLA* 29 (1914): 93–128.

3. Robert M. Jordan, *Chaucer and the Shape of Creation: The Aesthetic Possibilities of Inorganic Structure* (Cambridge, MA: Harvard University Press, 1967).

4. Frederick J. Furnivall, "A Temporary Preface to the Six-Text Edition of Chaucer's *Canterbury Tales,*" Part I, ChauS, 2nd series 2, no. 3 (London, 1868), pp. 25–26, 35.

5. In discussing the interaction of Miller and Host in the Prologue to the Miller's Tale, Alfred David treats some of the festive precepts to be examined here; see his *Strumpet Muse,* pp. 92–95. My argument owes much to it, as well as to Mr. David's comments and suggestions.

6. C. L. Barber, *Shakespeare's Festive Comedy: A Study of Dramatic Form and Its Relation to Social Custom* (Princeton: Princeton University Press, 1959); Mikhail Bakhtin, *Rabelais and His World,* trans. Hélène Iswolsky (Cambridge, MA: M.I.T. Press, 1968).

7. In addition to Bakhtin, see Natalie Z. Davis, *Society and Culture in Early Modern France* (Stanford: Stanford University Press, 1975), pp. 97–123, 152–87; Emmanuel Le Roy Ladurie, *Carnival in Romans,* trans. Mary Feeney (New York: Braziller, 1979).

8. Among Chaucer's contemporaries and acquaintances connected with these events are Othon de Graunson, John Gower, and Sir John Clanvowe, whose poems on Valentine's Day are similar to Chaucer's; Jack B. Oruch, "St. Valentine, Chaucer, and Spring in February," *Spec* 56 (1981): 557. Eustace Deschamps's name is found on one of the membership lists of the *Cour Amoureuse;* he also wrote a floure and leafe ballade in honor of Philippa, daughter of Chaucer's patron, John of Gaunt. Chaucer's possible links with the Pui are sketched by John Fisher in *John Gower: Moral Philosopher and Friend of Chaucer* (New York: New York University Press, 1964), pp. 77–83; his connection with the Floure and Leafe is most thoroughly examined by Kittredge, "Chaucer and Some of His Friends," *MP* 1 (1903–4): 1–18.

Although Chaucer died the year the French *Cour Amoureuse* was instituted, he may have participated in an English version of the celebration; indeed, Oruch believes that Chaucer's "Parliament of Fowls" represents the beginning of the Valentine's ritual. Lydgate and Charles d'Orleans also mention lovers' lotteries on Valentine's Day (Oruch, pp. 534–65).

9. EKC 1:274–335 discusses the feast of fools; the quotations in this description are found on pp. 292 and 294.

10. Thomas H. Riley, *Munimenta Gildhallae Londoniensis*, 2 vols., Rerum Britannicarum Medii Aevi Scriptores, no. 12 (London, 1860), vol. 2, pt. 2, pp. 216–20, 589–90; Fisher, *John Gower*, p. 78. Similar powers were granted the Lord of Misrule; see EKC 1:411–12.

11. *Oeuvres complètes de Eustache Deschamps,* ed. Marquis de Queux de Saint-Hilaire, SATF (1884), vol. 4, *ballade* no. 765 (my translation).

12. Arthur Piaget, "La Cour Amoureuse: Dite de Charles VI," *Romania* 20 (1891): 452 (my trans.); the poet, Amé Malingre, was a "squire" of the *Cour Amoureuse.*

13. EKC 1:391; the Boy Bishop was also fully invested, as real-life bishops were.

14. *Les Cent Ballades: Poème du XIVe siècle,* ed. Gaston Raynaud, SATF (1905), pp. xvi–lxviii.

15. EKC 1:177, 223.

16. Bakhtin, p. 7.

17. EKC 1:56.

18. Piaget, "Cour Amoureuse," p. 451; R. Howard Bloch, *Medieval French Literature and Law* (Berkeley: University of California Press, 1977), p. 153.

19. Piaget, "Un Manuscript de la Cour Amoureuse de Charles VI," *Romania* 31 (1903): 602 (my trans.).

20. Richard F. Green, "The *Familia Regis* and the *Familia Cupidinis*," in *English Court Culture,* ed. V. J. Scattergood and J. W. Sherborne (New York: St. Martin's, 1983). Green sees the poetic allusions to punishment as generally fictional in nature.

21. The opinion that the plays moved to the spectators, rather than vice versa, does not have universal support. Anna J. Mill gives a brief summary of the debate in "The Miracle and Mystery Plays," part 12 of *A Manual of the Writings in Middle English,* general ed. Albert B. Hartung, vol. 5 (New Haven: Connecticut Academy of Arts and Sciences, 1975), pp. 1317–18.

22. *Records of Early English Drama: York,* ed. Alexandra F. Johnston and Margaret Rogerson, 2 vols. (Toronto: University of Toronto Press, 1979), 2:22–44.

23. Many examples of the formal nature of local pilgrimages in fourteenth-century France are found in RV, pp. 125–74.

24. Piaget, "Un Manuscrit," p. 601; EKC 1:286. A measure of piety is shown even in the burlesque "Prose of the Ass"; the Beauvais "missal" of this service (c. 1160) directs the congregation to bray, but also has them sing the pious *Vincit* and pray for their ecclesiastical and political leaders.

25. Piaget, "Un Manuscrit," pp. 599–601; Riley, *Munimenta* 2, pt. 2, pp. 216–20, 589–90.

26. Le Roy Ladurie's *Carnival in Romans* details inter-class conflicts in a sixteenth-century Mardi Gras; for medieval parallels, see EKC 1:305–315; RV, pp. 54–57.

27. EKC 1:305, 315.

28. Johnston and Rogerson 1:32–33 (for the Skinners' offenses), 158–59, 162–63, 166–74 (for the Cordwainers'); cf. EKC 2:331–32.

29. Richard F. Green presents the courtly model for such refined obsequiousness, provides a few examples, and presents some explanations for its pervasiveness in *Poets and Princepleasers,* pp. 112, 131–32, 204.

30. *The Waning of the Middle Ages,* trans. F. Hopman (New York: St. Martins, 1949), p. 72.

31. Thus the titles "Queen" of the "Floures," "Prince du Pui"—and "Bishop," *Archepiscopus,* and *Dominus* for the Boy Bishop.

32. The wage scales and gilds assigned the various roles and plays are recorded in EKC 2:117–18, 131, 139, 341; for the order of the torchbearers at York (1415), see Johnston and Rogerson, p. 24.

33. Bakhtin, p. 10; emphasis mine.

34. RV, pp. 22–25.

35. H. M. Gillett, *Shrines of Our Lady in England and Wales* (London: Samuel Walker, 1957), p. 308.

36. Alfred David (*Strumpet Muse,* pp. 92–95) has analyzed the Miller's behavior in terms of "holiday rights."

37. *Canterbury Tales* 1.3860–64, 3909 (Reeve); 1.4325–28 (Cook; Roger does indeed speak to the Host later in the poem [1.4365ff.], but only after the Host has slandered him); 3.1665–68 (Summoner).

38. EKC 2.279–82; my trans.

39. David shows how the depicted action (*Strumpet Muse,* pp. 220–21) and even the literary style (pp. 215–31) of the *Tales* breaks down in the poem's final sections; the increasing diffuseness of the action is in a way quite realistic, reflecting the logical consequences of the Host's violations of festive decorum. The breakdown of style offers an interesting artistic parallel.

40. As Figure 2 indicates, Boccaccio's *Decameron* and Sercambi's *Novella* are literary creations of Chaucer's time which observe, to some extent, the rules of folk festivals. But these works reproduce only parts of the festive pattern that Chaucer renders in full; see Lindahl, "Festive Form," pp. 558, 566.

5. THE SUBSTANCE OF THE GAME

1. Linda Dégh, "Adatok a mesekeret jelentöségéhez," *Ethnographia* 55 (1944): 130–39; idem., *Folktales and Society,* pp. 82–83.

2. The ending related briefly here is found most often in versions of "The Maiden without Hands" (AT 706). Other representative narratives which, when told in Hungary, feature the tale-within-a-tale include AT 408, 480, 517, and 707. See Dégh, *Folktales and Society,* pp. 299–300, 305, 307, 311–12.

3. The Merchant's mention of the Wife of Bath has puzzled critics for decades. The standard explanation is that the Merchant interrupts the speech of Justinus for an aside to his audience (Robinson, p. 715). Early in this century, John S. P. Tatlock proposed, as I do, that the Merchant places the comment on Alison in the mouth of the fictional Justinus: *The Development and Chronology of Chaucer's Works,* ChauS, series 2, no. 37 (1907), p. 204.

4. Robert K. Pratt, "Was Robin the Miller's Youth Misspent?" *MLN* 59 (1944): 47–49.

5. The pilgrims may be assembled inside the inn or just outside it; see G. G. Sedgewick, "The Progress of Chaucer's Pardoner," in *Chaucer Criticism I: The Canterbury Tales,* ed. Richard Schoeck and Jerome Taylor (Notre Dame: University of Notre Dame Press, 1960), pp. 199–201.

7. David, p. 195; Sedgewick, pp. 198–99, 208–11.

8. *The Complaynt of Scotlande,* ed. J. A. H. Murray, EETS, e.s., nos. 17–18 (1872) 1:29.

6. THE SOCIAL BASE OF ANGRY SPEECH

1. Indeed, slander is often legally classified as a category of trespass; see, e.g., Mary Bateson, *Burrough Customs,* vol. 1, Selden Society Pubs., no. 18 (London: Quaritch, 1904), pp. 78–80.

2. *CPMR* 2:2.

3. Oswald S. Hickson and P. F. Carter-Rock, *The Law of Libel and Slander* (London: Faber, 1935), p. 6.

4. A good description of London's local legal system is found in Charles Pendrill, *London Life in the Fourteenth Century* (New York: Adelphi, [1925]), p. 226.

5. The records include 45 cases (dated 1291–1418) from the London *Letter Books* as extracted in *ML*, and 66 from *CPMR*, vols. 1–3 (vol. 1 is represented by 5 cases, spanning the years 1328–1364; vol. 2 by 25 cases, 1364–1373; vol. 3 by 36 cases, 1383–1386). I include all cases that could be construed as slander during the years spanned; the total comes to 111, but I do not consider the 3 cases that led to acquittal. The great majority of actions date from Chaucer's lifetime; in fact, the number recorded in the years of his maturity (1360–1400) is far greater than that for the first half of the fourteenth century or the early years of the fifteenth. This indicates that political and social upheavals toward the end of Richard II's reign made verbal abuse a particularly serious and relevant topic for the man who wrote and the audience that first heard the *Canterbury Tales*.

6. The two quoted cases: *ML*, pp. 425, 479; cf. p. 454.

7. *CPMR* 3:40.

8. Some of the cases in which the plaintiff intercedes on behalf of the defendant: *ML*, pp. 81, 275–77, 433, 460–62.

9. My translation of pounds to dollars is based on John Gardner's calculations: *The Life and Times of Chaucer* (New York: Knopf, 1977), p. 321. I stress that all such estimates are speculative.

10. *CPMR* 3:2; a defect in the ms. is the cause of the defendant's anonymity.

11. *Ibid.*, 2:181.

12. *ML*, p. 41.

13. *CPMR* 2:210; a second case occurs on the same page.

14. *ML*, pp. 526–27.

15. *CPMR* 2:210.

16. *ML*, p. 433.

17. *Ibid.*, p. 662.

18. *Ibid.*, pp. 425, 454; *CPMR* 2:149.

19. The three cases in which servants are offenders: *ML*, pp. 352, 385–86, 576–77; nobles appear as plaintiffs in only 15 cases.

20. Barbara A. Hanawalt, "Community Conflict and Social Control: Crime and Justice in the Ramsey Abbey Villages," *MS* 39 (1971): 418–19.

21. Among the earliest surviving legal contracts between the city and various trades are those of the Turners (1310) and White-tawyers (1311); *ML*, pp. 78, 85. As time passed, the contracts became increasingly complex, and by Richard II's reign the gilds were charged with writing their own self-regulatory ordinances, then submitting them to the mayor and aldermen for approval (pp. 405, 438–42). For search and seizure clauses, see pp. 539, 541, 546, 556.

22. This is the phrase most often used by the city in passing judgment on trade fraud; *ML*, pp. 438, 446, *et passim*.

23. *Ibid.*, p. 549; cf. p. 541.

24. George Elkington, *The Coopers: Company and Craft* (London: Sampson Low, [n.d.]). I use these records because they are the fullest available and the only ones containing sufficient slander cases to allow general conclusions. I must add a caution: though they are among the earliest trade gild rolls I could find, they nevertheless date primarily from the fifteenth century and may not represent with total accuracy the typical self-governing measures of gilds in Chaucer's time. Slander is the third most common offense, after absence from meetings and trade fraud.

25. The two cases cited: *CPMR* 2:46; *ML*, pp. 415–17.

26. *CCR*. I rely principally on the 140 cases recorded 1325–1340; these earlier records give a detailed picture of the events preceding the deaths, while later accounts—heavily couched in legal jargon—seldom mention the language that spurred the crimes.

27. *CCR*, pp. xxi–xxii.

28. The ratio of intertrade to intratrade murders is 41:14. This figure may not seem to present overwhelming evidence for my hypothesis. For any given trade practiced in London in the fourteenth century, there were perhaps 75 others against which a tradesman could vent his anger (Unwin [p. 370] prints a list of 76 London trades compiled by the Brewers Gild in 1421). Thus, the proportion of intratrade murders may seem outrageously great. However, two qualifications must be considered. First, fourteenth-century London was divided into "occupational neighborhoods": people who plied the same trade lived and worked in the same district, and it was the rule rather than the exception for an apprentice to live in the house of his master. Second, the great majority of violent crimes, then as now, were perpetrated by people who were well acquainted with their victims, and the scene of the crime was usually the criminal's own neighborhood (Hanawalt, p. 414). When these facts are balanced against the figures the proportion of intertrade crime is quite great.

29. *CCR*, cases E2, E34, G34, H34.

30. *Ibid.*, case F1; even so, the small percentage of assaults on superiors may still be misleadingly high, for in at least two of the cases in which lessers killed betters, they stepped into quarrels which had been started by their masters. In 1322, as a cornmonger argued with a clerk (case B18), the cornmonger's servant intervened and wounded the clerk. It is nearly certain that the servant was acting on the behalf, and perhaps even at the urging, of his master. In a similar case (A27) a quarrel between two citizens grew violent, and the servant of one man killed the other; the record states that the master "abetted" the servant, provoking the murder and sharing legal responsibility for it. Thus, even in those cases where inferiors attacked superiors, they were often provoked by the superiors whom they served. Servants were used by their masters as tools to rectify intraclass disputes. This "use" of servants also supports the idea that the trades and other small family-like social groups possessed a solidarity that overcame class boundaries in many situations. There is no case in which a servant killed his own master, and only one in which, with no apparent provocation from his master, a servant killed another man's master (G36). On the other hand, it was not rare for a servant to kill *for* his master.

31. *CCR*, case C5.

32. Bertrand H. Bronson, *In Search of Chaucer* (Toronto: University of Toronto Press, 1960), p. 61.

33. In my survey of the pilgrims' direct discourse in the *Tales,* I counted 319 speech acts; only 19 are direct insults. For a detailed account, see Notes to Chapter 7 below.

34. For a general discussion of trade insults in postmedieval London, see Robert J. Blackham, *The Soul of the City: London's Livery Companies* (London: Sampson Low, [n.d.]).

35. See, for example, Robert A. Pratt, "Was Robyn the Miller's Youth Misspent?" *MLN* 59 (1944): 47–49; Robert M. Lumiansky, *Of Sondry Folk: The Dramatic Principle in the Canterbury Tales* (Austin: University of Texas Press, 1955), pp. 49–53.

36. These words are attributed to the nineteenth-century robber baron, Jay Gould.

37. D. W. Robertson, Jr., *Chaucer's London* (New York: Wiley, 1968), p. 101.

7. THINE OWN TONGUE MAY BE THY FOE

1. Froissart, *Chronicles,* trans. Charles Brereton (New York: Penguin, 1968), pp. 404–5; cf. pp. 406–8.

2. *Le Livre des faicts du Mareschal de Boucicaut,* p. 326.

3. Barbara Tuchman, *A Distant Mirror: The Calamitous 14th Century* (New York: Knopf, 1978), p. 426.

4. Some thirty-five English-language courtesy books are edited by Frederick Furnivall in *BB*. The six poems here analyzed for references to speech acts are "Stans Puer ad Mensum" (c. 1430), pp. 27–33; "Of the Manners to Bring One to Honour and Welfare" (c. 1430), pp. 34–35; "How the Wise Man Taught His Son" (c. 1430), pp. 48–52; "The ABC of Aristotle" (c. 1430), pp. 11–12; "The Young Children's Book" (c. 1500), pp. 17, 19, 21, 23, 25; "Vrbanitas" (c. 1460), pp. 13–15. The speech acts have been broken down and counted roughly according to Furnivall's marginal commentary.

5. This was a very important injunction, for in the absence of the perpetrator of a slanderous rumor, medieval courts would arrest and punish the party who repeated it; see Sir James Fitzjames Stephen, *A History of the Criminal Law of England* (reprinted in New York: Burt Franklin, 1964) 1:301.

6. Huizinga, *Waning of the Middle Ages,* p. 74.

7. Several pilgrims—including the Prioress (1.123) and Friar (1.237)—are identified as tasteful practitioners of *artistic* diction. The Squire, for example, is a fine *writer* of poetry (1.95). But the four studied here are noted for their nonartistic communicative skills. Chaucer does say that the Man of Law has "wise" words (1.313), but this is ironic, for the poet suggests later (1.327) that the lawyer's speech rambles.

8. Cf. *BB*, p. 81; "Of the Manners," lines 25–26. The Parson censures those who utter oaths (2.1170–72); the Knight (1.75–76) and Clerk (1.840–41) are noted for humble appearance; the Clerk and Prioress speak only when addressed politely.

9. The Clerk's criticism of Petrarch (4.53–55) and his put-down of the Wife of Bath (4.1169–72) show that he has mastered *gentil* criticism. Yet, significantly, his negative remarks are aimed either at or from within artistic forms.

10. *ML*, p. 53; cf. pp. 592–93, where a servant is put on the pillory for praying that "hell might devour" a certain alderman. Only when there is a great social distance between insulter and insulted do such curses make it to court. Even in ecclesiastical courts, blasphemy was punished mildly unless uttered in church to church officials: W. Hale Hale, *A Series of Precedents and Proceedings in Criminal Causes, Extending from 1475 to 1640* (London, 1847), cases 35, 96, 108.

11. Sylvia Thrupp, *The Merchant Class of Medieval London* (Ann Arbor: University of Michigan Press, 1948), p. 166.

12. On closer examination the punishable ethnic slurs found in the records are really political in nature. All concern the Scots: "banyshed Scot," "rough-footed Scot," "Robert Bruce." "Scot," in Chaucer's time, was synomynous with "traitor." Citizens were required to "purge themselves by a solemn oath from the injurious suspicions of being Scots and therefore enemies to the realm" (Coulton, *Chaucer and His England,* p. 6). These "ethnic slurs" are no metaphors, but concrete accusations.

13. Sir Frederick Pollack and F. W. Maitland, *The History of English Law Before the Time of Edward I* (Cambridge: Cambridge University Press, 1895) 2:535–36. George C. Homans finds some cases in manorial courts where truth was not a defense, but more investigation is required to confirm his findings; *English Villagers of the Thirteenth Century* (New York: Russell, 1941), p. 237. Of the cases I examined, there is only one *possible* instance in which truth was no defense. This is a clear case of *scandalum magnatum;* the offender has slandered "the estate of aldermanry"; *ML,* pp. 502–3.

14. Robinson, p. 763, s.v. "wyne ape."

15. Robertson, *Chaucer's London,* pp. 133, 152, 193.

16. The most extended and perceptive *in vivo* studies of indirect insult are by Claudia Mitchell-Kernan: "Signifying," in *Mother Wit from the Laughing Barrel: Readings in the Interpretation of Afro-American Folklore,* ed. Alan Dundes (Englewood Cliffs, NJ: Prentice, 1973), pp. 310–28; *Language Behavior in a Black Urban Community,* Monographs of the Language Behavior Laboratory, University of California at Berkeley, no. 2 (1971), pp. 87–129.

17. *The Poetria Nova and Its Sources in Early Rhetorical Doctrine,* ed. Ernest Gallo (The Hague: Mouton, 1971), lines 450–54.

18. *Ibid.,* ll. 1550–53.

19. Betsy Bowden, *Chaucer Aloud: The Varieties of Textual Interpretation* (Philadelphia: University of Pennsylvania Press, 1986).

20. Quoted by J. M. Manly, "Chaucer and the Rhetoricians," *Proceedings of the British Academy* 12 (1926): 95–113; my trans.

21. *Blameth Nat Me: A Study of the Imagery of Chaucer's Fabliaux* (The Hague: Mouton, 1970), p. 69 [emphasis mine].

22. For saga parallels to the deflected apology, see *Brennu-Njáls saga, IF* 12, ch. 112; also Snorri Sturluson, "Magnus Erlingson," in *Heimskringla,* trans. Samuel Laing and ed. Peter Foote (London: Dent, 1951) 2:408, 412.

23. See Chapter 2, note 14 for a discussion of the identity of the speaker of this passage.

24. Frederick Tupper, "The Quarrels of the Canterbury Pilgrims," *JEGP* 14 (1915): 263–64.

25. Behavioral comparisons of a different sort appear in exegetical analyses; Bede cites, for example, the epithet "King of the Jews" (Matthew 27:42) as an instance of sarcasm: *De schematibus et tropis,* trans. in *Readings in Medieval Rhetoric,* ed. Joseph M. Miller et al. (Bloomington: Indiana University Press, 1973), p. 118. Though behavioral comparisons are relatively rare in medieval literature, they appear with some frequency in German romance; D. H. Green, "On Damning with Faint Praise in Medieval Literature," *Viator* 6 (1975): 117–70.

26. *ML,* pp. 502–3; behavioral comparisons from sagas include *Hoensa-Thóris saga, IF* 11, ch. 5; *Njáls saga,* ch. 123.

27. Richardson, *Blameth Nat Me,* pp. 41–42.

28. Even the "lowest" Continental art forms eschew the simile. Among thirty-six medieval analogs to Chaucer's *Schwänke* printed in BA, I found only two examples of simile used in dialogue (121, 144); both are German. Chaucer certainly did not know them, though all three poets may have had similar oral sources. Simile is common in the sagas: "Thorsteins Tháttr Stangarhǫggs," *IF* 11; *Grettis saga,* ch. 15; *Laxdoela saga, IF* 2, ch. 29.

29. Thrupp, p. 166; cf. p. 165.

30. For the use of similar techniques in Germanic tradition, see *Gísla saga, IF* 6, ch. 34; *Laxdoela saga,* ch. 62; D. H. Green, "Damning with Faint Praise."

31. Priscian the Grammarian, *Fundamentals Adapted from Hermogenes,* in *Readings in Medieval Rhetoric,* pp. 55, 57.

32. John C. Messenger, "The Role of Proverbs in a Nigerian Judicial System," *Southwestern Journal of Anthropology* 15 (1959): 64–73.

33. Wibaldus of Stravelot, in *Readings in Medieval Rhetoric,* p. 210.

34. *Gísla saga,* ch. 32; the same proverb is applied to similar situations in *Hoensa-Thóris saga,* ch. 3, and *Njáls saga,* 17; cf. *Laxdoela saga,* ch. 23.

35. *Beowulf,* ed. Fr. Klaeber, 3rd ed. (Boston: Heath, 1950). The two cited speeches are, respectively, lines 247b–48a; 250b and 272b–280 (my trans.). Saga parallels include *Laxdoela saga,* ch. 24; *Njáls saga,* ch. 87.

36. *Poetria nova,* partially trans. in Richardson, *Blameth Nat Me,* pp. 68–69; I have filled in the lacunae in her trans.

37. *Hoensa-Thóris saga,* ch. 2; cf. *Njáls saga,* ch. 87, 112.

38. *ML,* pp. 502–3.

39. See, e.g., Froissart, pp. 237, 332.

40. "Chaucer and the Rhetoricians," *Proceedings of the British Academy* 12 (1926): 95–113.

41. Robert O. Payne, *The Key of Remembrance* (New Haven: Yale University Press, 1963).

42. Robert A. Pratt, "Was Robin the Miller's Youth Misspent?" *MLN* 59 (1944): 47–49; Robert M. Lumiansky, *Of Sondry Folk* (Austin: University of Texas Press, 1955), pp. 49–53.

43. Homans, pp. 285–86; Muriel Bowden, *A Commentary on the General Prologue of the Canterbury Tales* (New York: Macmillan, 1948), pp. 246–55; and, for folk stereotypes of millers, Werner Danckert, *Unehrliche Leute: Die Verfempten Berufe* (Bern: Francke, 1963), pp. 125–45.

44. Homans, p. 225.

45. The grain was most often tallied by the miller, though Tupper ("Quarrels," p. 267) claims the contrary; see Homans, pp. 285–86.

46. Tupper ("Quarrels," p. 268) cites Hone's *Manorial Records* as evidence that carpenters received quittance of rent in return for services. Homans (p. 287) finds evidence of carpenters on rural manors, but does not find proof of their special trade status.

47. Tupper, "Quarrels," p. 268. See the description of the reeve's function in Homans, pp. 297–306. As he states, the more egalitarian parts of his description were slightly out of date in the thirteenth century—and, I add, even more anachronistic in the fourteenth, after the plague, the Statute of Laborers, and the Peasant's Revolt had reduced the peasant population and created widespread class antagonism. In the fourteenth century, the reeve was still often recruited from the villeins, but with the passage of time he was less likely to be elected by them.

48. Tupper, "Quarrels," pp. 256–70; Lumiansky, pp. 60–61.

49. *The White Book of the City of London,* trans. and ed. T. H. Riley (London, 1856), pp. 395–96.

50. See, for example, *Select Cases Concerning the Law Merchant, Volume I: Local Courts,* ed. Charles Gross, Selden Soc. Pubs., no. 23 (London: Spottiswood, 1908), pp. 13, 17, 23, 30, 33, 57, 71, 84, 85, 91.

51. All three characters receive special abuse in the General Prologue, where the poem's "innocent, ignorant" narrator reveals things he shouldn't know or say about them: the Man of Law seems busier than he is; no one knows the Merchant is in debt; and the Summoner's Latin is like a trained parrot's.

52. Lumiansky, pp. 129–31; see also Muriel Bowden, *Commentary,* pp. 265–68. A historical overview of the status of friars in Chaucer's time is presented by Arnold Williams, "Chaucer and the Friars," *Spec* 28 (1953): 499–513. A contemporary view of the moral ugliness of friars, who abjure their vows of poverty to strive for temporal wealth, is found in Gower's *Vox Clamantis,* book 4, ch. 17–23.

53. The seating charts are supported by the estates satire tradition; Jill Mann, *Chaucer and Medieval Estates Satire: The Literature of Social Classes and the General Prologue to the Canterbury Tales* (Cambridge: Cambridge University Press, 1973). Of 21 satires in Mann's appendix A, eight list friars. Of the eight, seven clearly rank the various estates in hierarchical order, and the friar is listed as the lowest *clerus* in six (the one exception, *Le Dit de Patenostres,* places friars in a separate category from clerics). *Sermones nulli parcentes* places friars at the very bottom, after "gamblers, thieves and pimps; peasants; and women." Gower's *Vox* and *Mirour de l'omme,* among the most influential satires in Chaucer's time, both place friars at the very bottom of religious society, beneath clerks, monks, and (in *Vox*) nuns.

54. The phrase "false friar" had proverbial status: cf. Wycliffe's title, "Tractatus de Pseudo-Freris."

55. Roger D. Abrahams, "Playing the Dozens," *Journal of American Folklore* 75 (1962): 209–20.

8. LICENSE TO LIE

1. The two exceptions are the Merchant's and Shipman's tales. As I discuss later in this chapter, *gentils* do not use the *Schwank* to full effect. The Manciple's Tale,

identified by some as a *Schwank,* is in reality an *exemplum*—though, as I will also show, this tale is used in much the same way the *Schwank* is.

2. Linda Dégh, "Folk Narrative," in *Folklore and Folklife: An Introduction,* ed. Richard M. Dorson (Chicago: University of Chicago Press, 1972), pp. 70–71.

3. Hermann Bausinger, "Schwank und Witz," *Studium Generale* 11 (1958): 699–700; Klaus Roth, *Ehebruchschwänke in Liedform: Eine Untersuchung zur deutsch- und englischsprachigen Schwankballade* (Munchen: Fink, 1977), pp. 225–50.

4. Siegfried Neumann, "Schwank und Witz," *Letopis* 6/7 (1963/64): 331 [my trans.].

5. Bausinger, "Bemerkungen zum Schwank und seiner Formtypen," *Fabula* 9 (1967): 135 [my trans.].

6. Kurt Ranke, "Schwank und Witz als Schwundstufe," in *Festschrift Will-Erich Peuckert,* ed. Helmut Dölker (Berlin: Schmidt, 1955), pp. 41–42 [my trans.].

7. Siegfried Neumann, *Der Mecklenburgische Volksschwank* (Berlin: Akademie, 1964), pp. 91–102, presents the strongest argument that the *Schwank* is primarily a tool of social criticism. Roth (pp. 225–50) takes the more balanced view that social criticism is one of many important *Schwank* traits.

8. Kurt Ranke, "Kategorienprobleme der Volksprosa," *Fabula* 9 (1967): 4–12.

9. By 1965 oral analogues to Chaucer's churls' tales had been collected in the following numbers: Miller's Tale (AT 1361), 73 versions; Reeve's Tale (AT 1363 and 1544), 148 and 197 versions respectively, for a total of 345; Friar's Tale (AT 1386), 49; Manciple's Tale (AT 1422), 11, with further analogues under AT 243 and 1380. These totals were computed by Francis Lee Utley in "Some Implications of Chaucer's Folktales," *Laographia* 22 (1965): 598. Utley found the variants in many sources, but primarily in Thompson's *The Types of the Folktale,* Folklore Fellows Communications, no. 184 (1961). Utley could find no oral analogue for the Summoner's Tale, a fact he imputed to its obsenity (595), but I have found one oral parallel from France: Frank Hoffmann, *Analytical Survey of Anglo-American Traditional Erotica* (Bowling Green: Popular Press, 1973), p. 256. Like Utley, I believe more parallels will surface now that the ban on obscene folklore has been lifted. The oral tales are probably far more popular than these figures indicate, because the *Schwank,* scorned by folklorists throughout the nineteenth century, was not sought out until recently. So little documentation existed that even Thompson believed that the history of the *Schwank* was primarily literary; see *The Folktale* (New York: Dryden, 1946), pp. 216–17. It has since been shown, however, that the *Schwank* is among the most vital oral art forms.

10. Joseph Bédier, *Les Fabliaux* (Paris, 1893).

11. Per Nykrog, *Les Fabliaux: Étude d'histoire littéraire et de stylistique médiévale* (Copenhagen: Munksgaard, 1957), p. 18.

12. Muscatine first advanced his thesis in *Chaucer and the French Tradition* (Berkeley: University of California Press, 1957). After Nykrog's book appeared, Muscatine altered his approach; cf. "The Social Background of the Old French Fabliaux," *Genre* 9 (1976): 1–19.

13. D. S. Brewer, "The Fabliaux," in *Companion to Chaucer Studies,* ed. Beryl Rowland (Toronto: Oxford University Press, 1968), p. 248.

14. Walter M. Hart, "The Summoner's Tale," in BD, p. 276; Archer Taylor, "The Friar's Tale," in BD, pp. 269–74; BA, pp. 3–77.

15. Brewer, "The Fabliaux," p. 249.

16. John M. Manly, "Chaucer and the Rhetoricians," *Proceedings of the British Academy* 12 (1926): 95–113; Earle Birney, "English Irony before Chaucer," *University of Toronto Quarterly* 6 (1937): 538–57; John Speirs, *Chaucer the Maker* (London: Faber, 1951), pp. 21–26; Janette Richardson, *Blameth Nat Me.*

17. Jurgen Beyer, *Schwank und Moral: Untersuchungen zum altfranzöischen Fabliau und verwandten Formen* (Heidelberg: Winter, 1969), p. 73 *et passim.*

18. BA, pp. 10–77; Thompson, in BD, pp. 106–23.

19. See notes 3, 5, 7, and 38 of this chapter for references to major recent works. Reviews of *Schwank* scholarship appear in Thompson, *The Folktale,* pp. 216–17; Peuckert and Lauffer, p. 177.

20. Klaus Roth devotes an entire monograph to analyzing the dynamics of social competition at work in one type of *Schwank:* "The Clerical Lover in German and Anglo-American *Schwank* Ballads" (Master's thesis, Folklore, Indiana University, 1964).

21. In June 1980, I examined all transcribed variants of AT 1000 available at the C.É.L.A.T. archives, Université Laval, Québec; all feature the competition between *habitant* and *seigneur.*

22. BA (pp. 40–45) translates a portion of the *Ring.*

23. BA, pp. 46–59.

24. Dégh, "Folk Narrative," pp. 70–71.

25. The Latin text appears with a translation in BA, pp. 72–77.

26. This tale was related to me by the collecter, Luc Lacourcière, 19 June 1979 in the presence of folklorist Margaret Low, at Université Laval, Québec. The tale was not tape-recorded, and is here retold as I wrote it down immediately after the telling.

27. For example, Hale's *Precedents,* case 663: "Thomas Ellis, de Boreham. Detected, he hathe reported a ryme *upon names* of sundry men and women in our parishe. . . ."

28. *Before the Bawdy Court: Selections from Church Court and Other Records Relating to the Correction of Moral Offenses in England, Scotland, and New England,* ed. Paul Hair (New York: Harper, 1972), p. 74.

29. From an interview conducted by Robert Bouthillier, Vivian Labrie, and myself with Henri Sonier, Sheila, New Brunswick, 22 June 1979. M. Sonier's comments are transcribed in Collection Bouthillier-Labrie, no. 4210, p. 3, housed in the C.É.L.A.T. archives, Université Laval, Québec.

30. The idea that stereotyping helps the typer make sense of strange new situations is common in psychological literature; see Robert A. Stewart, Graham E. Powell, and S. Jane Chetwynd, *Person Perception and Stereotyping* (Westmed, England: Saxon House, 1979), pp. 4–5, 215–36.

31. Over the past century Chaucerians have disputed the nature of the Canterbury pilgrims: are they individuals or types? For eighty years most readers have seen some truth in R. K. Root's judicious conclusion that they are very much both: "It is by their successful blending of the individual with the typical that the portraits . . . attain so high a degree of effectiveness"; *The Poetry of Chaucer* (Boston, 1906), p. 161. What I argue here is not to contradict Root, but to qualify his statement. The Prologue offers all sorts of individual and typical evidence, but the narrative persona, principally through superlatives, chooses to emphasize a certain consistent type in each portrait. In the portrait of the Prioress, for example, there is much evidence to show that she is an atypical nun, yet Chaucer the Pilgrim chooses to ignore her religious duties and make her a typical lady. My view owes much to Donaldson's concept of the naive narrator; see his *Chaucer's Poetry,* pp. 1038–41, 1044–45.

32. Roth, *Ehebruchschwänke,* pp. 436, 429.

33. *Ibid.,* songs D19, E45; Danckert, *Unehrliche Leute,* pp. 125–45.

34. Rainer Wehse, "The Erotic Metaphor in Humorous Narrative Songs," in *Folklore on Two Continents: Essays in Honor of Linda Dégh,* ed. Nikolai Burlakoff and Carl Lindahl (Bloomington: Trickster Press, 1980), pp. 223–32.

35. Danckert, pp. 130–31 [my trans.].

36. Earlier scholarship on the connection between Norfolk and the Reeve consists of a brief reference in Mann's *Chaucer and Medieval Estates Satire* (p. 284) and a

recent note by Alan J. Fletcher, "Chaucer's Norfolk Reeve," *Medium Aevum* 52 (1983): 100–103. Yet the Norfolk stereotype has been the subject of study for nearly a century; William A. Clouston, *The Book of Noodles* (London, 1888), pp. 17–20. My manuscript, "The Reeve and the Norfolk Stereotype," refers to over 40 tales, circulating from the twelfth to the nineteenth century, which caricature Norfolkers.

37. The *Descriptio Norfolciensium,* the work of a Peterborough monk of the twelfth century, has been edited in full only once: *Early Mysteries and Other Latin Poems of the Twelfth and Thirteenth Centuries,* ed. Thomas Wright (London: J. R. Smith, 1844), pp. 93–98. An excerpt, normalized from Wright's edition, appears in *Mediaeval Latin,* ed. K. P. Harrington (London: Allyn and Bacon, 1925), pp. 511–13. An English translation of the entire poem appears in my "Reeve and the Norfolk Stereotype"; portions of that translation appear in this Chapter. I thank Prof. Paul Alessi and Joanne Harrison for their assistance with the text.

38. Walter Clyde Curry, *Chaucer and the Mediaeval Sciences* (New York: Oxford University Press, 1926), pp. 71–75.

39. Mann, pp. 161, 282; Mark Azadovskii, *A Siberian Tale Teller,* trans. James R. Dow, Center for Intercultural Studies in Folklore and Ethnomusicology, monograph 2 (Austin: University of Texas Press, 1974), pp. 15–16.

40. "The Idiom of Popular Poetry in the Miller's Tale," in his *Speaking of Chaucer* (New York: Norton, 1970), pp. 13–19.

41. Tupper mounts his argument in "The Quarrels of the Canterbury Pilgrims," *JEGP* 14 (1915): 256–70. Thompson (BD, p. 108) is among those who believe that earlier medieval tales may have featured a carpenter as dupe; he offers the cuckold of *Violi e li suoi amanti* as evidence for his claim. But BA (pp. 28–29) correctly renders Masuccio's "omo lignaiuolo" as "wood-worker"—after all, this character's "trade consisted solely in making wooden shoes."

So there are no carpenters among any of the early analogues. The Flemish *Schwank* most often cited as "the closest to Chaucer's probable written source" features no cuckold husband at all, but three suitors who visit an unmarried woman (BD, p. 106). In other variants, nobles, farmers, merchants, a shoemaker, and a smith figure variously as dupes. The only plot-related significance served by Chaucer's carpenter is the typological connection between the cuckold John and the biblical carpenter Noah. Yet references to Noah are made in several of the analogues in which the dupe is not a carpenter; and Chaucer does not develop the connection between John and Noah.

42. The closest version to Chaucer's, *Le Meunier et les II Clers,* makes the dupe a miller and features the episode of the missing horses and the stolen wheat. The five other extant medieval analogues lack these two elements; BA, pp. 72–73.

43. Danckert, pp. 130–33; Roth, *Ehebruchschwänke,* texts D18, D19, D42, E10, E34, E57. Compare these to the ballads cited under note 37 above, in which the miller is portrayed as an adulterer.

44. "Chaucer and the Medieval Miller," pp. 3–15.

45. Roth, *Ehebruchschwänke,* types D18, D42, E34; Danckert, p. 130.

46. John Gardner, *The Poetry of Chaucer* (Carbondale: Southern Illinois University Press, 1977), p. 260.

47. Arnold Williams, "Chaucer and the Friars," *Spec* 28 (1953): 499–513; Roth, "The Clerical Lover."

48. Neumann, *Mecklenburgische Volksschwank,* p. 94.

49. Robert Dudley French, *A Chaucer Handbook,* 2nd ed. (New York: Appleton, 1947), p. 284.

50. Archer Taylor, "The Friar's Tale," in BD, pp. 269–74; "The Devil and the Advocate, *PMLA* 36 (1921): 35–59; "Der Rihter und der Teufel," in *Studies in Honor of Hermann Collitz* (Baltimore: Johns Hopkins University Press, 1930), pp. 248–51.

51. Beyer, *Schwank und Moral,* pp. 61–63.

52. Walter Morris Hart, "The Summoner's Tale," in BD, p. 276.

53. Gardner, *The Poetry of Chaucer,* pp. 271–73.

54. From William Fitzstephen, "A Description of the Most Noble City of London," trans. H. E. Butler in *The World of Piers Plowman,* ed. Jeanne Kochalis and Edward Peters (Philadelphia: University of Pennsylvania Press, 1975), p. 27.

9. BACK TO COURT

1. "Chaucer and the Custom of Oral Delivery," *Spec* 13 (1938): 413–22.

2. "The Audience of Chaucer's *Troilus and Criseyde,*" in *Chaucer and Middle English Studies in Honor of Rossell Hope Robbins,* ed. Beryl Rowland (London: George Allen, 1974), pp. 173–89.

3. Edmund Reiss, "Chaucer and Late Medieval 'Hearing' and 'Reading,'" paper presented to the MLA annual convention, 1979.

4. Jack Goody and Ian Watt, "The Consequences of Literacy," in *Literacy in Traditional Societies,* ed. Jack Goody (Cambridge: Cambridge University Press, 1968), pp. 27–68. On the importance of memory in classical and early medieval culture, see Frances Yates, *The Art of Memory* (Chicago: University of Chicago Press, 1966).

5. *BB,* p. 2.

6. Froissart, *Chronicles,* p. 276.

7. *Le Livre des faicts du Mareshal de Boucicaut,* p. 326.

8. "A Collection of Materials for a Study of the Literary Scene at the End of the 14th Century" (Dissertation, New York University, 1970); the cited quotes are on pp. 10, 17.

9. *In Search of Chaucer* (Toronto: University of Toronto Press, 1960), p. 87.

10. Thrupp, pp. 158–63; Judson Allen, "Reading and Looking Things up in Chaucer's England," *Chaucer Newsletter* 7, no. 1 (1985): 1–2.

11. Derek Brewer, introduction to his ed. of the *Parlement of Foulys* (London: Nelson, 1960), pp. 3–7.

12. *Poetria Nova,* ed. Ernest Gallo (The Hague: Mouton, 1971), lines 2036–70.

13. Gervase Mathew, *The Court of Richard II* (London: Murray, 1966), p. 14; F. R. H. Du Boulay, "The Historical Chaucer," in DB, pp. 33–36.

14. Mathew, p. 19; cf. Daniel Poirion, *Le Poète et le prince: L'Évolution du lyrisme courtois de Guillaume de Machaut à Charles d'Orleans* (Paris: Presses Universitaires de France, 1965), pp. 21–22.

15. Translated in A. F. Schoot, *Every One a Witness: The Plantagenet Age* (London: White Lion, 1970), p. 59.

16. Hallmundsson, p. 17.

17. The characteristics of oral narration described in this discussion are summarized from the following: Dégh, *Folktales and Society,* pp. 63–119, 165–285; James H. Delargy, *The Gaelic Storyteller* (London: British Academy, 1945); Azadowskii, *Siberian Tale Teller;* Roger D. Abrahams, "Personal Power and Social Restraint in the Definition of Folklore," in *Toward New Perspectives in Folklore,* ed. Américo Paredes and Richard Bauman (Austin: University of Texas Press, 1972), pp. 16–30.

18. Haldeen Braddy, *Chaucer and the French Poet Graunson* (Baton Rouge: Louisiana State University Press, 1947), pp. 65–66; idem., "The French Influence on Chaucer," in *Companion to Chaucer Studies,* ed. Beryl Rowland (Toronto: Oxford University Press, 1968), p. 126; James Wimsatt, "Chaucer and French Poetry," in DB, p. 118; Brewer, *Parlement,* pp. 131–32.

19. "Originality, Controlling Purpose, and Craftsmanship in Chaucer's Man of Law's Tale," *PMLA* 68 (1953): 572–616.

20. *BB,* p. 49.

21. *ML,* p. 507.

22. *Ibid.,* p. 526.

23. CS 1:1–56; my survey includes all entries listed to 1475.

24. A. C. Spearing, *Medieval Dream Poetry* (Cambridge: Cambridge University Press, 1976), pp. 11–16.

25. *Le roman de la rose,* ed. Felix Lecoy, 3 vols. (Paris: Champion, 1970). A cursory reading uncovered 20 direct insults, including 5 charges of lying, one curse, and the following 14 abusive names: *vassaus, traistre, deable, dam orde, orde garce, ribaude, vilains, garce recreue, thief, fole.*

26. See "Gamelyn," in *Middle English Verse Romances,* ed. Donald B. Sands (New York: Holt, 1966), pp. 154–81. Various characters brand each other "fool" (line 22) and "liar" (line 297) and exchange curses (lines 114, 131) and imprecations (line 484).

27. P. K. Kean, *Chaucer and the Making of English Poetry* (London: Routledge, 1972) 1:20.

28. Fisher, *John Gower,* p. 243.

29. Margaret Galway, "The 'Troilus' Frontispiece," *MLR* 14 (1949): 174. See also Fisher, pp. 113, 243.

30. Adapted from the text and translation presented by Fisher, p. 244.

31. Sir James Fitzjames Stephen, *A History of the Criminal Law of England* (London, 1883) 1:301.

32. See, for example, the apologies of two of Chaucer's contemporaries: Gower's *Vox Clamantis,* in *The Major Latin Works of John Gower,* trans. Erik W. Stockton (Seattle: University of Washington Press, 1962), p. 50; and Thomas Usk's Prologue to the *Testament of Love,* in *Complete Works of Geoffrey Chaucer,* ed. W. W. Skeat (Oxford: Oxford University Press, 1897) 7:1–3.

33. The first four quoted terms are found, respectively, in CS 1:481, 449, 271, lxiii. The final two quotes are used by Larry Benson to describe typical nineteenth- and early twentieth-century critical views of Chaucer: DB, p. 340.

Index

Aarne, Antti: 5n
Aarne-Thompson Folktale Types: AT 510A ("Cinderella"), 40, 180; AT 706, 5, 43, 63, 182 (see also Man of Law's Tale); AT 756 and 756A, 42; AT 763, 43 (see also Pardoner's Tale); AT 888, 42; AT 974, 42; AT 1000 ("Bargain Not To Become Angry"), 127–28, 132; AT 1361, 5, 188 (see also Miller's Tale); AT 1363, 188 (see also Reeve's Tale); AT 1422, 188 (see also Manciple's Tale); AT 1423, 5 (see also Merchant's Tale); AT 1544, 188; other tale types, 180, 182, 188
Abrahams, Roger D.: 176n3, 187n55, 191n17
Amplificatio: 91, 93
Anonymity, in indirect insult: 131–32, 147
Appeal for consensus: 107, 112–14, 116, 120. See also Folk rhetoric
Aquinas, St. Thomas: 160
Arundel, Archbishop: 37
Arundel, Thomas, Earl of: 169
Augustine, St.: 6
Audience: Chaucer's, 1, 161–65, 172; participation of, in folktale, 40–41, 63; aural, 1–2, 19, 159–61; of festival, 45–46, 50. See also Community, Context, Folk Performance, Folktale
Aural entertainment: 6–7; at Richard's court, 159–64

Bailiffs, medieval: 111
Bakhtin, Mikhail: 45, 50, 57
Barber, C. L.: 45
Barry, Phillips: 175
Başgöz, Ilhan: 175
Bausinger, Hermann: 125
Bédier, Joseph: 125–26
Behavioral comparison: 100–101, 116, 121, 169. See also Folk rhetoric
Benson, Larry D.: 174n16, 190n41, 192n33
Beowulf: 105
Block, Edward A.: 164
Boccaccio, Giovanni: 62, 70, 182n40; *Decameron*, 49
Boucicaut, Jean, Mareschal de: 34, 50, 88–89, 161
Bowden, Betsy: 97
Boy Bishop's ceremony: 46–61. See also Festivals, medieval
Brembre, Nicolas: 73, 77, 165
Brewer, D. S.: 4–5, 162
Bronson, Bertrand S.: 4, 83, 162
Burns, Robert: 11

Canon: on slander, 84; insulted by Canon's Yeoman, 93, 100; insulted by Host, 105–106; mentioned, 109
Canon's Yeoman: social status, 22, 24; insults Canon, 93–94, 100; mentioned, 84
Canterbury Tales: as oral performance, 2–3, 13; "dramatic principle" of, 3; retold by Scottish Shepherds, 7, 70; combines piety and play, 30. See also Clerk's Tale, Frame tale, Friar's Tale, General Prologue, Knight's Tale, Man of Law's Tale, Manciple's Tale, Merchant's Tale, Miller's Tale, Pardoner's Tale, Physician's Tale, Prioress's Tale, Reeve's Tale, Shipman's Tale, Summoner's Tale, Wife of Bath's Tale
Capgrave, John: *Mandeville's Travels*, 38
Carpenters, medieval: 112
Carruthers, Mary: 177n12
Chambers, E. K.: 50
Chaucer, Geoffrey: as aural artist, 1–2, 159; portraits of, 2; family background, 12; folk rhetoric of, 12, 167–71; criticisms of social system, 31; life in London, 29; professional life, 164–65; social position, 26, 161–66; legal troubles, 77, 165; described by his contemporaries, 166; described by modern critics, 1–2, 172; literary intent and philosophy, 13, 19, 31, 35–37, 42, 147–51, 155, 166–72. See also Chaucer the Pilgrim
Chaucer, Philippa: 26
Chaucer the Pilgrim: 14, 22–23, 45, 58, 102; insulted, 107; folk rhetoric of, 108; quoted, 21, 170–71
Child, Francis J.: 4
Chirchman, John: 165
Chrétien de Troyes: 13
Churls: standing in middle class, 22–24; in parish gilds, 27; factional competition of, 55–57, 86; seize "holiday rights," 56–58, 110; speech of, 78–80, 84–86; rhetoric of, 96–97, 103, 109, 110; portrayed in *Schwank*, 128–32. See also *Gentils* and churls
Churl's tale: 129
circumlocutio: 97
Clanvowe, Sir John: 180
Clare, Countess of: 34
Class status: determinants of, 20–21; of Chaucer's pilgrims, 22–24; within parish gilds, 27; and festive behavior, 54–61; influence of, on slander rulings, 78–80; and crime, 82–83, 184; and narrative, 147–50. See also Churls, *Gentils*, *Gentils* and Churls, Middle class, Three estates